DIVISIBLE

A Novel
By Robert Oliynik

Novels also by Robert Oliynik:

Unfortunate Cure

Fates And Fortunes

Dedication

This book is dedicated to all American voters who put aside partisan politics, vote their conscience, and do what's right and just in support of the greatest country in human history.

My third work, like the two before it, is a novel. In fact it is the most "novel" of all three books, and when first conceived, it was more fantasy than anything.

The day I conceived this story, Donald Trump was 40 days from his inauguration in what was likely to be the most unusual and unpredictable presidency in the history of our republic. Clearly, the pendulum of public sentiment had swung from, a Barack Obama presidency that was rooted in globalization with America merely co-existing as citizens of the world, to a Trump presidency whose foundation was built on nationalism and American exceptionalism.

Now as I sit here nearly a year from when I began this story, I am more amazed each day with the political divide that exists in our country. The ideology has almost become irrelevant, the policy differences of little or no consequence. What seems of greatest importance to those locked in a never ending partisan battle of disingenuous propaganda is simply making the other side seem small, self-serving, and ignorant.

And to what end? For quite simply, power, political power. Political power has now become the aim, and the only thing that seemingly matters.

Just look at any news story today that involves someone in politics engaged in something controversial. Within the first ten seconds, you typically will learn the party affiliation of the offending person.

Moreover, if the offender is Republican, and the story is airing on MSNBC, you will know immediately that the offender is a Republican. Likewise, if the offender is Democratic, and the story is airing on FOX News, you will know immediately that the offender is a Democrat. This is a certainty.

If you follow the passage of laws through our Congress, you will see a parallel theme. Laws now seemingly pass solely on a pure party line basis. I can't remember the last time a major social or economic bill passed the Congress with solid bi-partisan support.

Sure there are bills that pass with both party supporting them, but those are typically bills dealing with an enemy of the U.S., like Iran or North Korea, or a topic involving unfathomable human suffering, like hurricane, fire, or earthquake relief. Those are topics everyone seems capable of getting on board with, regardless of political ideology.

But it's the social or economic issues of the day that seem to divide us against each other; liberal versus conservative, rich versus poor, black versus white, citizen versus non-citizen, young versus old, and man versus woman.

Having lived as a voter through 11 Presidential campaigns, I can say unequivocally, it hasn't always been this way. It has gotten much worse in the last 20 years. I distinctly remember President Reagan working with Speaker of the House Tip O'Neill for the betterment of the country. I remember President

Clinton working with Speaker of the House Newt
Gingrich to balance the budget.

These men were political rivals, but they were
not adversaries.

Such cannot be said today. Today it is about
discrediting the other side to the point where you have
ultimate power. And I for one believe it is damaging
to us and to the future of our country.

So I wrote a story, far-fetched indeed, but not
inconceivable given our present political environment.
Call it what you will. Some may call it a thriller; some
may call it a satire. Some may even find humor in it.
But my hope is that you as the reader, will call it
simply a warning; a warning of a place none of us wish
to go.

Prologue
January 20, 2021

    The President stands ready. He is prepared to take the oath of office and be sworn in for his second term as the 46th President of the United States. He is a tall man. He is broad and powerful, but not athletic. In fact he is approaching mild obesity as the long days and stress of his first term have added weight, and more age to his face than his 72 years would suggest.

    It has been a contentious four years to say the least. Since day one, he had been at odds with the news media and the opposition party, whom he both held in low esteem, and blamed for the policy failures of his first term.

    But despite those failures, mainly in the areas of social programs like social security, Medicaid reform, and education, the U.S. economy had flourished. Gross domestic product growth had averaged between 3 and 4 percent for the last 8 quarters. The unemployment rate is hovering around 4 percent, and the labor participation rate is at an 8 year high. In the recently released December labor statistics, it had been revealed that the economy had added another 300,000 jobs for the latest month, and all told over the four years of his first term, the President had presided over an economy that had added 15 million new jobs, 8 million of which were added in the manufacturing sector.

    Tax reform implemented now more than 3 years ago, had reduced the corporate tax rate to 22%.

When this had occurred, it began an influx of jobs returning to America from places like, China, Mexico, Singapore, and Ireland; all the most significant tax havens of the last 30 years.

The "repeal and replace" campaign promise relating to the Affordable Care Act of the prior administration had never been fully realized. After eighteen months of partisan rancor, and outright disagreement within the Republican Party on how to reform the law, a watered-down version of a modified ACA was finally passed and signed into law. It maintained the pre-existing conditions, and coverage for children up to age 26 on their parents' insurance features of the ACA, but did little to reduce the overall cost of medical insurance

Competition had been increased across state lines, and some tort reform had been instituted, but the savings associated with those actions had been more than consumed by removal of the individual and corporate mandates requiring that people and companies purchase health care insurance. Many small companies no longer provided health insurance forcing their employees to the open market for coverage; and the vast majority of young healthy people opted out of insurance altogether.

All of the social woes of the past four years were of little consequence during the President's re-election campaign. The economy was doing well, people were employed as jobs returned to America, and people felt safer than ever before as border security and immigration controls had been restored.

So no one was terribly surprised when President Oliver Stanton easily won re-election capturing both the Electoral College with 342 votes, and the popular vote by more than 5 million votes.

The Democrats had pinned their hope on the extreme leftwing of their party by putting forth an extremely liberal candidate, Victoria Cheshire, the junior Senator from Massachusetts. The extremely vocal and socialist fringe of the party had hijacked the more moderate base and forced Cheshire as the candidate claiming a return to a more socially civil temperament and inclusive society.

The message never resonated. The majority of the country had money in their pockets and felt safe in their homes. Little else mattered on Election Day.

So here stands Oliver Stanton, confident, and sure in his convictions of where he will take America in the four years that lie ahead. It will be more of the same of the previous four years, much to the dismay of the Democrats.

It's a gray day with temperatures in the mid-twenties. The air is damp with the smell and feel of an approaching snowfall. The ground and area surrounding the Capitol building is already covered with a layer of snow and coated on its surface with a thin shell of ice. The weather this winter has already been harsh; harsher than the previous few winters, and the mood is hopeful, yet cautious. Many in the crowd that is gathered within plain view of the capitol steps and the impending ceremony wonder if the day's weather is a foreshadowing of the new America that is coming. Almost incredibly, the country is even more divided than it was four years ago fueled in large part by a media that dislikes the President and everything he stands for. Over the past four years the percentage of news stories that portray the President in a negative light is hovering around 90% with little credit given to the President for anything positive that has happened in America. Incredibly, left leaning cable news spends nearly 70% of its time fixated on the Russian hacking of the Democrats' emails and voter registration roles that had occurred during the 2016 election. It is the only thing that keeps their viewership pacified about the still unbelievable election loss of their candidate of destiny, Elizabeth Morley.

America in 2017 was divided, yet hopeful. There was talk of bringing jobs back to America, cutting taxes, spurring economic growth, securing borders, defeating terrorism, and making America again respected in the world.

President Stanton had won an impressive, yet surprising victory in the 2016 election. A victory very few saw coming, in places where no republican had won in decades. Places like Pennsylvania, Ohio, Michigan, and Wisconsin had surprisingly voted republican, while stalwart states like Texas, Arizona, and the southern states from South Carolina to Louisiana, were clearly and solidly in the Stanton camp. So much so, that Stanton easily won the Electoral College vote with more than 300 electoral votes. Liberal bastions like California, Illinois, New York, New Jersey, and Massachusetts had voted overwhelmingly for Stanton's opponent by nearly a 2 to 1 margin resulting in a huge number of popular votes. So much so that Stanton's opponent, Elizabeth Morley, in her bid to become America's first ever woman President, had amassed over three million more popular votes than Stanton.

Morley was supposed to have won in a landslide. At least that's what all the polls had indicated in the days and weeks leading up to the election. She was the chosen one. She was popular, if not unexciting. She was experienced, but ineffective in her roles as both a U.S. Senator and Secretary of State. Her policy failures, particularly with regard to the Middle East, had led to increased terrorism in the region that had spilled over into Europe and eventually found its way onto U.S. shores. In addition one personal scandal after another had dogged her political career causing some of her supporters to question her honesty and integrity. But she had always managed to escape responsibility. There was always an excuse and plausible deniability. Like many politicians she accomplished little but made the most of it with an organization that insulated her from scrutiny, and a media that adored her, so much so that they had unwittingly become partisan supporters, though they would never admit to it. She was a frequent guest on all the late night talk shows as well as Saturday Night Live. At 59 years of age she was still young enough to be considered "hip" and she was admired by Democratic voters young and old, and particularly by the Hollywood elite who shamelessly endorsed her to no end.

Although divorced for nearly 20 years, after her then congressman husband, had taken up with a rather attractive Pharmaceutical lobbyist, she had dedicated herself to service to her government, and always appeared to be a tireless worker and advocate of all people. That is, as long as your world-view happened to coincide with hers.

She was uncompromising, and like the man she looked to succeed as President, she was downright obstinate when it came to matters of policy. This, as it had turned out, was the source of frustration for a lot of voters in 2016, which viewed government as totally ineffectual in solving the problems of the everyday American.

She had expected to become the 45th President of the United States. Many thought she believed she was entitled to it, that it was her time. It was time for a woman to occupy the most powerful office on Earth, and rightfully so. But in the end she was a flawed candidate and the wrong woman. She had ignored a large portion of the population and believed that the loyalty of her coastal constituents, liberal elite, and otherwise loyal, but downtrodden democratic voters would win the day for Elizabeth.

And when Stanton had won the Oval office with a decisive Electoral College victory, it stunned the political world.

Oliver Stanton was a businessman, and a successful one. He had made his fortune in the mining industry, copper specifically, but his companies also mined silver and coal. At 68, he had amassed a fortune some estimated at $5 billion. He was blunt, impolite, and accustomed to always getting his way. This is how he had run his companies and he paid no mind to those who had objected. He was confident, shrewd, and had a razor sharp mind, but lacked decorum and social grace. Such qualities were completely unnecessary in his view and he had little use for those who possessed those qualities, but otherwise were mediocre at their jobs.

He didn't believe in catching more flies with honey versus vinegar. He'd just as soon smack them with a swatter when they weren't looking. But above all, he was smart and loved his country and its people. And this came through to his constituents who were fiercely loyal. And they rewarded Stanton with the Presidency.

No matter that his opponent had won the popular vote. That was not the way America elected its President.

But now in 2021 things were indeed different. The Stanton administration had become a juggernaut, and with resounding wins in both the House and Senate, the Republicans would continue to dictate policy in the country, and the Democrats bristled at the thought.

Many Democrats had seen the writing on the wall years earlier. Their view of America had not taken hold. Although kinder and more-gentle, as well as benevolent and inclusive, it was also more expensive, less safe, and perched on the principle of taking from those who had produced and giving to those who had little.

This was resented and flatly rejected by the majority of voters, particularly in Middle America and the suburbs, who had worked hard to achieve what they had. While many were compassionate, their compassion only went so far, particularly when the Democrats looked to re-distribute the wealth they had worked so hard for.

People in the northeast, far west, and certain urban centers were more sympathetic to the principles of the far left, as many were quite happy to have the government provide a better way of life for them. After all, anyone doing better than them could certainly do fine with less. And big companies making billions in profits should be made to pay their "fair share", as long as some of that fair share wound up in their pockets.

So a great movement began shortly after Stanton's election in 2016. It began in California and quickly spread to places like Oregon and Washington. The movement took hold and gravitated eastward to New York and Massachusetts, and eventually back west to Illinois, and Colorado. Many of the blue northeast states followed suit, and looked to a new political strategy, one that would go deeper than mere policy. This new strategy looked to turn the status quo on its ear, and would change the fabric of the country forever.

Secession. Yes, *secession.* But not the kind that had occurred in 1860 that triggered the Civil War, but a legal secessionist's movement. Done in a way that would be perfectly logical, and constitutional, and rational in the minds of those who conceived it.

First, it would occur by individual state referendum, then by a vote of Congress, and finally through ratification of all the state legislatures.

The movement grew and gained momentum throughout Stanton's first term. So much so that by the time the 2020 election rolled around, a public question on secession had been approved by voters in 13 different states.

All that remained to do would be to obtain congressional approval and the vote of 38 of the 50 state legislatures. The 13 had banned together and decided that the triggering event for their secession and formation of a new country would be the re-election and inauguration of Oliver Stanton for a second term.

That day had come.

Part I

STORM CLOUDS

Four Years Earlier

Chapter 1 – Washington D.C.
January 30, 2017

Oliver Stanton frowns as he studies the front page of the New York Times. The headline reads: "Country In Chaos Over President's Executive Orders."

"Humph," he says to Chief of Staff, Kenneth Latimor, who is seated on one of the sofas opposite the President in the Oval office. "That's an opinion Ken. That's not news reporting." The President leans forward from the other sofa and retrieves his morning coffee from the table that separates the two men.

"Yes Mr. President. There's been a lot of that the past week. A lot of opinion pieces trying to be passed off as fact. And it doesn't help that the media is playing up a few thousand overly loud protesters when over 60 million people who wanted a change from the status quo voted for you."

The agreement from Latimor is little solace for the President who is beginning his second week in office after having been sworn in as the 45th President of the United States on January 20, 2017. Stanton began his administration with a flurry of executive orders that he signed during his first three days in office.

It was not unusual for an incoming President, particularly one from the opposing party, to begin his show of power with executive privilege and a pen. In

Stanton's case, he had campaigned to undo many of the policies of the previous administration, and in fact, that is just what he had done the previous week. No one on the Republican side was surprised, just politics as usual. But the Democrats were definitely feeling the sting. They were still reeling in shock and disbelief over Stanton's surprise upset victory over Elizabeth Morley. It had been almost three months since Election Day, and many of the Democrats and their constituents were having trouble accepting the election results.

All the pundits and all the polls had strongly shown that Elizabeth Morley was destined to become the first woman President of the United States. Few gave Stanton any chance whatsoever.

With a week to go until the election, Morley held a lead in the national polls of almost 9 percentage points, and commanding leads in virtually all the battleground states, with the exception of Florida and Ohio. But the voters in the large urban centers of Miami, Orlando, and Jacksonville, Florida, along with those in Cleveland, and Cincinnati, Ohio were expected to turn out and make the difference. They never did. And Stanton captured those states, plus Pennsylvania, Michigan, and Wisconsin, which no one saw coming.

The popularity of the outgoing President, William A. Prentice, was not nearly enough to make up for what many, in retrospect, were now calling a flawed candidate, who was out of touch, and insensitive to the joblessness or underemployment of the middle class in those largely industrial states.

Stanton's populist message had resonated significantly, albeit quietly with many of those voters. And now he sat in the Oval office by virtue of the biggest political upset in U.S. history.

"If the media wants to sensationalize every one of our setbacks and say the country is in chaos, let them. I've had only one of my appointments run into a snag and the media runs wild with it. I guess they forgot that the last guy had *four* of his appointments run into problems and that they had to be replaced. Where were they when that was happening? What about this order on the temporary banning of immigration from terrorist hotbeds? It was perfectly within my constitutional authority, so I criticize the judge and they make me out to be some kind of dictator that doesn't understand separation of powers. I guess they forgot when Prentice delivered his State of the Union address and criticized the Supreme Court for the Citizens United ruling. He got a pass on that one because they loved the guy. No matter. I promised to do certain things when I got into office and I've done them."

Done them indeed. The three most significant orders were issued swiftly only hours after his swearing in on January 20th.

First, he signed an order indicating that the U.S. would not enter into a major trade deal with Asian and Latin American countries that had been sponsored by the previous administration.

Next, he signed an order that called for easing the regulatory burden of the previous administration's signature legislation relating to healthcare.

Finally, he issued an order strengthening the southern border by hiring thousands of border guards, and potentially removing funding from dozens of U.S. cities that failed to support immigration officials in arresting and deporting undocumented workers who had committed violent crimes.

There were dozens of other orders Stanton had signed in his first seven days, but these three were particularly noteworthy as they went after three key areas that many felt were a significant part of the previous President's legacy.

No doubt, this incensed the liberal wing of the Democratic Party, and their sympathizers at media outlets like the New York Times, Washington Post, CNN, and MSNBC. So much so, that the usual media bias against the Republicans had become much more amplified over the past week, and Stanton was bearing the brunt of it, while Republican leaders in Congress tried to stay out of the crossfire.

Chapter 2 – Washington D.C.
February 2, 2017

Marcus Pilfery stared down the end of his nose and peered over the top of his reading glasses at the former Secretary of State and now defeated Democratic candidate, Elizabeth Morley. Morley was still stinging from her election upset at the hands of Oliver Stanton nearly three months earlier and was seated in Pilfery's Senate office.

She was meeting with the Senior Senator from New York today to plead her case to be the Leader of the National Democratic Party. Morley, after the election, suddenly found herself out of a job. She had put everything she had into her failed campaign and now was nothing more than a private citizen. She had gone for broke by vying for the Presidency—and lost, and now she was desperate to hold onto some vestige of power. She shifted nervously in her seat.

"Marcus, I've still got a lot of support across the country. I'm still viable. We wait for Stanton to screw things up and self-destruct and I go hard at him and what will certainly be a failed record in four years. I'll only be 67, still young enough. Hell, I'll still be younger than Stanton was when he got elected. I've still got the drive."

Pilfery was skeptical. At age 42, Marcus Pilfery was an up and comer in the Democratic Party. He was young by comparison to many of the aging dinosaurs in the Party that had failed to convince the voters that they had the vision to deliver good-paying full time jobs to the American economy. Many of the jobs the prior President had claimed to create were part-time minimum wage jobs in the non-manufacturing industries, like hospitality, fast food, and retail. Families were barely able to survive on those salaries, and many opted not to work at all due to the fact that they could enjoy a better standard of living on public assistance rather than taking some menial job at eight bucks an hour. Those folks were not stupid. They had run the numbers and discovered that through rent subsidies, food stamps, and other forms of assistance, they were better off staying at home.

In many ways the Democrats preferred this to prosperity as it assured them a steady stream of voters who were beholden to the government for their very existence. The "Nanny State" had run amuck, and the elite Democrats couldn't care less, as long as they continued to be re-elected by those who were indebted to their failed policies.

All the while, the Democrats laid the blame at the doorstep of a Republican controlled Congress, who was demonized by both the Democrats and the news media for resisting even more handouts that would keep voters dependent on the federal government for their very existence.

Pilfery was now part of a new breed of "take no prisoners" Democrats who, like their Tea Party Republican counterparts of eight years earlier, had adopted a scorched earth policy of flat out obstructionism. The extreme right leaning Republicans had blocked President Prentice at every turn. They had made preventing Prenctice's re-election their primary goal, rather than working with the President for the betterment of the American people. It was not a particularly attractive approach when practiced by either party, but it always aroused their base supporters, who were the most vocal and demonstrative. And it was done for one purpose only, to gain and hold political power.

Pilfery was clearly the leader of the new Democratic movement. He had come up through state politics in New York starting first in the State assembly. Six years as an assemblyman, led to his first Senate run in 2006, which was wildly successful. The country was war-weary and the storm clouds of the impending financial crisis were forming when Pilfery took his Senate seat in Washington.

He had slowly, yet methodically risen to power within the Senate and had become Majority Leader in 2012 with the Democratic President's re-election. He was smart, brash, eloquent, and a tireless campaigner for the President and others in the Party. He built many alliances and had entertained running for President himself in 2016. However, the President talked him down from that insisting that it was indeed Elizabeth Morley's time. She had paid her dues as a Senator and Secretary of State and, in the opinion of many in the Party, deserved to make history by becoming the first woman to be elected President. Besides, Pilfery was only 42 at the time, and the President assured him his day would come, most likely in 2024 after Morley served her two terms.

Pilfery conceded, grudgingly, yet amicably to the President's wishes.

Pilfery grew up in Buffalo, the son of a factory worker father, and E.R. nurse mother. He grew up with his three younger brothers in a modest lower-middle class home, played sports, chased girls, and got into the occasional scrape with the law, usually for some petty offense like knocking down mailboxes or drinking beer on a Saturday night. He was a tough kid, and physically large at six foot three, and 200 pounds, and could hold his own in a fight, so as a result he was feared more than respected.

Upon graduation from high school in 1992, he decided to escape New York, at least for the time being, and attended the University of California-Berkeley majoring in Political Science. There he underwent a metamorphosis in terms of his political ideology. As a result of his upbringing, he had been fairly conservative in his thinking. He believed in hard work, loyalty, and perseverance. But once at Berkeley, he quickly succumbed to liberal university groupthink and his world-view changed radically. He was taught to distrust capitalists who dwelled on productivity and profits at the expense of social justice. He developed sympathies for the underprivileged — so long as they didn't get in the way of his own aspirations for success. Upon graduation in 2000 ran for State Assembly, and amazingly at age 23, was elected. He was the youngest person to ever serve in New York's State Assembly, and toiled there loyally for nearly nine years.

He was personable, smart, shrewd, and knew how to both give and take favors.

His Senate campaign was rough and tumble as he barely edged out the long time incumbent Democratic Senator, who was laboring under some dubious, nonetheless serious conflict of interest accusations, in a hard fought primary. By the time he got to the general election in November, it was no contest as extremely "dark-blue" New York turned out for the 32 year-old, up and coming, no nonsense, tough kid from the streets of Buffalo.

So, now at the age of 46 he sat across the desk from the woman who three months earlier many believed would become the leader of the free world, but suddenly was nothing in the Democratic sphere of influence in Washington. Pilfery was in control. He held all the cards. He knew it and Elizabeth Morley knew it.

He stared at her for what seemed like a long time to Morley, so much so that she broke eye contact with Pilfery and looked down at her hands folded in her lap.

Finally Marcus Pilfery spoke. "We've got something else in mind for you Madame Secretary." Pilfery was brash and sometimes condescending, but he was always respectful of those who had come before him. He acknowledged Morley's standing by addressing her as Madame Secretary, for the last position she held in government, namely Secretary of State.

Elizabeth was buoyed by Pilfery's show of respect, but at the same time deflated by his dismissal of her for the Leadership of the National Democratic Party. She held her breath as she waited for Marcus to elaborate.

"There's a movement coming. Something unprecedented and colossal, and I'm not overstating it." Pilfery paused to get a read on Elizabeth's reaction, of which there was none. She sat staring blankly at the Senator.

"A movement for which you can be extremely invaluable. A movement so different, and so groundbreaking, that many would consider it radical, or even seditious." Pilfery paused again waiting for a reaction. This time he got it. Morley sank back into her chair frowning, eyes darting nervously from side-to-side. "What the hell was this all about?" She thought to herself. She couldn't imagine what Marcus Pilfery was about to reveal.

She composed herself and calmly asked, "What are you trying to say?"

Pilfery smiled and stood up from his chair. He walked around the desk and sat on the corner of it facing Elizabeth. His frame was normally imposing, but propped on the edge of his desk with Elizabeth only a mere three feet away sunken back in the low club-style chair, he was downright ominous.

He continued. "Madame Secretary -- may I call you Elizabeth?" All decorum had gone out the window.

"Ah, yes," she stumbled to get the words out. "Yes, by all means."

He nodded and smiled approvingly. "Good. Elizabeth," he paused again and smiled with self-satisfaction. "Elizabeth, when a people or a movement go through the normal process or protocol to effect change and they are unsuccessful. And I don't mean unsuccessful like losing an election or two. No, indeed. I mean when they can't get the greater citizenry to accept their leaders or enact their policies to the point where they are completely ineffectual to the point of being rendered irrelevant. When a Party, like the Democratic Party, loses hundreds of seats in Congress and thousands of State government seats, and dozens of Governorships, what options do you think remains for that Party?"

Elizabeth thought for a moment, still not knowing where this was going, but she decided to engage Pilfery in his little diatribe. "Well, I suppose you can either change the people delivering the message or the message itself."

Pilfery smiled again, nodding slightly. "Yes. Yes. I knew you would say that. Yes. That's what we've all been taught. Change the message. Change the people. That 's what we've all been led to believe. Led to believe by those who taught our Political Science courses. Let to believe by those leaders who've preceded us. Led to believe by what our experiences have shown us." Marcus paused, allowing those thoughts to sink into Morley's head so as to stimulate some other thought, which at this moment in time, Morley was completely incapable of rendering.

He went on. "But you know, there is another pathway."

He rose from the desk and walked across the room and stood in front of the large map of the United States that hung on the wall in a beautiful mahogany frame. She turned to see what he was doing and rose from her chair to face him as he studied the map before him.

"You know what you do?" He asked her, glancing over to her and locking on to her eyes as they met his.

She dreaded the answer, yet didn't know why. "No, what?"

She swallowed hard.

He firmed his jaw and glanced back at the map. "You form a new country."

He turned toward her, smiled and shrugged.

Chapter 3 – San Francisco
February 2, 2017

Horace Dettinger groggily makes his way down the hallway to the kitchen of his Napa Valley cottage in the quaint town of Yountville. Congressman Dettinger arrived back in San Francisco the night before, touching down in his home district at a little past 11 pm.

The limousine was waiting curbside just outside the doors by the baggage carousel for United Airlines. Dettinger had left Washington D.C. the previous afternoon and was now tucked into his cozy home in the quiet confines of the Napa Valley. He also kept a small apartment in downtown San Francisco, but Yountville was where he called home.

At 68, Dettinger was a career politician, having served nearly 36 years in the U.S. House of Representatives. He was first elected in 1982 during the Reagan administration, and had easily won re-election 17 times. If ever there was a walking testimony to the need for Congressional term limits Horace Dettinger was it.

His district, the California 12th, is contained entirely within San Francisco, and is one of the most liberal in the country. It is nearly 80% Democratic. If Jesus Christ himself were to run as a Republican, he'd have little chance of unseating Dettinger or any other Democrat.

His constituents were fiercely loyal and Dettinger, for fear of compromising that loyalty, would never vote against any of the most liberal legislation regardless of its cost or how much it might trample on the liberties of the average citizen. He was determined to stay in office as long as he were alive, as he knew nothing else nor was capable or prepared to perform any other type of job. Unlike many of his counterparts in Congress, he was not a lawyer. So he possessed no marketable job skills of any kind.

He grew up in the bay area, the son of college professors who taught at Stanford in the tumultuous sixties. His father taught Political Science and was a disciple of activist Abby Hoffman and others who formed the Youth International Party, known as the "Yippies". His mother was less politically active, and taught Art History at Stanford.

Horace's political beliefs were established very early in life due to the influence of his father, and he attended Stanford where he majored in Political Science.

He graduated in 1970 at the height of the Vietnam War, and during the spring of Kent State. He had been drafted into the army but fortunately for Horace, due to a medical issue with his back, was declared 4-F, and was unable to serve.

He went to work in San Francisco as a community organizer and helped spearhead the movement that secured civil rights for the Gay and Lesbian community. He wrote and frequently spoke on topics that concerned the gay community like health care, fair housing rights, and workplace discrimination. He was a tireless champion for the community, and in 1982 at the age of 34 he ran for and secured the 12th district seat in Congress.

In 1984 he married a fellow community activist, Pamela Carter, who remained active in the community, so much so that they never took the time to start a family. At age 40, Pam was diagnosed with breast cancer, and battled the disease on and off for nearly 12 years before succumbing to the illness in 1996.

Horace was devastated by the loss, as Pam was the only woman he had ever truly loved. When she was gone, Horace re-dedicated himself to his work in the 12th and began aggressively championing the cause for woman's health and reproductive rights.

Over the next 20 years he had become a fierce supporter of progressive thought in Congress and would eventually become one of President Prentice's most vocal supporters of his landmark healthcare law approved by the congress in 2009.

No doubt Dettinger was committed to his beliefs, so much so that he believed the Republican Party was the enemy of his people and downright evil. He was personally crushed when Stanton was elected President as he campaigned tirelessly for Elizabeth Morley.

Since the election he spoke often about resisting the new President and his policies and had become very active with the newly founded California movement for secession from the United States. He envisioned California as an independent country and believed he and his constituents would thrive in an environment of like-minded progressive thought. He had little or no patience for the folks in Middle America or the south and believed those people were irredeemable when it came to social justice and civil rights.

So on this quiet, cloudy, cool morning in Northern California, Dettinger flips on his Keurig coffee maker and tunes his television to CNN for the latest news on what the Stanton administration is up to.

Stanton had been up to plenty. In addition to nearly two dozen executive orders, which in Dettinger's opinion undermined the civil rights of most Americans, Stanton had been aggressively pushing for confirmation of his Cabinet nominees.

Stanton had also been making loud overtures, for the benefit of his base supporters, about repealing and replacing the current healthcare law, reforming the income tax system, and securing the U.S. border through an enhanced vetting process aimed at refugees from the war-torn Middle East, and also Africa.

Dettinger watched with interest as the CNN reporter droned on with obvious disdain about each of Stanton's policy objectives. All of it strikingly in line with what Stanton had campaigned on.

Amazingly, Dettinger thought to himself as he sipped black coffee, Stanton was doing exactly what he said he would do. To Dettinger, and his counterparts in Washington, this was unprecedented. A politician doing exactly what he said he would do, and the media trying to make sense of it.

It had always been Dettinger's approach to campaign hard left, secure his votes, and then back-off to a more moderate position in order to get things done with the Republicans. The last four years, however, had been quite different. There had been no backing off and cooperating with the Republicans. Ever since 2012 when the Tea Party movement had wrestled control of the House away from the Democrats, there had been no compromise in Congress, and little meaningful legislation had been passed. Then when the Senate fell under Republican control in 2014, President Prentice and the Democrats all but gave up on passing legislation. Instead, Prentice charted a course for one Executive action after another precipitating a cry from the right that the President was now dictating policy.

Congress was virtually at a standstill, and the country more divided and partisan than ever before in its history.

Now under Stanton, in Dettinger's view, it would only become worse. Despite the fact that for the first time since the nineteen twenties, Republicans controlled the White House and both houses of congress, the margin in the Senate was slim enough that to achieve any meaningful legislation, it would require eight Democratic Senators voting along with the Republicans, to get anything done.

Dettinger was not optimistic. He, along with other liberal democratic leaders like Marcus Pilfery, was thinking about an alternative America. He was

thinking about an America that didn't include Stanton
and his Republican cohorts.

Chapter 4 – Washington D.C.
February 2, 2017

Elizabeth Morley was stunned. Was the Senate Minority Leader talking about revolution? Was she certain about what she had just heard?

"What exactly are you saying Marcus?" The former Secretary of State asked soberly.

Pilfery turned again to the map and shook his head while chuckling softly. "You're not quite getting it are you Elizabeth?"

This struck a nerve with Morley who rose from her chair and walked over to Pilfery who was scanning the map.

"Revolution? Is that what you're advocating? Revolution?"

Pilfery's tone changed immediately. He was no longer seeing the humor in Morley's reaction and resented the premise of her question.

He turned and glared at her. "No. Not revolution. Secession. Legal secession in an orderly and constitutional manner. It is possible you know, if done correctly, and," he paused for effect. "And with your help."

Elizabeth felt a chill and then a rush of heat to her face as her adrenal glands released a wave of adrenaline that quickly coursed through her veins. "What kind of help?" She asked cautiously.

"Look at this map Elizabeth. What do you see?" Pilfery asked.

Morley focused on the map. It was a standard Rand McNally map of the United States. Nothing too fancy, but nonetheless functional. It was approximately 50 inches wide by 32 inches high, done in full color.

On this particular map though, there were a series of different colored pushpins. First, there were red pushpins in each of the states that had voted for Stanton in the election. Next, there were blue pushpins in each of the states that had voted for Elizabeth Morley. No great revelations there. But in six of the blue states, California, New York, Illinois, Washington, Oregon, and Colorado there were also white pushpins. In California, there was also a yellow pushpin. Off to the side on the map there was a collection of green pushpins.

Morley decided to play along with Pilfery. "I see the map divided up by red states and blue states. So what?"

"Look more closely. What else do you see?"

Elizabeth looking bothered glanced back at the map and studied it for a few seconds. "Ok, I see some other colored pins. What do they mean?" She asked impatiently.

"Very good. I'll tell you what they mean." Pilfery continued with a more urgent, business like tone to his voice. He now had Elizabeth's undivided attention. "The white pins represent states where there is an active campaign underway statewide to put a referendum on the ballot to vote for secession from the United States. The yellow pin in California designates that the referendum is in place and that it will be voted on in the next statewide election in 2018."

Morley was silent. She searched her innermost thoughts for how she felt and how she should react. She was having difficulty processing what Pilfery had just described.

The only reaction she could summon was one of disbelief. "You're serious about this? You really believe there can be a secessionist movement that's successful in modern day America?"

"I am. Or, I should say, we are. There are a number of us already on board in several of the States. Dettinger from California is on board. So is Diane Mitchell from Illinois, Michael Simmons from Washington, and Angela Gutierrez from Colorado."

Morley glanced back at the map noting the white pins in the states for all the members of Congress Pilfery had just mentioned.

Morley thought for a moment. "This can never work. How do you expect to form another country? There are a million details. What about all the complications around federal programs, defense, economics. How do you even begin to address all that?"

"We've been thinking about it since November 9th. It's moving quickly and has momentum. We met several times over the past two months; marathon sessions, all day, all night, discussing the things you just raised. We have a framework. I can describe it for you. It will take time to fully formulate. But we have time. We have four years if necessary. If we defeat

Stanton in 2020, then we don't need it, but if he gets re-elected that's the trigger. So we need to be ready."

"You said earlier you had something else in mind for me. What exactly did you mean by that?"

"Please Elizabeth, come sit down." Marcus moved back to his chair and took his seat behind the massive oak desk. He was re-establishing his authoritative command over Elizabeth and the desk and its prominence was a key element in his posture.

"We know you are still very popular around the country, particularly in the blue states, especially in the far west and the northeast. Your efforts in helping to rally the sentiment for secession will be of critical importance. In fact, we need you in order to be successful."

Now Elizabeth was feeling a sudden resurgence of confidence; of self-worth, that had been badly needed since her defeat in November. It was perhaps time to use her popularity as leverage.

"Where do you see me fitting into the new government?" She asked with her now famous, trademark smirk.

"Oh Madame Secretary. We see you at the very top of the new government. No one would be more deserving or more capable to lead our new country."

Elizabeth Morley liked the sound of that, as she smiled confidently.

"Tell me Marcus," as she glanced back to the map. "What are those green pushpins for? The ones that aren't located in any state right now. I count a total of 13 of them."

Pilfery sat back in his chair looking self-satisfied. "Oh those. Simple. Thirteen pins, thirteen states of the new Union. Historically, relevant and fitting, don't you think?"

Morley processed that and smiled. "Indeed. Yes, indeed."

President Stanton's first five weeks in office had come and gone, and never before had the Washington political scene nor the American people seen such a whirlwind of activity.

Stanton had set a blistering pace. A pace that was unprecedented at the federal government level. The long-time Republicans in congress were dizzy from the activity. The Democrats in congress were exhausted. The news media was on its heels having been publicly dressed up and down by President Stanton in two marathon press conferences that went on for hours.

The first such news conference was somewhat impromptu on a Friday afternoon in mid-February in which the President took the media to task for their negative-toned reporting relating to several of Stanton's Cabinet appointments that had been expedited through the Senate despite Democrat filibusters that went all day and in a few cases all night before a largely vacant Senate meeting room. It seemed only a few thousand insomniacs watching on C-SPAN had any interest or knowledge about what was being said about the President's nominee for Treasury Secretary and Head of the Environmental Protection Agency. But despite that, it took nearly three weeks for those appointments to be confirmed strictly across party lines.

And then there was Russia.

For months now the democrats were screaming that the Stanton administration had formed some sort of unholy alliance with Russia's Borzov government.

It began with the Russian hack of the Morley campaign and the release through Wiki Leaks of hundreds of damning emails written by Elizabeth Morley's campaign director, Scott Garrett.

There was everything in those emails. From the bias against, and sabotage of opposing Democrats' primary campaigns by the Leader of the Democratic National Committee, to the Campaign Director's sniping against his own candidate and Morley's apparent failure to connect with millions of working class voters.

It certainly seemed like the Russians were meddling in the American electoral process, yet there had been no evidence presented by any of the 17 U.S. intelligence agencies that a single vote had been altered or hijacked. Yet there was clear evidence that the Democrats had been attacked while somehow the Republicans had been spared. Was it poor security by the Democrats versus airtight security by the Republicans? It was likely never to be known for sure.

But one thing was sure. Plenty of scrutiny had been placed on the Stanton administration and their contacts with the Russians by the media since his election.

Stanton's National Security Director was particularly active in the months leading up to inauguration day and was caught in a series of half-truths and omissions that invariably led to a loss of confidence in him by Stanton.

The President figured it was best to cut his losses so on February 17th, the National Security Director was forced to resign leading the media to begin a feeding frenzy with regard to Stanton's relationship with Russian President Borzov.

It dominated the news for a week while leaders in Congress on both sides of the aisle called for investigations by both the Justice Department, and the Congress. This became the lead story on every news outlet, but dominated the airtime on CNN as the news shows airing all day and night suddenly became opinion shows. There was a steady stream of Democratic partisans both from the CNN news staff as well as former Prentice staffers, and Ex-Congressional members now turned political news pundits.

It finally came to a head on Friday February 24th when President Stanton announced he would hold a news conference in which he proposed the following. He would allow the attendance of one reporter from each of the over the air networks, ABC, CBS, NBC, plus one reporter from each of CNN, FOX, MSNBC, Univision, BBC, and a dozen or so major U.S. newspapers including the New York Times, Washington Post, and the Wall Street Journal.

The news conference convened around 1 pm and President Stanton took the podium and announced the ground rules for the news conference.

"I am here today to answer all of your questions on one topic and one topic only, namely

Russia and my administration's dealing and relationship with President Borzov's government. All other topics are off limits. And I have one additional rule I would like to impose, but only with your total agreement. I will stay here and answer your questions for as long as you like. But there is one condition. Once you leave the room, you or another member of your news outlet may not re-enter the room today to continue the conference. When you leave, you are done. When the last of you have left the room, the news conference is over and you report that I stayed as long as you liked and answered all of your questions on this topic. Then there will be no further questions to my administration on this topic until the joint Congress/Justice Department investigation is concluded. Then, we will convene for a follow-up news conference in which I will answer all of your questions once again. Is that agreed?"

There was a low rumble in the briefing room as the media members mumbled to one another discussing the terms of the President's proposal. After about a minute, the reporter from CNN, Josh Cantwell stood and asked to be recognized by the President.

"Yes, Josh Cantwell," the President said pointing in the direction of the CNN reporter.

"Mr. President. Just to clarify, you will stay as long as we stay and as long as we have questions. But once we leave the room, our role in the news conference is over."

"Yes. That is the idea. No bathroom breaks. Once you leave, you're done; you're satisfied. No re-admittance."

"And once we agree that you've answered all our questions, we will withhold any further questions until the investigation by the Justice Department and Congress is complete?"

"Yes. That is the proposal."

Cantwell looked around the room as, to a person, each of the media members present nodded and agreed. Clearly, many of those in attendance thought that when the President stopped to take a bathroom break, they would do the same. Surely, he would not deny them that and risk appearing to apply a double standard.

"Very well Mr. President. We will abide by your rules."

"Good. Since we are going to be here a while, I've arranged for some light refreshments for you. Notice in the back of the room there is a table with bottles of water, cups, and ice. Please help yourself and let's begin."

The questioning began at 1:20 pm.

The questions came fast and furious from every angle and addressed every aspect of Stanton's history with Russia, all the calls that had occurred between Stanton's team and anyone in the Russian government since Stanton had announced his candidacy nearly a year-and-a-half ago. There were follow-up and re-follow-ups and re-re-follow-ups. Nothing was off limits. Everything was surfaced. During the second hour of the conference, many of the reporters stepped to the back of the room for water, and quickly returned to their seats for more questions.

President Stanton himself went through two bottles of water in the first two hours.

When four o'clock rolled around, the conference was still going strong. None of the television networks covering the event, specifically CNN, MSNBC, and FOX had broken for commercials. This was truly an historical event in the making. After five o'clock, NBC, CBS, and ABC went on air to cover this most unusual of Presidential news conferences. At a little after 5:30 eastern time, after just over four hours of non-stop questioning, the first reporter, an older gentlemen from FOX News excused himself to use the bathroom. He was not re-admitted and the news conference continued.

At 6:20 pm three more reporters urgently left the room and sought out the nearest bathroom. They were done.

By 7:10 pm eastern time, the President was still standing answering questions, and sipping water. Amazingly, he was still fresh, alert, and in control. It had been going for nearly six hours without a stoppage, and the media members were quickly wilting.

At eight o'clock, the original cast of reporters that had numbered 36, had dwindled to four. All that remained were the BBC reporter, two of the newspaper reporters, and Josh Cantwell from CNN, who had not had anything to drink in the last two hours, hoping that his young strong, 38 year old prostate would outlast the President's 68 year old, but recently repaired prostate.

Cantwell, to see him, was clearly under stress, as he pleaded inwardly for the President to propose a bio-break. But it was not to be. The President kept calling on the remaining reporters. Eight thirty came and went. Seven hours now of continuous questioning, and there stood Stanton with barely a hair out of place, top button still buttoned, bright red tie firmly in place.

At 8:54 pm eastern time, the President called for the next question from the New York Times reporter and Josh Cantwell. The two looked at each other. They had had enough.

"We have no further questions Mr. President," the Times reporter said with obvious fatigue in his voice.

Stanton took a sip of water, and shot a glance to his Director of Communications, Charles Ryan, who had been in and out of the room on several occasions over the past few hours.

"Thank you gentlemen. I've enjoyed our time together. I'm glad that I was able to answer all of your questions. I wish you a very good weekend."

Stanton waited at the podium until the two exhausted reporters left the briefing room. As the door closed, Stanton gave a nod and a smile to Ryan, who smiled back with obvious pride.

How had he done it, wondered Ryan. Here was a man his age standing for nearly seven-and-a-half hours, drinking water, with no bathroom break. This had to be more than just shear will power.

"Charles, why don't you take a walk with me to the residence?"

The two moved through the hallway leading to the West Wing, through the Oval Office, where the President checked his desk for phone messages, and picked up his schedule of events for Saturday.

He scanned through the 15 messages waiting for him. Grabbed five of them that he felt were important enough to answer this evening and headed off to the residence with Charles Ryan in tow.

When he arrived in the residence, Chief of Staff, Ken Latimor was waiting with the President's personal physician, Vice-Admiral John P. Stevens.

The President sat down on the end of his bed in the Presidential bedroom that had been used by Lincoln, FDR, Kennedy, and Reagan.

Showing no emotion or expression Stanton unbuttoned his trousers and lowered them revealing a urinary bag that was strapped to his right thigh. At 750 milliliters, the bag was nearly full. At the top of the bag a tube extended up inside the leg of his boxer shorts, that he methodically dropped to his ankles.

He lay back on the bed as the Navy Surgeon went to work removing the urinary catheter he had implanted in the President of the United States nine hours earlier.

The President grimaced for only a second as the catheter came out. The urinary bag was removed and

disposed of by a Navy corpsman who was standing by
to assist the doctor.

"Thank you very much Admiral," was all the
President said as he pulled up his trousers.

"Thank you, Mr. President," replied the
Admiral as he and the corpsman left the residence.

The President left the bedroom and took a seat
on the sofa in the living room, glancing at his schedule
for Saturday, as the Chief of Staff, and Director of
Communications looked on slack-jawed.

Without so much as looking up from the
schedule, the President calmly uttered, "That'll teach
'em not to fuck with me."

Chapter 6 – Naples, Florida
March 4, 2017

Relations with the press cooled even more after the Stanton news conference of the week before. The President's physician and the corpsman assisting the doctor were both loyal republicans and were especially loyal to Stanton so they needed no urging by the President's Chief of Staff to remain silent about the President being catheterized for the news conference. Besides, both being soldiers, they were not about to jeopardize the chain of command, which in this case extended all the way up to the Commander in Chief. And as if that weren't enough as far as they were concerned it was strictly a medical matter, and confidential between doctor and patient. No one would ever know.

The press had been put in their place, at least temporarily, and was now on notice that Stanton could match wits with them and play hardball when he felt it was worth his while. It had been in this case. Stanton felt it was time to show the press he would not wilt under the unrelenting questioning. Furthermore, it demonstrated to Stanton base supporters that he was not a person to be trifled with. He was just as tough as the press, and Stanton's supporters ate it up.

Now on a warm breezy winter morning at the President's vacation home in the Port Royal section of Naples, Florida, the President was sipping coffee with his Chief of Staff, Ken Latimor.

"Ken, I've reached a decision on my Supreme Court nominee."

Latimor looked up from his copy of the New York Times, and leaned forward to give the President his full attention.

"I want Vasquez. I'm going to announce on Tuesday."

Vasquez was Antonio Vazquez. Judge for the 11th Circuit Court covering Florida, Georgia, Alabama, and the Virgin Islands appointed by George W. Bush in 2002. He was the perfect pick in Stanton's estimation. The son of Cuban exiles, who had fled Cuba just prior to Castro coming to power, Vazquez was born in the U.S. in Miami in 1962. He was conservative, but not flaming, as he tended toward more moderate views. He was Harvard educated, and a strict constitutionalist.

"Great pick, Mr. President. He'll keep the court conservative by a 5 to 4 margin. He favors a woman's right to choose, but is not personally in favor of late term or partial birth abortion, but will obviously uphold the law of the land. And he's also okay with marital rights for LGBTQ. So he'll withstand Democratic scrutiny on those two hot button issues. There's no chance he'll put Roe v. Wade at risk, which is good for you politically, and good for the country."

"Yes. He's a solid second amendment advocate, tough on crime, and because his parents came in to the country and became citizens through the normal legal process, he's big on border security and proper vetting of immigrants," Stanton added.

The President looked out over the waters of the Gulf and expressed some concerns though. "I'm bound to take some criticism though on his Nationality though."

"What makes you say that? He's Latino. Why would you be criticized for that?"

Stanton smiled, and glanced over at Latimor. "You know they're going to say something negative whatever I do. If I pick a Latino, they'll say, oh he's pandering, or why didn't he put more Latinos in his cabinet, or oh he's trying to make up for slamming the Latino judge in Indiana back during the campaign. If I don't pick a minority, they'll say oh he's just continuing his steady stream of white elitists. Isn't it obvious that no matter what I do, it will always not be enough, way too late, or due to an ulterior motive."

"Yes, Mr. President. You're right. That's the way the media works. They're biased. It's obvious. Everyone knows it—except them, and their loyal viewers on the left. They don't want to admit it for fear of having their objectivity questioned, or worse being accused of going easy on a sitting President. Look what they did with Prentice. They'd always throw a few tough questions his way, but he'd stall them with some long-winded non-specific answer that sounded good and statesmanlike, but had no real substance to it. But then there were always the puff pieces with 60 Minutes, or Oprah, and of course his and the first lady's appearances on the late night talk shows. Those were always love fests with the cool kids, and the media ate it up and so did the public because they wanted to be cool too." Latimor paused to give his boss a chance to digest those thoughts. Then he continued. "So the best you can do is show them with action, not words. Your words are never going to convince them. But if you bring jobs and grow the economy, and make Americans safer, that will be difficult to ignore or spin negatively to the American people. So let's just keep moving ahead and delivering on what you promised."

The Chief of Staff's words buoyed the President. It was what he needed to hear this morning six weeks into his Presidency with many of the polls showing his approval rating below 50%.

"All right Ken. What's next?"

"Your most important issue, Mr. President. Health care reform."

"Good. Where are we?"

Chapter 7 – Brooklyn, New York
March 4, 2017

Marcus Pilfery surveys the streets of Brooklyn out the taxi window as the cab snakes its way along Flushing Avenue. He had left his Brooklyn brownstone in the upscale neighborhood of Brooklyn Heights 15 minutes earlier.   He is on his way to a dinner meeting with his long-time friend Seth Dudley.

Pilfery and Dudley met at Cal-Berkeley and became fast friends and college roommates. While Pilfery chose a political career after Berkeley, Dudley chose Madison Avenue and a career in Advertising.

Dudley in a word is smooth. He is also shrewd and streetwise, but was not much of student. What he lacked in smarts he more than made up for with attitude and guile. He had grown up in Brooklyn a poor working class kid but had a blazing fastball, and wicked curve ball that lead him to Cal-Berkeley on a baseball scholarship.

There he met Pilfery. At first Dudley thought Pilfery strange, downright weird in fact. Here was this guy, a student of politics, and a real straight arrow. But Pilfery possessed something else, namely a knack for getting people to listen to him, and more importantly follow him. This was a guy, Dudley thought, who was going to go far, if not in politics, then in something else just as impactful. Dudley decided that Pilfery would be worth knowing in the future. And Pilfery decided that Dudley would be worth knowing also. Pilfery could see from Dudley's attitude toward him that Seth would be a loyal friend and would do anything he could to help him succeed. They decided to keep in touch after graduation.

Upon graduation they both returned to New York, Pilfery to Albany to begin his career in State Politics and Dudley back to Brooklyn where he landed an entry level Advertising position in a prestigious Madison Avenue Advertising firm that specialized in consumer products, especially in the area of sports and leisure.

Dudley had hit it off with one of the Account Managers during his interview process, who liked Dudley's jock persona. He felt the young graduate, with a marketing degree, and a real passion for all things sports, would be a valuable asset in developing advertising campaigns that were directed at young people with similar interests.

Seth worked directly under the Account Manager on ad campaigns for Gatorade, Nike, and Under Armor.

Seth quickly established himself as a clever marketer and became well liked in the firm and rose quickly through the ranks.

He was now directly managing five different clients, including Nike, and at 42 was one of the highest paid account managers in the firm.

All along he and Marcus Pilfery had stayed in touch as each built impressive, yet very different careers.

They spoke often and they and their families had vacationed together on several occasions to places like Disney World and the Outer Banks in North Carolina.

They often joked about how each of them would change careers with the other with Seth entering the world of politics and Marcus becoming an advertising mogul. Neither was serious as Seth was too much a capitalist to give up a lucrative career that allowed him to buy a million dollar brownstone in Brooklyn. And Marcus was too hell bent on achieving political power to throw away what he had in favor of writing ads for sports drinks or athletic shoes. Besides, he had inherited his grandmother's house in Brooklyn, which he updated and made his home when he was not in D.C. The home was convenient to the area airports and he could make the flight to Washington in less than an hour.

Now, however, each man was en route to a dinner meeting at the famous Brooklyn Steakhouse, Peter Luger's. A meeting that would change both their lives in a way neither had ever envisioned.

The cab made the turn northward onto Bedford Avenue and within ten minutes came to a halt in front of the restaurant.

Marcus paid the fare and headed through the front door for his date with destiny.

Chapter 8 – Brooklyn, New York
March 4, 2017

Seth Dudley had arrived early and was already seated at a four top in a quiet corner of the busy restaurant. The Saturday night crowd, largely comprised of groups of young professionals and couples enjoying a date night, was energetic and lively. Waiters smartly dressed in crisp white shirts and black neckties efficiently delivered plates of sizzling steaks and endlessly uncorked bottles of fine wines.

There were occasional bursts of laughter as the diners were enjoying a casual evening in the company of their well-healed contemporaries. Elections indeed did have consequences, but apparently not for this group of young progressives, who often spoke ill of the President and his capitalist agenda, but willingly fed from the same trough while consuming $200 bottles of French Bordeaux wine.

The clientele, many of whom were Morley voters and worked on Wall Street, had long gotten over the election of Stanton. After all they were the ones benefitting the most from the recent stock market rally since Stanton's election. Little had or would change in their worlds regardless of who ran Washington.

Pilfery scanned the room and spotted Dudley sipping a martini. He made his way across the room avoiding the path of a waiter carrying a tray of six plates of steaming food.

He greeted Dudley with a hearty handshake as Seth rose with a smile.

"Marcus! Long time no see," the affable Ad Exec said with just a tinge of sarcasm.

"Hello Seth. It's good to see you. Your looking well," Pilfery responded soberly.

"Yes. I've been spinning," Dudley said proudly.

"Spinning?" Pilfery said, looking puzzled. "What on Earth do you mean? Replied Pilfery, not focusing on the indoor cycling craze that continues to be all the rage.

Seth seemed disappointed that Pilfery had no appreciation for the rigorous exercise activity. "You know, riding a stationery bicycle, to music, indoors, with lots of other people."

The look on Pilfery's face indicated he was finally getting it. "Oh right, right. *Spinning.* Yes, of course. Well, it's working. You're looking fit."

The old friends sat, and the waiter was on them in a matter of seconds to offer drinks.

"Scotch, neat," Pilfery requested. Dudley ordered another martini.

"So Marcus, how long has it been? Six months? Last summer maybe? The Carolinas?"

Pilfery knew exactly how long it had been. It was last summer. The two families had been together in Corolla on the Outer Banks of North Carolina. Then came the election and the disappointment, and he and his fellow Democrats had gone into hiding over the holidays. Then after Stanton's inauguration, it had been a non-stop series of Senate confirmations involving the Stanton Cabinet. The two friends hadn't even spoken on the phone in two months.

"Yes. Corolla. Last summer," Pilfery replied quietly.

"You guys really took a beating in November, huh?" Dudley stated matter-of-factly while downing the last of his martini. "My God. What a shock? Stanton? I still have a hard time believing it. What the hell happened?"

"Yeah. Shit happens, huh? In this case a lot of it."

"I'll say. Morley must be inconsolable. Have you seen her?"

"Yeah. She's stunned. We all are." Pilfery stared out across the room, letting the words hang in the air during an uncomfortable silence.

The waiter arrived with the drinks and left menus as well.

"So what's on your mind Marcus?" Dudley said to break the funk that had suddenly invaded the conversation.

Pilfery took a sip of his scotch and held it in his mouth for a few seconds before swallowing it. The liquor soothed his throat and warmed him as it settled into his stomach.

"I've got a job offer for you Seth. Probably the most important job offer you've ever gotten."

The Ad Exec looked surprised. "Really. What kind of job offer?"

Pilfery looked Dudley straight in the eye. "One that could change the direction of this country forever." Pilfery's eyes fixed on Dudley while the Ad Exec tried to imagine what this could possibly be.

Pilfery looked away and prepared to take another sip of his drink. "Take a good long drink of that martini, and I'll tell you all about it."

The waiter returned for their dinner order. "Give us some time will you please?" Pilfery asked the waiter. "I'll flag you down when we're ready."

"Very well, sir," said the waiter as he headed off to his other tables.

For the next 40 minutes Marcus Pilfery explained the secession plan the Democratic leadership had devised. Dudley listened intently; at times visibly straining to process the myriad of reasons why the Democrats had believed this is what it had come to. It was as if he and Marcus were the only two people in the restaurant, yet he still looked around to see if anyone was listening to what Pilfery was explaining.

"Marcus, I understand the why, believe me I do. But do you think it's really going to be necessary? I mean Stanton is a loon. He'll never get through his first term, let alone be re-elected. Why plan this? How can you possibly do this? How do you even divide up a country as complex as the United States?

The look on Pilfery's face was stone cold. All good questions he thought to himself. "We underestimated Stanton once. We sure as hell are not going to do it a second time. We need to be prepared. And believe me it's going to take every bit of the next four years to become prepared. I'll tell you how we'll do it, but not here. Let's have dinner, but then go back to my place and I'll lay it out for you. But first I've got to know—will you help us?"

Dudley looked perplexed. "How? How could I possibly help you?"

"Listen Seth, this is going to be all about how we position this and present it to the people in the states we want to take with us. It's complicated, and scary. We have to sell the idea, make people want to do this and become passionate about it. That's where you come in. You can develop the communications plan and help us push this through the states legislatures. California will be easy. Probably places like Oregon, Colorado and Washington will be too. It's all the other states that are going to be the harder sell. It'll take a well-coordinated campaign to deliver the message and drive a groundswell of support. It'll take you to make that happen."

Dudley was concerned but intrigued. "Supposing I help you and you're successful, what does that mean for me? I mean what do I get besides, say money?"

Pilfery leaned forward in his chair and was virtually eyeball to eyeball with his long-time friend. "Power. Quite simply more power than you could ever imagine." The look on Pilfery's face was all it took to convince Dudley.

"All right. I'm in. I want to know more."

Chapter 9 – Naples, Florida
March 4, 2017

The President did not like what he had heard that morning about the Health Care bill from his Chief of Staff. Fringe elements on the right in the party had seemingly hijacked what the President had hoped would be a quick and effective repeal and replacement of the previous administration's signature health care law.

Stanton had sincerely wanted a health care law that would protect all Americans, especially the most vulnerable, while lowering the cost for all. But his proposed law had quickly become a political football for all concerned. The far right simply wanted to first gut the existing law and return to what simply hadn't worked prior to eight years ago. They argued first there should be a complete scrapping of the existing law and then a fresh start should be made on a new law. But they knew in their hearts that new law would never come to pass. It was merely a ploy to curry favor with their constituents by fulfilling their own campaign promises and ensure re-election. With a slim four-vote margin in the Senate, it would take eight Democratic Senators to enact a law that would be meaningful, fair, long lasting, and stand up to public scrutiny. The issue had become so politicized, that both sides would scarcely be able to look their constituents in the eye unless they each got exactly what they wanted. Compromise had long since faded from the political landscape in Washington.

Conversely, the Democrats were determined not to cooperate *at all* with the Stanton administration. They found themselves in exactly the same position that the Republicans had found themselves in eight years earlier. They would obstruct Stanton at every turn just as the Republicans had made it their very public goal to make President Prentice a one-term President. When they failed to do so in 2012, they essentially shut down any hope of meaningful legislation two years later by gaining control of both the House and Senate. President Prentice saw the writing on the wall and effectively withdrew from the legislative process with Congress, and proceeded to govern through executive fiat. As he had stated to the public on several occasions, "I have a pen and a phone," implying that he didn't need a dysfunctional congress in order to move his agenda forward.

So now the Democrats were merely returning the favor and Stanton was becoming increasingly frustrated with how governing worked, or didn't work, in Washington.

It was going on midnight and Stanton was sitting across from his Chief of Staff Ken Latimor. The two were sharing a drink in Stanton's Port Royal home. Earlier that evening the two had had dinner with their wives at the Stanton residence.

Prior to his election, Stanton and Lidia had frequently enjoyed dining out at Truluck's on fifth-avenue. But now as President, he was forced to remain at home while in Naples, as it had become too difficult to secure a radius around the popular fine dining spot in the heart of Naples' tourist district.

The foursome had dined on baked, locally caught grouper while they engaged in light, non-political banter throughout the evening.

Now, the two men had retired to the President's study for a nightcap, while the wives wandered off to enjoy the balmy night air by the pool out back. There they sipped Far Niente Dolce while enjoying fresh berries and imported cheeses.

The President was pensive, yet troubled about the pace of how things were progressing with his health care law.

"Ken, I don't like how Carlson and Prescott have come out and criticized my bill so publicly. It's not good for the party or the country. We look divided, not in sync, and the Democrats and their pals from CNN and MSNBC are jumping all over us." Carlson was Senator James Carlson; Republican from Texas and Prescott was Senator Harlen Prescott Republican from North Carolina. Both had sought the Republican nomination that Stanton would eventually secure through a dirty and hard fought campaign that had included lots of name-calling. Now both Senators were pandering to their constituents, as they were both up for re-election in 2018.

Latimor tried to soothe the President's ego, which was of above-average size. "Mr. President, this is just how the game is played in Washington. They're both taking the extreme case because they know their counterparts on the left are going to do the same thing.

It's all for show. They'll work with you. They just
need to demonstrate to their voters that they're looking
out for their interests. At the end of the day, the bill
will achieve all the objectives you set out on the
campaign trail."

"Well it better. I've got to deliver on those
campaign promises or people will say that I'm just
another politician who doesn't do what he says he will
do. What the hell do they want anyway?" Stanton
asked becoming more agitated by the moment.

Latimor paused and thought making sure to
carefully choose his words. "Mr. President, they are
trying to remove any remnant of the current law.
Their hope is to fully discredit the previous
administration's attempt to deliver quality, affordable
health care to all Americans. It's actually more
important to them to do this than to develop an
alternative solution. Their opposition to Prentice is
what got these guys elected in the first place back in
2012. The replacement of the law is secondary."

Stanton scoffed at the notion. "What crap," he
seethed. "This is exactly what is wrong with politics
and our congress. They only care about being re-
elected. Not about doing the right thing. This is why
we need term limits on these people in Congress. Hell,
they've got them on mayors, governors, and me. Why
the hell not on Congress?"

Latimor squirmed in his chair at the thought of
the President's suggestion. Term limits in Congress
had been brought up dozens of times over the years
but had never gotten any traction. And although

Latimor had never served in elected office, who in their right mind, he thought, would legislate themselves out of a job? And a pretty cushy job at that. At least, that's the way it appeared to the average citizen.

Congress was off the entire month of August and another month at Christmas. Then there was the spring recess. Not to mention the fact that congress was rarely in session on Friday. Monday was typically a travel day back to Washington from the home district. Even when congress was in session little seemed to be accomplished. No wonder congress's approval rating was worse than the President's.

If you were a House member and kept your nose clean in terms of scandals and towed the party line with your votes, you had the backing of your political party and more importantly political donors, and that meant money. Money to get re-elected, time after time. Some in the house had served a dozen or more two-year terms and if they chose could remain for a lifetime.

John Dingell, a Congressman from Michigan served a whopping 59 years in the House before retiring in 2015. The current longest serving Congressman is John Conyers also from Michigan who is in his 53rd year in office.

The "people's house" was not exactly what the founding fathers had in mind. When the nation was in it's infancy the notion of the House was that it was to be comprised of ordinary citizens coming from all walks of life. It was made up of farmers, ranchers, tradesmen, lawyers, engineers, doctors, teachers, and others of a variety of occupations who were there to represent the interests of the people from their home districts for a period of two years. Representation was done in a proportional manner meaning the more populous a state was, the more representatives it was allotted in the House. House members were there to bring forth new ideas from the people and act on their behalf by introducing bills to create laws. After serving, they were to return to their home district and were to be replaced by their neighbor who would then take a turn in government. That's why it was a relatively short two-year term. It wasn't meant to become a be-all, end-all career. Spend your two years, contribute to the nation, and return to your job.

No one, absolutely no one viewed it in those terms in modern America. It had evolved into a career and more alarmingly a place to become comfortable---and complacent.

The Senate is no better in terms of its members getting "dug in" for a lifelong career. The Senate was designed to function in an "advice and consent" role meaning it voted on and confirmed the laws the House had put forth before it went to the President for signature into law. The Senate could also establish treaties and confirm appointments of Cabinet members made by the President. As such, it gave equal representation and say to each state regardless of state size or population. A Senator's six-year term was established to provide for more continuity in terms of the advice and consent role, but despite this longer term, many Senators viewed their participation in government as something they could choose to do as long as they liked.

Senator Ed Markey from Massachusetts and Senator Orin Hatch from Utah, both currently serving, have each been in office for over 40 years.

And these are by no means exceptions to the general rule. As of 2015, there were 79 members of Congress who had each served for more than 20 years in office.

There is no doubt that if George Washington and Thomas Jefferson were alive today, they would be appalled at how Congress had evolved into its current state.

Latimor attempted to get the President back on point, meaning the proposed health care law. "Mr. President, I've been assured by the majority leader that it will just be a matter of a few days for the Senate version of the health care bill to be put up for a vote. He is confident that it will contain all your most important asks and that it will even win some Democratic support, enough to get to 60 votes."

Stanton was skeptical. "Well, we'll see. If it doesn't I'm going to have to visit the states of those Senators who want to block the will of the people and call them out."

Once again Latimor felt the uneasiness and was fearing the worst, as the Democrats seemed help bent on resisting Stanton at every turn and Stanton was not a man used to being told no.

Chapter 10 – Brooklyn, New York
March 4, 2017

By the time Marcus Pilfery and Seth Dudley got back to the New York Senator's brownstone it was going on midnight. They had stopped at a local Starbucks for coffee as Pilfery assured Dudley it would be a long night and require every bit of Dudley's concentration for what was to come.

The two made their way into Pilfery's study just off the massive hallway of the 100 plus year old home. The study was bordered on three sides by floor to ceiling bookcases. Opposite the door was a large window looking out into a side yard, and beyond that another newly renovated brownstone. On either side of the window were two, large, winged back leather chairs with a small table in between that held a dimly lit tiffany lamp.

"Please Seth, make yourself comfortable. Join me in a cigar?"

Dudley took a seat cradling his large coffee in his hands. "No thanks, maybe later."

Dudley watched as Pilfery prepared the cigar by using a clipper to remove the end and then light it with what seemed to be an overly powerful butane lighter. The cigar's tip glowed in the low light of the study as Pilfery took a series of long puffs. Smoke filled the air as Dudley sipped his coffee. They were both silent for a few minutes when suddenly Pilfery spoke up.

"So I've given you our reasons for a secession plan. Do you understand why it has to come to this? Why we have no other option?"

The look on Dudley's face spoke volumes. He didn't understand. He couldn't fathom why such an extreme measure was the only option for the Democrats at this point. Pilfery knew it was going to take more, much more in the way of background and explanation to get Dudley as firmly committed to the notion as he was.

He began. "First of all, remember, this is a contingency plan, but an extremely complicated, yet well thought out one. Because of the complexity of it and the numerous steps involved, we have to begin now, almost four years in advance of when we might have to invoke it."

He next took Dudley through the process. "First, there's getting on each target state's ballot for a referendum. That takes time. For most states we are aiming for November 2018. For a few where the sentiment for secession isn't as strong, namely New Jersey, Rhode Island, Maryland, and Delaware, we'll go for November 2019. Once the question is on the ballot and it passes, and you can rest assured it will pass, the rest of the country will see the resolve that we have. Many moderate Democrats will be aghast and incredulous. There's no way they'll go along. States like Ohio, Pennsylvania, Iowa, Michigan, and Wisconsin, which more times than not go Democrat in national elections will be opposed. But that will be of no consequence. We don't need them and we're not counting on them. However, places like Texas, Georgia, Florida, Tennessee, Kentucky, Kansas, and Indiana; that's who we're counting on."

Dudley looked puzzled and Pilfery could see it. He went on. "These are states that are either traditionally more conservative or are becoming more conservative, like Florida for example. Where do you think the majority of retiring baby boomers are going?" Pilfery paused giving Dudley a few seconds to consider the question. "They're going to Florida, in droves. And why? Well, put the weather aside for a moment. They're going because there's no state income tax. They're going because the government doesn't meddle in the lives of its citizens. Did you know Florida doesn't require you to wear a helmet when you're riding a motorcycle?" Dudley frowned in obvious disbelief. "It's true," continued Pilfery. "The citizens there don't want a nanny state. Don't want the government telling them what to do, and that sentiment grows stronger with each passing day as conservative boomers retire there. It's states like Florida, in addition to the obvious ones like Texas, that we're counting on."

Dudley leaned forward. "Counting on for what?"

Pilfery smiled as Dudley was going precisely were he was leading him. "For secession, we're going to need two thirds of the congress to agree to our plan. We'll obviously have California and its 53 house votes and New York and its 27. When you add up all 13 of our target states for secession, we figure we'll have

158. That's 36% of the total of 435. When you add in states like Texas, Florida, and the others I mentioned that adds up to another 96, which gets us close to 60%. We'll only need about another 30 or so representatives to get us to the two thirds. With conservative strongholds like Utah, South Carolina, Alabama, Louisiana, Arkansas, Oklahoma, and Montana, we'll easily get there."

Dudley was still skeptical. "What makes you think all those representatives are going to agree to let you secede? They won't want to see the republic carved up like a Thanksgiving turkey."

Pilfery re-lit his cigar while he seemingly pondered the question. But he was already prepared to answer such a question before the two men sat down. He puffed the cigar and took a long drag before expelling the smoke straight up. "Right now the Republicans control 52 Senate seats. Even if they were to gain another six in the next election cycle, which is highly unlikely, they'd still only have 58. To pass any meaningful, long lasting legislation they're going to need 60. No Democrat is going to support any Stanton sponsored legislation, so the Stanton agenda will be frustrated at every turn. Oh sure, he'll get some watered down bills passed as part of reconciliation, but to do what he really wants to do, like immigration reform and infrastructure spending, he's going to need money. And to get money, he's going to need Democrats. And he won't get them. I'll see to that."

Dudley offered yet another challenge. "I still don't think you can get enough Republicans to go along with breaking up the United States. I mean, after all, it's a pretty radical idea. They are going to need more of an incentive."

"That's where you come in Seth. We need you to spearhead a campaign that will make the Republican led congress, as well as their lemming constituents, want to, no make that, *beg* us to secede."

Dudley gave a crooked look at the Pilfery. "And how would I do that exactly?"

"With the right information. The right *selective* information."

Seth looked puzzled. He was not getting it.

Pilfery explained. "Seth, can I ask you to think like a Republican for a minute, a conservative Republican?"

"Sure, I guess so."

"Good. Now what are the most important issues of the day to you, ah, as a Republican, putting aside say jobs, the economy, and defeating terrorism. Everyone thinks those are important. So what are the issues that really divide the parties?"

"Oh. Ok," Dudley pondered the question for a few seconds and began to rattle off the issues. "Border security and immigration, second amendment rights, abortion, welfare reform, school choice, military spending, limited government—"

Pilfery cut Dudley off. "Ok, ok, that's good, you got it, you got it."

"Got what?"

"Those are the issues. Those are the wedge issues. Those are the issues we use to incite

Republican sentiment to push for our secession plan.
You construct a well-orchestrated campaign focusing
on those issues to capitalize on and build Republican
outrage against the 13 secession states."

Dudley was nodding now. He was beginning
to see it.

Pilfery continued. "So let's take border security
and immigration. Where are the majority of sanctuary
cities in the U.S.?"

"California, Oregon, Washington, Colorado are
probably a lot of them. Some in Iowa, New Mexico,
New York, New Jersey, Maryland, Massachusetts,
some in Florida."

"Ok, stop right there. How many of our
secession states did you name?"

Dudley thought for a few seconds and counted
on his fingers, I think it was eight."

"Yes. It was eight. And you know damn well
the other five have them as well."

"Yes Marcus, that's true, but so do a lot of red
states as well like Georgia, Louisiana, hell even Texas
does."

"Yes that's true Seth, but they're typically in
urban centers that vote blue. We don't care about
those for our purposes. We care about the ones in the
secession states. That's what we have to create more
awareness about with the average Republican voter."

"Ok. I see where you're going. We can craft
similar messages around the other wedge issues like
which states have the toughest gun laws, and the most
liberal abortion guidelines," Dudley reasoned. "So the

ads you want me to create will ideally raise Republican sentiment for allowing secession."

"Exactly. And in some places that sentiment already exists. We just want to intensify it, like California for example. Hell, a lot of Americans already consider California to be on the radical fringe anyway, what with Hollywood and all. It's spilling over into Oregon and Washington as well. Your aim will be to create an ad campaign that will make the average American think that maybe they'd be better off with two separate Americas. Better for them, and better for the new country."

Dudley didn't react. He just stared at Pilfery, expressionless.

He now understood. Then he spoke. "It sounds far-fetched."

"Does it? Was it far-fetched to think Stanton could turn the Republican Party on its ear and get elected President by defeating Elizabeth Morley?

Dudley had no response. Pilfery finished the scenario up for Dudley. "Once we have the congress, then we'll need the approval of 38 of the 50 state legislatures. That will be enough to secure the secession plan. By the way do you know how many state legislatures are Republican controlled?"

"Ah, no, not sure but I'd say about 30," Dudley guessed.

"32 to be precise. And do you know how many of the 13 secession states' legislatures are controlled by the Democrats?"

"All of them?"

"Close. In fact it's 10," said Pilfery with confidence.

Dudley did the math. "32 plus 10."

Pilfery cut him off before he could say it. "Sounds like 42."

"Sounds like enough." Dudley looked at the ashtray on the table. "I'll take that cigar now."

Chapter 11 - Wichita, Kansas
May 26, 2017

Benjamin Goodwin is up early this Friday morning before Memorial Day weekend. At 6:45 am the sun is already up and lighting the flat Kansas landscape as if it were the middle of the afternoon. The Republican junior Senator from Kansas takes a gulp of coffee and sets down the Kansas Jayhawk mug on the kitchen counter and heads out the back door for a morning run.

It is cool, but clear this morning and Goodwin is in good spirits having just returned from Washington, D.C. the night before for a long holiday weekend recess. He left wife Jennifer still sleeping at home as he set off for an hour of solitude on this brilliant Kansas morning verging on summer.

The last of President Stanton's cabinet nominations had been approved the three weeks earlier, leaving the Senate to focus on approving Stanton's nominee to the Supreme Court just last week.

The President's pick was not a particularly controversial one, but the Democrats, who were in the business of opposing *everything* Stanton did these days, made it controversial by dragging out, for public criticism, every circuit court ruling Judge William Canfield had ever made that supposedly trampled on the rights of the little guy.

After three days of tenacious questioning by the minority party, the Republican Majority leader in the Senate invoked the so-called "nuclear option" and ended a Democratic filibuster that prevented a vote on the Supreme Court nominee. As a result, the Republican leader called for a straight-up vote on Canfield requiring only a simple majority for his confirmation. Under this option, used just four years earlier by the Democrats to break a Republican filibuster on President Prentice's federal court judicial appointments, Canfield landed on the Supreme Court by a 52-48 vote. The vote furthered the animus felt by the Democrats since Stanton's election the previous November and sent the Senators home for a much-needed break from partisan politics.

As Goodwin made his way through the shady and winding streets of his suburban Topeka Kansas neighborhood, feet lightly pounding the asphalt, he replayed the events of the last four months in his mind.

President Stanton's bias toward action was unprecedented in Washington politics. The establishment had *never* seen anything quite like it. Washington was accustomed to politicians talking a good game on the campaign trail but then maintaining the status quo when they landed in office. Those few who were not simply content to maintain the status quo, but wanted real meaningful change, like Stanton's predecessor William A. Prentice, quickly learned how politics in Washington bogged down the best of intentions. For the first two years of Prentice's first term he had a Democratic majority in both houses and was able to get some things done, even without the support of Republicans. But once the House went Republican and the Senate followed, Prentice was paralyzed. His entire second term was ineffectual and was highlighted by a string of executive actions, which now Stanton was in the process of cancelling.

In addition to this Stanton was plowing ahead and calling for legislation from the Republican congress with respect to securing the border with Mexico, reforming health care, rolling back controls on financial organizations, and lowering tax rates for individuals and corporations with the hope of stimulating the economy. These were all issues on which he campaigned and was now pressing for in his first year in office.

Coming from the private sector, Stanton was accustomed to moving quickly and getting his way. Such was not the case in Washington and, Stanton was frustrated at the pace by which government moved. So, while the Republicans continued to fight amongst themselves on legislation, Stanton continued to do what his predecessor had done the four previous years, namely to effect change where he could through executive order.

First, there was the ban on immigration from countries in the Middle East which had unstable governments and which had been known terrorist hot spots. This action was quickly stymied by an activist federal court system that prevented enactment of the order leading Stanton to take his case all the way to the Supreme Court. Much to the dismay of the Democrats, the Court ruled five to four in favor of Stanton, with newly confirmed Justice Canfield breaking the tie in what otherwise would have been a four/four deadlock.

What was particularly disturbing for the Democrats was the fact that the Supreme Court ruling came a mere three days after Canfield's confirmation. The Court had been deadlocked on the issue for nearly six weeks, and Canfield's first order of business was to break the tie. This was a serious setback for the Democrats as it hardened the border and opened the door to potentially limit the flow of immigrants, undocumented or otherwise, into the country from all countries. Immigrants, who in most cases under any sort of eventual amnesty program leading to citizenship, would have been courted to become Democratic voters.

Next, the President threatened to reduce funding to so-called "sanctuary cities" for failure to cooperate with immigration enforcement officials in the apprehension and deportation of immigrants who had illegally entered the country. This further antagonized the Democrats as it reduced their political power and potentially struck a blow to their voter base.

And finally there was the Stanton order that withdrew the U.S. from the Paris Climate Accord. On the campaign trail, Stanton had called climate change a hoax invented by the left for their own political purposes. Although the data was irrefutable, Stanton refused to acknowledge that man-made activity, in the form of carbon dioxide emissions, was the primary reason for the warming of the planet and the rise of the oceans. No one really knew what he believed as he wavered between calling it a complete hoax, and sometimes saying the climate was changing but who knew how much was due to human interaction.

In any case, he didn't like the provisions of the Paris Accord as it called on the U.S. to immediately, albeit voluntarily, reduce its carbon emissions, while for example, a country like China will continue to increase its carbon emissions until 2030 before voluntarily beginning to reduce them. The accord also called on the U.S. to provide a disproportionate amount of funding relative to GDP to the Green Climate Fund relative to other polluting nations such as China and India. This, and a host of other inequities in the accord, caused Stanton to back out of the deal struck by his predecessor. He argued that it hindered the competitiveness of the U.S. in world markets and in turn hurt job growth in the U.S. This decision infuriated the Democrats, as Stanton was seemingly dismantling President Prentice's legacy at every turn.

As Goodwin turned for home concluding his five-mile run his head was swimming with the events of his first four months as a newly elected U.S. Senator.

Ben Goodwin is 52 years old, and an actively practicing Eye Surgeon serving in the U.S. Senate. After serving as a Medical Corpsman in the Marines and now nearly a 25-year career in medicine where he was able to make a difference in the lives of his patients, he embarked on a new mission where he believed he could make an even bigger impact on behalf of his fellow Kansans.

A graduate of Kansas University and Johns Hopkins Medical University, Goodwin is a model citizen. Married for 20 years to Jennifer, the couple have three children, two girls ages 16 and 13, and a boy aged 9. Goodwin has had a solid medical career as an Ophthalmologist in suburban Topeka with three other doctors.

Two years ago while attending a local Rotary Club meeting he had the pleasure of meeting his long time Congressman, Russell Chambers, at the gathering. Chambers was immediately struck by Ben Goodwin's intellect, charm, and likeability. So much so, that Chambers eventually put the bug in Goodwin's ear about running for the Senate. Then current U.S. Senator Robert Rollins was retiring in 2015 at the age of 83, after 36 years in Washington, and Chambers and his largely Republican colleagues from Kansas were looking for some new blood to come onto the political scene in Kansas.

The political landscape across the country was becoming more populist all the time and with the increasing distrust in Washington of Congress, it was becoming more important than ever to put forth candidates who were more like ordinary citizens. They had to be smart, likeable, squeaky-clean, and most importantly, they had to appeal to the ordinary citizen. This was particularly important in conservative Kansas where family values and a solid work ethic were important to voters. He was good-looking, tall at six-foot two, athletic, and soft-spoken. He reminded people of Kevin Costner with his kind of Field of Dreams, aw shucks, homespun charm. He was not brash but exuded confidence and this enabled him to quickly gain the confidence of his patients. Ben Goodwin fit the bill in every way—except one.

He believed in term limits for members of congress. In fact, he campaigned on that basis. His position was he would *run for* one-term. Six years to serve the people of Kansas in the U.S. Senate. He vowed not to actively campaign for a second term. If he did a good job and was true to his beliefs, he believed the people would recognize that and return him for a second term. But he would not waste his time or theirs by spending a year or more on the campaign trail. He would vote his conscience and would not pander to special interests or big money contributors. He was grateful to the voters who gave him a chance and he was determined not to violate that trust. He was truly unique to the political landscape of Washington.

The Republican establishment at first resisted this notion, but realizing his popularity, they agreed to look the other way. He won the office in a landslide against a career democrat from the state legislature. Goodwin had garnered nearly 82% of the popular vote in a conservative state where any previous Republican Senator had never won more than 70% of the vote.

When the voters felt he no longer was serving their interests, they would vote him out and he would go back to his practice. Ben Goodwin was perfectly fine with that and slept well each night knowing that he owed no favors to anyone.

When Goodwin made it to the kitchen door, he caught the aroma of bacon wafting through the warm morning air. Jennifer was up and busy making breakfast for herself and the three children.

"Hey Marathon Man, just in time for breakfast," she cheerfully remarked.

Goodwin smiled as he stood in the door way as he greeted his family. "Hey Jen." He looked at her fondly, leaned in and kissed her while she tended to what was on the stove. She gave him a contented smile as he turned to the kids. "How is everyone doing today?"

Goodwin was immediately greeted by the thirteen year old, Amanda. "Daddy!" The middle child hugged Ben around the waist as he entered the kitchen. He was clearly the apple of her eye, and she was quite clearly Daddy's girl.

"Hey slugger, how are ya doin'? Ready for the big game today?"

Amanda was already in her softball uniform. Today was her softball game, which Ben had always made it a point to attend before his election to the Senate. But since his election with much time spent in Washington, he had missed far too many of her recent games. Today would be different and he looked forward to taking her to the local middle school for her 10 am game.

"Hi Daddy!" 9 year-old Justin gushed as he looked up from his Cinnamon Toast Crunch cereal. Justin was also a ballplayer but his little league team was off today so he'd be accompanying Dad and Amanda to her game today.

Sixteen year-old Taylor casually looked up from her ubiquitous cell phone and the stream of text messages that were flowing from her gaggle of friends after school had ended for the summer the day before. "Hey Dad," she said with the understated cool of most sixteen year olds. Taylor absolutely adored her father, but like most kids her age, she didn't demonstrate it overtly.

"Good morning sweetie," Ben said earnestly. While Amanda was more demonstrative with her affection for her dad, which Goodwin loved, he would always have a special place in his heart for his number one daughter.

Taylor was a preemie. Born two months early in April of 2001. Jennifer was young and strong and working nights as many new nurses tended to do when just starting out. She had planned to work right up until the baby came, which was supposed to have been June 20th. But Taylor had decided that April 12th was as good as any day to be born. So she came early.

Initially she struggled physically as she weighed just a bit less than four pounds at 32 weeks. But after an extended stay in the NICU and under the watch full eye of many of Jennifer's colleagues at Stormont Vail Medical Center in Topeka, she went home after three weeks.

Having a surgeon for a father and an acute care nurse as a mother, Taylor progressed nicely in terms of her physical development over the coming months. By the time she reached her first birthday, she was in the 60th percentile for both weight and length. She was clearly a fighter. A trait, she no doubt had gotten from her mother.

Jennifer Perkins went to work as an operating room nurse at Stormont Vail right out of Kansas State University in 1995. It was there she met Ben Goodwin who was fresh out of residency and now working as an ophthalmologist, splitting his time between the hospital and the practice he had entered with three other eye specialists.

Unlike Ben Goodwin, who came from a solid upbringing in a traditional family, Jennifer Perkins had grown up in a series of foster homes. Her parents had died in a car crash when she was only five and the little girl was devastated. Left without siblings and no family that was capable of raising her, she floated through the foster system for thirteen years. She was fortunate to have had some decent families care for her over the years that gave her a good sense of values and an excellent work ethic.

She was very bright and attended K-State on an academic scholarship and became a registered nurse. She worked frequently on many of Ben's surgical cases and the two began dating shortly after they met. They were married in the spring of 1997 and four years later Taylor came along.

Amanda was born three years later, and with each of their careers now in high gear, the two decided to make Topeka their home for the foreseeable future. This would be where they would put down roots and raise their family.

Ben grabbed another cup of coffee and sat down at the table with the kids.

"Bacon and eggs, hon?" Jennifer offered.

"You bet. Thanks," Ben answered as he sipped coffee.

"The game is at 10 daddy. Will you be ready to go?" Amanda asked her Dad with wide eyes.

"Wouldn't miss it for the world," the junior senator from Kansas said looking proudly around the table at his beautiful family.

Chapter 12 – Washington, D.C.
June 21, 2017

Marcus Pilfery peers at the front page of the Washington Post and scowls. "Another congressional loss," he says shaking his head. "That makes four since Stanton took office. This has got to stop." He shakes his head again. "What the hell is our message anyway? What are we selling?" He says with frustration to Seth Dudley sitting across the desk in Pilfery's Senate office in the Capitol building.

Dudley is dumbfounded. He hesitates then answers. "Beats me. I don't know what you guys stand for. Probably just the opposite of anything Stanton wants."

Pilfery folds the paper and tosses it in the garbage can next to his large mahogany desk. He stands and steps around the desk and slowly begins to pace. "You know we used to have a very good message. It was clear and concise and compassionate. It was all about the little guy, the ordinary citizen. We cared about the ordinary citizen. Now," he shook his head and let out a disgusted laugh under his breath. "Now, we care about gender neutral bathrooms, and college safe zones, and all kinds of politically correct bullshit that the average guy doesn't give a rat's ass about. All he wants is a job that pays a living wage, and to feel safe in his home and community. That's what he wants and that's what Stanton promised him. And they believed him!" Pilfery stops pacing and

89

looks across the room toward the map, the secession map.

"When did we lose them? I don't even know. It just happened. Maybe it was during Prentice's second term. We should have seen it. We had no one waiting to succeed him. Just a collection of geriatric fools whose time had come and gone twenty years ago."

He approached the map and stared at it. Dudley sat in silence waiting for Marcus to finish venting and come out of his funk.

"It's too late now," he said somberly staring at the map and the multi-colored push-pins scattered across it. "This is our future, a new nation. A new nation comprised of people who share our vision, our values." He scanned the map noting the progress that had occurred in each of the thirteen states.

The secession question was already on the ballot in four states: California, Oregon, Washington, and Colorado. Petitions were circulating in four others: Illinois, Vermont, Rhode Island, and Connecticut, with approval for a ballot question expected by the fall.

The remaining states would be more difficult. In New York and New Jersey support was inconsistent. Although they were very blue states on a federal level, there were bastions of Republicanism in both states. In New Jersey, the northwest and north central counties, as well as some sections along the shoreline were Republican strongholds. The state had a history of electing Republican Governors, although the state legislature was usually staunchly Democratic. So New Jersey could be a coin flip depending on the mood of the citizenry, who were always laboring under the burden of some of the highest property and state income taxes in the country. Retirees with means were fleeing the state in droves for places like Florida and Arizona. But those with more modest means and deep family roots were destined to remain. And those were the people who a more socially sensitive government would appeal to. A government that favored the middle class senior and went after corporations was the key. Hell, they didn't care about jobs or schools anymore. All they wanted was to be comfortable in retirement.

New York was another questionable call. New York City was extremely liberal and the average person there wouldn't think twice about secession if they thought it meant the government would provide them more in the way of entitlements. In fact, New York had just passed a law providing for free college tuition at State Universities and the citizens were absolutely euphoric over the program. Upstate was a different story, at least in the rural areas. Those folks tended to be a bit more conservative, worked hard, and like their New Jersey counterparts were heavily taxed and unwilling to pay more. They'd be more distrustful of government, especially a new government that would be committed down the path of Nordic style socialism. Fortunately, those folks were severely outnumbered by the liberals in the urban centers, who were either wealthy enough that they didn't care if they paid a bit more in the way of taxes, or were part of the group that was happy to be living in an entitlement state and would be equally happy to take more handouts. New York would come around, but would take a different kind of messaging. Seth would figure that out, thought Pilfery.

Maryland and Delaware were questionable as well, but with the vast numbers of progressives living in the urban centers, there would probably be enough sentiment to swing them toward at least putting the question on the ballot for public consideration. Once it was on the ballot, there'd be no doubt the voters could be convinced that it was in their best interests to get out from under a Stanton presidency.

Then there was Massachusetts, cradle of the revolution. Home to John Adams, Samuel Adams, John Hancock, Ben Franklin, and Paul Revere. This state was a real dichotomy. On the one hand, the citizens were first and foremost patriots. They loved America and they loved their state even more. It was here during the battles of Lexington, Concord, and Bunker Hill that America set itself on the path to liberty. From one standpoint it would be difficult for the average person from Massachusetts to imagine themselves not being part of America. The abolitionist, woman's rights, and temperance movements all had their roots in New England with Massachusetts being in the forefront.

However, somewhere along the way during the mid-20th century, the intellect of the citizenry had been high-jacked by the ideologues who professed to care deeply about the working class and the puritan ethic, while at the same time they rode around in limousines, sailed yachts, and spent summers in fine mansions at places like Cape Cod or Martha's Vineyard. This misappropriation of the state's political conscience grew out of control with numbing swiftness fueled in large part by a university system that promoted its own liberal agenda while tolerating no other by crushing dissent. This created multi-generations of like-minded liberal thinkers who were unwilling to consider world-views other than those of the progressive establishment. It was an establishment that was becoming more extreme and unwavering everyday.

Pilfery thought long and hard about Massachusetts and what it would take to swing them into the secession movement. He had concluded that it would take an appeal to the patriot spirit in every citizen of the state. They must be convinced that a new revolution was upon them and that Stanton was in fact King George III, a modern day oppressor of sorts. He loved the romance of the notion and the obvious analogy, and was quite confident the people would as well.

So there it was. The goal was to have the public question on all thirteen states' ballots by no later than November 2018. That date, would be a "pre-trigger" point of sorts for the movement. Obviously with all 435 House of Representative seats up for grabs, failure by the Democrats to regain control of the House would be a green light to move the secession plan to the next step, namely beginning to lobby the congressional delegations for secession and formation of a new nation of thirteen states.

Chapter 13 – Washington, D.C.
June 29, 2017

"The ayes are 52, the nays 48. The motion passes."

The words of the clerk of the Senate hung like a shroud over the few remaining Democratic Senators who sat in disbelief in the Senate chamber. When the aye vote had reached 50, the majority of the Democrats swiftly and angrily rose from their chairs and quickly exited the chamber. It was the first time anyone could recall a Senate vote where all 100 Senators had actually taken their seats at the same time.

The bill under consideration was the repeal and replacement of the existing Affordable Care Act that had been enacted by the Prentice administration seven years earlier. After many contentious weeks leading up to the vote where extreme right-wing elements of the Republican Party had held up the bill because it did not go far enough in totaling dismantling the system President Prentice had put in place, the Senate had finally approved a new health care law.

The Democrats were furious while the Republicans were uneasy, but hopeful. President Stanton was downright boastful, tweeting within minutes of the bill's passage how he had accomplished in six months something that had taken his predecessor two years to achieve.

This enraged the Democrats all the more as they had had it with Stanton's incessant tweeting.

The bill, while touted as a new dawn in health care coverage, was for the most part a scaled-back version of the ACA.

While it removed the requirement that individuals purchase health care insurance, and repealed a tax on the manufacturers of medical devices, it preserved the essence of the pre-existing conditions provisions of the ACA, so that no one who was ill could be denied coverage. It did however penalize individuals who opted out of coverage more than once as a means of avoiding paying insurance premiums. It also preserved the coverage for children up to age 26 by remaining on their parents' policy.

The Medicaid expansion provisions, that provide federal matching funds, and had been a major concern for both Democrats and extreme right Republicans, had been revised to slow the rate of federal Medicaid growth by 2022. The agreed upon provision would only allow matching funds for existing participants with cost increases tied to the consumer price index. New entrants would have to be funded solely by the states without matching funds. It was this last provision that brought the rogue Republicans into the fold and allowed the bill to pass.

All of this was completely unacceptable to the Democrats as they maligned the bill by saying all the Republicans wanted was to throw millions of poor people off Medicaid. To the Republican's way of thinking it did nothing of the sort. All it did was slow the rate of *growth* in spending at the federal level and put the onus on the States for new participants after

2022. But in reality it meant the money would not be there for all new entrants who would have otherwise been eligible for Medicaid under the ACA. Those people would now have to be funded solely by the states, go to the open market for coverage, or do without.

Equally alarming to the Democrats was a provision that allowed a resident of any state to opt out of any specific insurance coverage that an individual deemed as unnecessary. So for example if a 60 year-old couple determined that they did not require maternity or family planning coverage, then they were not forced to buy a policy which offered that coverage. In essence, health insurance would become patient focused as opposed to a one size fits all.

And finally, the health insurance market was opened up to allow all companies to compete in any state they chose, creating more options for people and lower premiums with reasonable deductibles.

It remained to be seen if this last point would truly bring down costs, but companies like Aetna and Cigna were already talking about going back into markets they had left during the implementation of the ACA.

All told, the Congressional Budget Office had determined that the bill would save $200 billion over six years. And while the CBO had also estimated that 10 million fewer people would be insured over the next six years due to the slowing of Medicaid growth, Republicans had insisted that number was grossly overestimated due to the fact that many who were currently on Medicaid would find their way onto private policies that would now be just as affordable as a monthly cell phone bill.

The Republican Senator from Texas, James Carlson was quoted in the media as having said, "If a family of four can pay $200 a month so everyone in the family can have an iPhone, they should consider if it might be more important for that money to go toward health care insurance."

CNN had a field day with that quote as they assembled a panel of nine liberal commentators to lambaste the Senator for over an hour in primetime one Thursday night calling him insensitive and cruel.

The Democrat outrage over the passage of the Senate bill was more about the statement it made about the recent failings of the Democrats to influence policy, gain the confidence of voters, and win elections. President Prentice's signature legislation was now dead, and all it would take to bury it was for the House to approve the Senate bill, which was a virtual certainty according to the House Speaker and those in the most conservative wing of the House Republican party.

Marcus Pilfery along with his Democratic Senate colleague, Victoria Cheshire from Massachusetts, sat in utter shock as the Senate chamber began to empty.

Pilfery saw this as a watershed moment in the secessionist movement that was beginning to take hold across coastal blue state America.

"What do we do now? There's no stopping Stanton now. This will give him incredible momentum. Next is tax reform, then immigration reform. He's doing everything he said he'd do. How is this happening?" Victoria Cheshire forlornly asked Pilfery turning toward him.

Pilfery let some time pass to allow Cheshire to process her own questions. She was stunned and he saw this as the right opportunity to bring up the subject of secession.

"Victoria, can we meet in my office? I have something I want to share with you."

Cheshire studied the look on Pilfery's face and knew something profound was about to occur. She could not have imagined what was about to follow.

Chapter 14 – June 29, 2017
Washington, D.C.

Marcus Pilfery's pitch for secession to Victoria Cheshire had been as swift and well rehearsed as a vacation time-share presentation. Within minutes, Cheshire's head was spinning with timelines and strategies and a dizzying array of political issues that would serve as the various triggers and sub-triggers for approaching the remaining thirteen states that needed to be won over for the plan to succeed.

Pilfery had specifically waited for the repeal of the ACA as the trigger to approach Cheshire. Years before, Massachusetts had lead the nation with a health care law that had set the table for the national health care law. Pilfery knew that repeal of the ACA would strike a chord with Cheshire and the people of Massachusetts.

Indeed, it had. By the time he had finished his appeal to Cheshire, she was so whipped up emotionally she was ready to secede right then and there.

"That bastard Stanton! He doesn't realize what he's doing to millions of people who rely on that health care law. There are hundreds of thousands of people in my state who are immediately going to feel the pinch. He can't be allowed to get away with this!"

"No Victoria, no. We won't let it stand! We can't and we won't!"

"Tell me Marcus, what's next? How do we move this forward?"

100

"It's really quite simple. You speak to the Governor and you let him know of a movement that is currently forming to put secession on the ballot in 2018. By the way, you should also speak to Senator Mumphrey. Convince him to come on board with us, but don't over-hype it at this point. Tell him it's just a public question for now. Nothing definitive. It's just a contingency if we don't gain back the White House in 2020. But we have to be ready to move. These things take time so we have to start now. I can speak to him with you if you like."

"No. That won't be necessary. Senator Mumphrey and I see eye-to-eye on most things. I'll make him understand."

"Good Victoria, I knew we could count on you," Pilfery said with a contented, knowing smile.

"The ayes are 55, the nays are 45. The motion passes."

For the second time in two months the Senate had passed a major piece of Stanton endorsed legislation. This time it was income tax reform. It was sweeping and dramatic to say the least, and this time three Democratic Senators had broken ranks and had come along with the Republican majority.

The three in question were all from states that Stanton had carried in 2016 and were all states where companies and jobs had been leaving steadily during the previous eight years of the Prentice administration. Not surprisingly, all three of the Senators had just been elected in 2016 and would not be up for re-election until 2022; plenty of time for the tax cuts they had voted for to hopefully bring back companies and jobs and make the voters forget they had voted with the Republicans.

First there was Thomas Kellerman from Pennsylvania whose constituents in the western part of the state were the hardest hit as many of the jobs related to coal and steel had dwindled over the years. Stanton had promised to bring jobs back to Pennsylvania and would do so with a major corporate tax cut. In fact, the Senate bill cut the corporate tax rate from 36% to 22%. This rate had ended up being a major point of negotiation all throughout the summer with the hard line Republicans pushing for 15% while the most left-leaning Democrats wanted to stand firm on 36% and not give the corporations any concessions. Most of the Republicans favored a 20% rate, but also felt it important to bring along some Democrats so they could show America that it was truly a bi-partisan effort. They finally settled on 22%, but the Republicans won a major victory with allowing corporations who had cash that had been earned overseas to be repatriated to the U.S. at a modest 15% rate.

But the most significant feature of the tax bill affecting corporations, and the final impetus that sealed the deal for the three Democrats, was the creation of a jobs tax credit. Many of the moderate Republicans as well as the three Democrats were concerned that merely cutting the corporate tax rate would only result in corporations using the benefit to buy back their stock, increase their dividend to shareholders, or simply pay their executives bigger bonuses. So to provide an incentive for job creation, the jobs tax credit was inserted into the bill.

It provided a 10% tax credit on every new job created and *maintained* for a period of four years. Quite simply if you hired ten new workers and paid them an annual salary of $50,000 each, for a total payroll increase of $500,000, then the corporation was given a $50,000 reduction in their income taxes. To prevent companies from taking the benefit and then firing the workers the next year, the four-year commitment string was attached. Failure to maintain the job for four years resulted in an immediate penalty of 20% of the full year salary. So companies would add jobs thoughtfully with an eye toward maintaining them over the long-term. Critics argued it wasn't perfect, and that companies would find a way to manipulate the outcome, but it directly tied a tax incentive to job creation. So the moderate Republicans went for it along with the three Democrats.

Kellerman came on board in the eleventh hour when these rates and the credit had finally been agreed to. Kellerman was only 52 and was serving his second term in the Senate, and was very much interested in serving a third term, so he climbed aboard the Stanton express and hoped to ride it all the way to retirement via the jobs the bill would bring back to Pennsylvania.

Then there was Julia Novak, the first term Senator from Ohio, which had also been decimated with job loss and a crumbling infrastructure, and which went surprisingly to Stanton in 2016.

Novak, only 43, had been a partner in a successful Columbus law firm and had been elected on the premise of bringing jobs back to Ohio, but just as importantly promised voters to repair and replace Ohio's crumbling bridges and roadways. In exchange for her support of the bill, she was promised a major voice in the President's upcoming national infrastructure legislation that would be up for vote in the fall of 2017. She hadn't yet come under the influence of the party loyalists, and like Kellerman, was insulated from election for another five years.

Finally, there was Richard Morgan from Michigan, the state that had put Stanton over the top in the election. Michigan, of all the so-called rust belt states, had been the hardest hit with job loss. In some of the urban centers of the state like Detroit and Grand Rapids, unemployment was as high as 20%. The tax base had shrunk and as revenues declined so did money for bridges and roads.

The state was teetering on bankruptcy, and Morgan, now in his fifth term as Senator, was desperate to save the state he had grown up in and served for over 35 years as both a State and U.S. Senator. He wasn't planning on a sixth term so he didn't feel beholden to the Democratic machine. Instead, he wanted to finally vote his conscience and do the right thing for the people of Michigan. That meant partnering with the Republicans to get something done that would finally set Michigan on the road to recovery.

He too, like Novak from Ohio, was offered a seat at the table when the infrastructure bill came up for vote later in the fall. It was amazing to Morgan how liberating it was to not be thinking about running for re-election, but instead to be creating legislation that would make a difference in his state.

The tax bill had also lowered tax rates across the board on all Americans, including those at the top. The lowest tax rate was now 8% on individuals earning up to $52,000. There were only three other tax brackets namely 12% for earnings up to $125,000; 20% for earnings up to $350,000; and 28% for individuals earning over $350,000, or couples earning over $700,000.

In addition, virtually all of the exotic tax deductions, particularly those related to passive investment losses had been eliminated. So it was no longer possible for those making millions of dollars to deduct huge losses on bad investments and avoid paying any tax. Those types of deductions had been eliminated in exchange for the lowering of the tax rates and ensured everyone paid some form of income tax that would be regarded as measured and rational.

The only deductions that survived were the mortgage interest, property tax, and state income tax deductions, along with the medical expense and charitable donation deductions, but even those were phased out for those earning more than $350,000 so as to prevent those who earned millions from making huge donations resulting in no taxes due.

Finally, the rules surrounding establishment of charitable foundations, trusts, and several other popular tax shelters in order to claim huge deductions were tightened up, so that *no one* who had any significant income could avoid paying taxes.

Everyone now had skin in the game, and what was even more impressive was that this tax bill was projected by the Congressional Budget Office to reduce the federal deficit by $800 billion over a six- year period.

Even the Senior Senator from Vermont, who was a self-proclaimed socialist, admitted in private that he liked the bill, although he couldn't bring himself to vote for it along with the Republicans. After all, even he had to save face with his constituents.

It was President Stanton's desire to put $400 billion of the savings, along with the $200 billion from the healthcare bill, back in to infrastructure, which was now the next thing on which he set his sights.

While the majority of both Republicans and Democrats now believed the tax code was much more simple and fair, many Democratic Senators and House Representatives, particularly those from the coastal blue states were uneasy. It was presumed their uneasiness was due to their fear of coming under attack by rival democrats who would look to unseat them in congress in the upcoming election cycle for not digging in their heals against the Republicans.

In actuality, the uneasiness was due to the fact that many of those coastal blue states were now starting to see the groundswell of public support for secession. By the time the President would sign the tax bill into law, a total of four states would have secession on their ballots for the upcoming November 2017 elections.

Chapter 16 – August 31, 2017
Washington, D.C.

The three men gathered in the Senate office wing of the Capitol Building are enjoying cigars. Smoking is strictly prohibited in the Capitol building, but this is a special occasion that warrants this slight breach in protocol.

Senator Harlen Prescott, Republican from North Carolina, and Senator Ben Goodwin, Republican from Kansas, sit across from the desk of Senator James Carlson, Republican from Texas, and Senate Majority Leader.

"Gentlemen, now that's the way to begin the Labor Day weekend. Congratulations on the passage of the Tax bill," Carlson says while he sends a puff of pungent smoke into the air above his desk.

Prescott, a hardline conservative, seized on the comment to gloat over yet another Republican victory early in Stanton's administration. "Did you see the looks on the faces of those Democrats when the tax bill passed with three of their own coming along. They were absolutely despondent, and I loved it."

Goodwin's reaction was more sober, if not conciliatory. "It's not wise to take too much pleasure in the defeat of our opponents. They are, after all just that, our opponents, not our enemies."

Prescott bristled at the apparent naiveté of the junior Senator from Kansas, and took the opportunity to enlighten him about what he and his fellow Republicans had lived through during the prior eight years of the Prentice administration. "They were the ones, Ben, who called *us* their "enemies" and shit all over us with their liberal agenda whenever they had the opportunity. First it was that ruinous health care bill, then the knee-jerk banking regulations, then the restrictions on energy exploration and the onerous environmental restrictions.

They never once took any of our positions seriously when they had the majority in Congress. What did Prentice say when he took office and called the Republicans up to the White House for a sit down? Elections have consequences."

Prescott seethed with indignation as he studied the cigar in his hand. "Well, he was goddamned right about that. Now the shoe is on the other foot and we have control. Time for them to deal with the consequences of last November," Prescott took a long drag on his cigar as Goodwin looked at him incredulously.

This, Goodwin thought to himself, was what was wrong with Washington. The partisanship and posturing for absolute political power to the point of destructive polarization was unrelenting. And for what, he thought, to placate the constituents to the point where getting re-elected was all that mattered.

Voting your conscience and doing the right thing was not the order of the day. Both sides were guilty of it, and Goodwin wondered if it would ever change. Probably not, he thought. Not without some cathartic event that would change the political landscape forever. Little did Goodwin realize that the country was on the path to that event and that the upcoming off-cycle, and otherwise insignificant, fall elections would set the table for such a change.

Chapter 17 – Washington, D.C.
November 8, 2017

Eileen Pilfery was up early this morning. Her husband Marcus had been up late the night before awaiting election results from California, Oregon, Washington and Colorado. It wasn't the election of anyone in particular, but more importantly the vote on the public question relating to secession on each of those states' ballots. It was all he, and Seth Dudley, had been obsessing about the past week. Dudley had stayed over and was now asleep in the guest room of the Pilfery's brownstone on this sunny, but cool November morning.

As Eileen pulled together a breakfast of scrambled eggs, bacon, toast, and coffee, Marcus was up, showered, and now dressing for his noon shuttle flight back to Washington. She heard him moving about upstairs, as the brownstone's hundred-year old floorboards creaked revealing Pilfery's movements around the bedroom directly above the oversized kitchen.

A small, LCD TV sat on the kitchen counter and was tuned in to one of the morning news shows. Eileen glanced at the set every now and then as she fried bacon in an electric fry pan.

The hosts were particularly upbeat this morning in stark contrast to their demeanor one year earlier when Oliver Stanton had upset Elizabeth Morley in the Presidential election. One host, in particular was extremely animated this morning as she gushed false concern about the results of the public question that had succeeded the night before in the four western states, calling it a vote of no confidence in the Stanton administration. She went on to comment ominously that this was yet another show of resistance to his conservative agenda and further evidence that President Stanton was tearing the country apart.

Her sidekick, was a bit more restrained, but was having difficulty containing his exuberance as he viewed the overwhelming rejection of the Stanton agenda in those states as affirmation of his own decision several years earlier to gravitate toward the Democratic Party.

The panel accompanying the morning hosts was the usual collection of progressive pundits and political malcontents who made it their regular practice to scoff and smirk at anyone or anything that didn't align with their worldview. This morning, after approval by four states to inch toward secession, their vitriol was particularly snarky as they feigned concern for the future of the republic. "Look at what President Stanton had driven the fair-minded people of California, Oregon, Washington, and Colorado to do in desperation in response to his hopelessly cruel and divisive agenda," one columnist from the Boston Globe commented as the others gasped in horror at the thought of a secessionist movement.

Another just shook his head and proclaimed this a truly sad day for the country, and wondered aloud what the founding fathers would say on this sorrowful morning.

While they all outwardly expressed their sadness and outrage, inwardly they were excited, no make that titillated, by the idea of a someday, separate Socialist United States of America. Yes, that's what it must be if they were to be forced to endure another seven years of Oliver Stanton, and thereafter, his Republican successor.

They had all come to the realization shortly after Stanton's election, that the Democrat's agenda was not resonating with most Americans. Most people cared more about having good jobs and secure borders than they did about green energy and gender-neutral bathrooms. And the Democratic Party, with each passing day was being hijacked by the extreme leftwing, and could not hope to gain back the confidence of the majority of the American people anytime soon, particularly with Stanton managing to push his agenda through Congress.

Employment was up, consumer confidence was up, jobs were coming back to the U.S. and the stock market bull rally was continuing to bolster people's 401K balances, and give them hope for a brighter future.

Eileen watched the panel with odd curiosity and couldn't quite fathom the direction in which the conversation had gone. Was secession really the right path? Were things really that bad under Stanton, or had we really become two separate countries?

Eileen McCormack had met Marcus in 2003 while he was serving in the New York State Assembly.

Eileen had graduated from the State University of New York at Albany with an Information Technology degree and had become a free-lance web designer. It was through her development of the State's web site that she had met Marcus. It was love at first sight for the two and they were married six months later. Two years later in 2005, their daughter Lauren came along just around the time Marcus was making his Senate bid. The two moved downstate to Brooklyn where Eileen continued her work as a web designer. Between his Senate salary and her thriving web-design work, they were able to buy the brownstone fixer-upper. Eileen divided her time over the next five years raising Lauren, juggling contractors, and building her design business. She was tireless, organized, and extremely bright.

Marcus spent the weeks in Washington, and was home on weekends, and also during the very lengthy congressional recesses.

They enjoyed life, each other, and their little girl. And as the years passed neither was too concerned with adding to their family. They loved their life style and were content to have it continue.

She listened intently with concern as the political pundits discussed additional movements now afoot in Illinois, Vermont, Massachusetts, Connecticut, New Jersey, and New York. Yes, her beloved state of New York. Buffalo, New York was where her parents had raised her and her two sisters to be proud, patriotic citizens. Her father was a retired Buffalo police officer and her mother taught sixth grade for 42

years and was now also retired. The two had left
Buffalo for warmer winters in Bonita Springs, Florida,
just north of Naples and the Stanton vacation home,
that now served as the President's weekend retreat.

What would her and Marcus' life become if this
incredible movement toward secession were to become
a reality? She couldn't imagine it.

She heard Marcus bounding down the stairs;
turn the corner and head toward the kitchen.

"Good morning sweetie!" Marcus Pilfery
beamed as he planted a kiss firmly on the lips of Eileen
as she leaned in toward her husband while holding the
rubber spatula away from Marcus's best dark blue suit.

"Well, you look extra special this morning
honey. Something big going on today?" Eileen said
with a smile.

"Yes, something very special indeed, but it's a
surprise," Marcus said with an air of mystery to his
voice, and a crooked smile.

"Oh really, what kind of surprise?" Eileen
played along, but Marcus was not showing his hand.

"Oh, you'll see," he said continuing to build the
suspense.

"Come on Marcus, what is it? Or else," Eileen
said as she playfully advanced the egg-laden spatula
toward the Senator's freshly shaved face.

"Hey watch it!" he laughed as he ducked out of
the way and moved aside to pour a mug of steaming
hot coffee. "Ok, ok," he relented as she stood smiling,
but still wielding the greasy spatula.

"Alright. Yes, you should know. I'll tell you," he said taking the spatula gently from her hand and setting it down in the pan.

They were now face to face and Marcus Pilfery's demeanor had changed to one of complete seriousness. He put his arms around her waist and pulled her in even closer. Eileen's face surrendered the smile and her eyes were now fixed firmly on her husband's face.

"Last night's vote, the secession question, was a test case. It was a test case to see if fair-minded Americans from all walks of life want an opportunity for a better life, a life where their government cares about them and their kids instead of billionaires and big business."

Eileen was deadpanned, listening, almost squinting, and trying to understand where Marcus was taking this.

"Eileen, most people don't realize what last night means to the country. This is not just some isolated group of fanatics talking about breaking away from the United States. This is a real movement, and it has momentum. Momentum we can build upon, that *I* can build upon, with you alongside me. I'll be giving a news conference today at 1 pm to talk about my support for the New York petition for secession.

Eileen now understood what it all meant, and her look became mournful. She gently looked away and retreated to the stove where she removed the pan from the burner and extinguished the flame. She turned back toward Marcus, her eyes now glazed with

tears. She knew now. For Marcus, and the country,
there was no turning back.

Chapter 18 – Washington, D.C.
November 8, 2017

President Stanton and Chief of Staff Latimor had been up late the night before watching the election coverage from the East Wing residency. Obviously, they had known well in advance about the public question on the ballot of the four states, the President now endearingly referred to as the "mutineers". But what he and Latimor had grossly misjudged was the populace's appetite for seceding from the country.

He and Latimor watched in astonishment as, county by county, for each of the four states, the votes were tallied, and the results reported with equal astonishment by the likes of Anderson Cooper of CNN, Rachel Maddow of MSNBC, John Dickerson of CBS, Megyn Kelly of NBC, and Brett Baier of Fox News.

No one, not even the most seasoned of political pundits from any of the news outlets had anticipated such a lopsided victory for the secessionist vote.

Colorado's vote was the closest as the public question was passed by a 53% to 47% margin. Washington and Oregon were decisive margins with the question passing 56% to 44%, and 59% to 41%, respectively. But the stunner of the night was the result in California where the measure passed by a whopping 63% to 37%.

Many of the Hollywood elite had come out in support of the public question. Several, who were quite politically active, appeared in commercial spots urging the citizens of California to get out and vote, and send a message to their representatives, and to the President, that Californians were not happy with the direction of their government. Privately, none of them actually believed in secession, or that it would even become an eventuality, but they couldn't resist the free publicity it would provide to each of them, nor the adulation it would surely deliver from the their legions of misguided, misinformed fans. They would be viewed as "hip" and "cool" to stand up and resist the Stanton agenda, and the fans loved that these larger than life stars seemingly cared about the average American and their welfare.

President Stanton had asked Latimor to gather the Republican Leadership in the Oval office just before 1 pm eastern to hear their reaction to the election results. Latimor also had become aware that the Senate Minority Leader Marcus Pilfery would be appearing on CNN at 1 pm with a major announcement relating to the election results of the night before, so Stanton wanted the leadership in his presence when the announcement came down.

So, now gathered in the Oval office are the President, Latimor, Speaker of the House Gordon Garrison of Kentucky, House Majority Leader, Brent Locker from Wisconsin, and Senate Majority Leader, James Carlson, from Texas.

The Congressional leaders relaxed on the two opposing sofas while the President and Latimor sat side-by-side in arm chairs just in front of the Resolute desk.

The Resolute desk was a gift of England's Queen Victoria to Rutherford B. Hayes in 1880. It was constructed from the timbers of the British Arctic exploring ship Resolute, and has been used in the Oval office by many U.S. Presidents including Franklin Roosevelt, John F. Kennedy, and President Stanton's predecessor, William A. Prentice.

A large, flat-paneled television is at the far end of the room opposite where the President is seated and is tuned to CNN with the sound on mute. The on-screen reporter is on the left side of a split screen with the right side showing an empty podium in the Capitol building. Reporters are gathered all around obviously awaiting the arrival of Senator Marcus Pilfery.

As usual, CNN has a panel of eight; count 'em, *eight* commentators gathered on the set. It is eerily reminiscent of their election night coverage when the nine gathered that night had anticipated an historical victory for Elizabeth Morley, only to be stunned into disbelief by Stanton's surprise win.

Today, they have been chattering incessantly about the astonishing election results last night out west, and they are eagerly waiting to hear what the Senate Minority Leader's comments will be.

Stanton begins the dialogue. "What exactly do you guys make of this situation?" he matter-of-factly asks while glancing at the T.V. nervously.

Senator Carlson is first. "Mr. President. This was the first desperate step by the opposition in a process with a result that will never see the light of day. It was a "feel good" moment for a bunch of crack-pot radicals that won't gain any traction whatsoever."

Stanton let the words hang in the air for a few seconds, nodded slowly, and seeing that Carlson had little else to say, looked next to Speaker of the House Garrison. "Gordon, what do you think?"

Gordon Garrison had been Speaker of the House for the last two years of the Prentice Administration and was a pragmatist who always looked beyond the surface. He assumed nothing and took nothing for granted. Eight terms in Congress with having to win re-election every two years will do that to you. He chose his words carefully and always guarded against coming off as arrogant or half-cocked.

"Mr. President. While I agree with Senator Carlson that it will be nearly impossible for this to lead to anything remotely impactful in terms of a widespread movement for a call for secession, I must caution us when it comes to being too sure about the will of the people in terms of deciding the political future of the country. Things can change rapidly, and profoundly, and seemingly without much warning. With all due respect, sir, you are testimony to that change. The country was ready for you and rejected the status quo. It can happen at any time."

The President stared blankly at Garrison expecting more, but getting nothing. He pressed the Speaker. "Gordon, what are you saying we should take away from the passage of this public question in these four states?"

Garrison shifted in his chair knowing that the President was on to him in terms of wanting to know what action should be taken in response to the situation, or at a minimum, what should the President say to the American people about the passage of the public question.

"Mr. President, I say we acknowledge it as a product of a free democracy where the voice of the people must always be heard and given weight. We don't criticize it, we don't reject it, and we don't, above all else, dismiss it. You accept it and you use it as incentive to work for the betterment of all Americans, especially the citizens of those four states. You acknowledge that you are accountable for winning the trust and support of all Americans, and you pledge to make the country more united than ever."

Stanton thought for a few moments, and gave his signature pout that he wore when he wanted to demonstrate that he was deep in thought and weighing his options. He mostly agreed with Garrison's assessment in that he must keep the country united, while acknowledging the right of the people to dissent, his inner voice was telling himself something altogether different.

He long felt the people of California were essentially a lost cause when it came to sharing his, or any other Republican's, view of the direction in which the country should taken. He never stepped foot in California during the campaign, and there were counties that were so hopelessly liberal and committed to liberal ideals, that no Republican, not even a moderate Republican, would ever stand a fighting chance in changing the minds of the electorate there.

California had casually talked for years about secession, but no one had ever taken the movement seriously, that is, until now.

The vote had been overwhelming, almost a full two-thirds of the electorate had voted to secede. Stanton couldn't help but ask himself would the greater United States be better off without California?

Stanton said nothing to Garrison. He next turned to Majority House Leader, Brent Locker. But as he did, the CNN coverage shifted to full screen coverage of Marcus Pilfery. Chief of Staff Latimor reached for the remote and turned on the sound. All eyes in the room shifted to the television image of Pilfery as he stepped to the podium.

Chapter 19 – Manhattan, N.Y.
November 8, 2017

Seth Dudley stood outside the office building on Madison Avenue he had been working in for the last sixteen years. Operative word, *had*. He had just given notice to his firm that he was resigning.

His last day would be the day before Thanksgiving. He would only need a few weeks to put his affairs in order and to transition his clients to the well-trained team of understudies he had always been grooming for such a day. Funny, he thought it would be the day when he had had enough of the advertising game, and had accumulated enough money so that he could go do something else. Whatever the hell he wanted is what he used to say to his wife of twelve years, Gretchen, when she asked him what he wanted to do next.

But he hadn't had enough yet, not of advertising. He still enjoyed it plenty. The power and the influence he wielded with his clients and the consumer was like an aphrodisiac and he was far from having had enough of that.

The money was another story. He hadn't accumulated enough yet. Although he had worked sixteen years in advertising, with the last eight being as a Vice-President on the most elite of accounts, he had managed to accumulate a portfolio of about only $300,000, not even enough to payoff the mortgage note on the Brownstone, which sat at $700,000. Not a bad nest egg for most 42 year olds with another twenty or so years of productive work ahead of them. Yet not nearly enough to support the lifestyle he, Gretchen, who also worked in advertising, and their son, Justin, age 9 had grown accustomed to over the years should he decide to pack it all in.

He had been earning over $300,000 a year the past five years. But first there was the Brownstone that set them back $1.1 million. Then, the renovations followed, totaling another $200,000. There were the elaborate vacations to places like the Outer Banks; skiing in places like Vail and Park City, summer vacations in Europe, cruises in the Caribbean, and annual pilgrimages to Disney with Justin. Next came the cars, his Mercedes 550S, and Gretchen's Porsche Cayenne SUV. Finally, there were the watches, the jewelry, and the wardrobe. Being an advertising mogul meant entertaining clients and that called for image, and image called for the best of everything.

So now, at the urging of Marcus Pilfery, he had given up a lucrative career and work he enjoyed for a chance at power. Political power, Marcus ensured him that would be significant. And that power would lead Seth eventually back to money. Money that would flow to a man who would now help Marcus Pilfery sell the notion to millions of Americans of a new country, a new United Socialist States of America.

It would be the greatest advertising campaign of his career and the most challenging. Instead of convincing people to buy an athletic shoe or a sport drink, he'd have to convince people to want to become part of a new country, a utopian country where all their needs would be met. It would begin with free child care, medical care, family leave, free college tuition, subsidies for every kind of social program imaginable, green energy, elder care, nursing care, end of life care. Complete cradle to grave care provided for by the government. Provided for by the government, but at the expense of the motivated, talented and productive members of that new nation.

And for successfully running such a campaign, Marcus assured Seth that there would be wealth to follow. There would be speaking fees, book fees, consultancy fees, and always the assurance of moving within the highest circles of political and economic power within the new country.

Until that day came, Seth would work as an aide on his Senate staff and earn a salary of $110,000. But there would be bonuses. Bonuses for each time a state looking to secede met certain milestone events. Getting the public question on the state ballot would earn Seth a $100,000 bonus. Successful passage of the public question to secede would earn him $250,000 per state.

If Seth hung on all the way to the finish line, sometime out in 2021, and secession were to actually occur, Seth would be paid a $1 million bonus.

Where this money exactly was to come from, Seth did not know. But Marcus assured him there were individuals, wealthy individuals, who were very interested in seeing this new society form. They came from a variety of areas, entertainment, sports, technology and others. And Marcus assured Seth that there would be plenty of money for those who enabled the achievement of the goal.

It was to be a long haul, and a risky one too, but Seth was confident in his abilities to persuade people to buy whatever his clients were selling. Marcus Pilfery was selling Utopia, and Seth was banking that the people would buy it.

Marcus Pilfery looked Presidential as he took the podium. Dozens of reporters gathered around, pens and pads at the ready to furiously scribble notes relating to what Pilfery was about to say. They didn't know what he would say. Up until recently the media rarely discussed secession. And when they did, it was casually dismissed as the notion of extremists who were merely looking to bring attention to whatever issue of the day had agitated them to the point of foolishly speaking of forming another country.

But now with the question miraculously appearing on four state ballots and even more miraculously passing on those ballots, the media was whipped into a frenzy like never before. No one had anticipated what was about to happen.

Pilfery began without salutations. "Last night was an historic election night in America. It was perhaps even more historic than election night one year ago. Four of our United States of America took a bold step forward on behalf of their beliefs in liberty and justice for all, and against repression and injustice by the current administration.

Repression and injustice exhibited by the actions of an administration that has recently passed legislation that would deny millions of Americans health insurance, give tax breaks to big corporations, and signed executive orders designed to restrict the free flow of immigrants to our shores in search of the freedom and liberty we cherish. The passage of a public question in Oregon, Washington, Colorado, and California to propose secession from the United States is a demonstrative reaction to the destructive and polarizing direction this administration has chosen to take the country in.

The fact that this movement, and it must now be regarded as a movement, has spread to four separate states lends credence to the notion that a broad cross-section of our citizenry have grave reservations about the future of a United States of America grounded in liberty and justice for all.

We have all seen news lately that this movement is not likely to be limited to these four states. At present, there are petitions circulating in five other states that will raise the possibility of a similar vote occurring in 2018.

Illinois, Rhode Island, Connecticut, Vermont, and my home state New York are all now considering the question of secession. The seriousness and gravity of this question is not to be taken lightly or hastily. The people are restless.

That is why today, I stand before you and announce my support and endorsement for secession by the state of New York from these United States of America."

The words cascaded through the microphones and crashed into the hearts and minds of all Americans listening at that moment like a wrecking ball. The press was stunned for a moment as they let out a collective gasp before spontaneously erupting into hundreds of questions simultaneously. Digital cameras were furiously clicking, as the reporters seemed to surge forward toward Pilfery as though they were riding a wave onto the shoreline.

The Senator raised his hands like a ring announcer at a prize- fight would to calm an unruly crowd moments before the introductions of two boxers. "Ladies and gentlemen, please, please, may I continue my statement? I will allow you ample time to ask questions."

The Senator's endorsement of such an act, an act of secession, was unprecedented in modern politics. Such an endorsement had not occurred since the days of Jefferson Davis and the confederacy.

Pilfery continued. "It has become more clear recently that the country has never been more polarized. Issues such as health care, taxes, immigration, education, and the rights of women and minorities have divided the country into two camps with a wide gulf between them.

At times it seems as though there are two countries and this was never more evident than during the 2016 election cycle. Somewhere in our recent history the people in our great nation decided to go two separate paths; two separate paths that go beyond the normal partisan politics. Two paths that are so divisive it seems like the two may never converge again. Each side being so firm in its beliefs that it seems there remains little room for compromise and working together, so much so that the current path we are on, in my opinion, and in the opinion of many within my caucus, as well as many of our constituents, is tenable at best.

To be more blunt, the divisive path we are on makes the success of, as Alexander Hamilton called it, "our grand experiment", unlikely."

Pilfery paused for dramatic effect, and glanced at the gathered crowd. "It is therefore perhaps time for an even grander experiment. And that is one that consists of two distinctly different Americas. One that adheres to the unfair and sometimes cruel ideology of President Stanton and his extreme Republican base, and one that is more fair, hopeful, inclusive, and above all progressive in its thoughts and actions to provide a better life for all its citizens.

In the coming months I will be meeting with my fellow Democrats to chart a course for a new United States of America consisting of states that share the vision I have just described. This will not be an easy course of action, but I believe it necessary to ensure the futures of all of the people of America. And with that I will take your questions."

Chapter 21 – Washington, D.C.
November 8, 2017

The silence in the Oval office was deafening. The President sat motionless and virtually expressionless. His only reaction was an increase in his usual pouty look that had become his signature since general election debates.

Latimor, seeing that the President was not inclined to speak first, broke the ice. "Absolutely ludicrous," he said shaking his head and leaning forward in his chair. "A new country? Is he serious?"

"The Congress, let alone the State Legislatures, will never go for it. It would be like Brexit on steroids. It would takes years, if not decades, assuming it made it through all the legislative hurdles. That asshole Pilfery is just grandstanding. He's probably setting himself up for a Presidential run in 2020."

Stanton listened but was content to let his Chief of Staff vent before the real serious conversation began. Latimor continued. "How would he propose to tear apart something that has been carefully constructed over hundreds of years? Can you imagine all the issues? Defense and the military, social security, Medicare, infrastructure management, border management, trade and currency; the issues would be endless."

House Majority Leader Brent Locker had been sitting quietly digesting and processing the events of the last 20 minutes, and above all choosing his first words carefully. "It could work," was all he said.

"What? Are you insane?" Latimor said turning to Locker.

Unlike Latimor, Locker was measured and calm. "I'm not saying it would be easy and it certainly wouldn't be quick. But there's a lot of benefit to what Pilfery is describing."

Locker's thought intrigued Stanton. "Go on Brent."

The Congressman sat forward on the sofa seizing the opportunity to have the President's ear. "Well, it would obviously be a very complex process but it could make legislating much easier if certain elements of the Democratic Party were no longer part of that process. Your agenda would sail through the Congress and your re-election would be a virtual certainty. That is, assuming it could all unfold over the next couple of years."

"Not much chance of that," Senator Carlson said with skepticism.

"Yes, I tend to agree with the Senator," Stanton said matter-of-factly. "There's a tremendous number of issues that would have to be settled, and that's assuming it received approval. Unless I'm missing something, I believe it would take a constitutional amendment, plus approval by three-quarters of the state legislatures."

"You're correct, sir," Locker confirmed. Brent Locker, an attorney and somewhat of a constitutional scholar, described the secession process to the group confirming Stanton's assessment.

Stanton pressed on. "So tell me Brent, how would you go about setting up a country within a country? I mean, what about defense and the military, social security, Medicare, currency and trade? It seems like an insurmountable task."

"Well sir, its not unprecedented in recent times. Look at the Soviet Union and its breakup, and then there's Yugoslavia, which was divided up into six independent nations. Its been done before. You just have to have the desire and the will.

Take the military for example. You could leave the existing military intact initially and then phase in a separate military over time with separate bases in the secession states. There could be mutual defense agreements like NATO, which I'd assume the new country would want to be part of. Or maybe not, who knows. But it could be arranged and paid for by both countries. The devil is in the details but if both countries wanted it bad enough, we'd make it work. Until we did, it would remain under your control.

As far as social programs, you divide the assets and liabilities up based on some logical measure, such as proportion of participants. You'd do the same for Medicare, welfare, food stamps. Hell, based on the states Pilfery was talking about as secession candidates, I for one would be happy to see those states not be part of our programs. They'd probably make everything free and run themselves into bankruptcy. Look at California and their state pension debt. They'll never get out from under that. It would be a big weight off of us."

Speaker Garrison, having been silent up until now was a bit more cautious though. "Yes, but take California for example, it's the largest producing state of GDP in the country. They actually generate much more GDP than the federal and state funds they consume. That would be a big drain on the U.S. treasury."

Locker was prepared for this argument. "Yes Gordon that's true, but a lot of that GDP is tied up in Silicon Valley. What you've got now in California is an increasing number of high tech millionaires and billionaires where the wealth is concentrated in a few large players. At the same time, the middle class is fleeing the state due to its enormous tax burden. What you've got left is a lower class that can't get ahead and can't afford to get out. It's becoming a two-class state consisting of elites and poor people. They want to secede, I say let them. They'll end up giving away all their GDP in free health care, childcare, and tuition just to keep the working class happy, and all the while not realizing their middle class won't stand for it. It'll end up looking like pre-French revolution France or modern day Venezuela."

Stanton was now genuinely intrigued. Locker was all in, while Carlson was warming to the idea. Garrison was still skeptical if not aghast at the idea of the United States being divided in two.

Stanton was still pragmatic. "Hell, let's see where this all goes. There are still an awful lot of hurdles for these jokers to get over before this thing gets any real traction. Meantime, Ken," said Stanton looking over at his Chief of Staff. "Why don't you commission a study of how one would go about partitioning the country in two. It wouldn't hurt to know more precisely how that would work."

Stanton always planned for the unexpected. It was exactly how he wound up in the White House, although he could not possibly have known how prophetic his request truly was.

Part II

TEMPEST

Chapter 22 – Washington, D.C.
September 6, 2018

In the aftermath of the Marcus Pilfery announcement expressing his support for secession by his home state of New York, the divisiveness amongst Democrats and Republicans reached a fevered pitch.

Many of the Senators from the blue states that had been circulating petitions to put secession on the ballot for vote, had come out in support of the notion.

Senator Diane Mitchell, the Democrat from Illinois, and Senator Peter Bollinger, the Democrat from Connecticut, while expressing grave concern about the idea of secession, nevertheless said the issue would be in the hands of the voters from their states, and ultimately the Congress, the State Legislatures, and the President.

Senator Simmons from Washington and Senator Gutierrez from Colorado had already gotten on board with the idea since their voters had resoundingly approved the question last fall.

The idea was gaining traction across the country in the bright blue states that tended to vote heavily progressive. The vast majority of Democrats who opposed President Stanton and who were absolutely appalled with the idea of him even being President in the first place, were enamored with the idea of a new breakaway republic that could become a bastion of socially progressive policies. The thought of such a new nation of like-minded progressive thinkers conjured up images of the revolutionary colonies standing up to the British crown. Commercials, print and online advertisements, and other forms of imagery depicted President Stanton sitting on a throne with a crown while he crushed the progressive resistance with the heel of his shoe.

And while the country was fracturing, the more moderate Democrats and Republicans were astonished to be witnessing what was unfolding before their very eyes. They were aghast with the idea of a separate United States of America consisting of highly progressive Democratic states. This resulted in some of their political action committees running counter ads depicting a highly socialized runaway republic that taxed innovation out of existence and re-distributed accumulated wealth right out from under those who had spent a lifetime building it.

While this was occurring, those on the extreme right of the political spectrum were quietly, but effectively delivering the message that it was indeed time to establish a separate United States that would strive to be more like the highly socialized countries of Scandinavia. Their attitude was effectively: "If they don't like the form of government that created the greatest and most prosperous democracy in human history, then let them go and create their own utopian existence." Senator James Carlson from Texas, the Majority Leader was among the most vocal and ardent supporters for the secessionists, as he would say privately, "throw the radicals out and give them just enough rope to hang themselves. We will be better off without them and accomplish more."

President Stanton projected an outward image of wanting to save the republic and create a more inclusive America that would cause the secessionist enthusiasm to subside. But his policies and the laws that his Republican congress had been able to pass in his first eighteen months in office had offered little comfort to liberal Americans. Privately, he admitted to his family and closest advisors that he wouldn't mind seeing the secessionist movement succeed, rationalizing that it would simply remove from the America he loved only the "most undesirable and non-productive citizenry".

Although he would never admit to it publicly, he despised the progressive left as misguided, entitled, and lacking in personal responsibility. He would no doubt hide himself behind the cloak of "doing what the will of the people called for", if he were ever called upon to sign into law a plan that allowed for secession. Besides that, he rationalized to himself that it would probably only be a handful of states; at most four or five of the most, as he put it "crazed and extreme states".

Meanwhile Stanton pressed on with his agenda. He had managed to sign into law back in the spring a national infra-structure spending bill that narrowly passed the Senate with the required 60 votes as he managed to bring along eight Democrats from more moderate states like West Virginia, Ohio, and Iowa. However he had been unable to see through the passage of a comprehensive immigration reform bill, despite the fact that Congress had agreed to and the

President signed into law the Deferred Action for Child Arrivals program making the program permanent and establishing a pathway to citizenship for its participants. This enraged the far right members of Congress but to no avail. Public sentiment was overwhelmingly in favor of the program and no Republican Senator whose state was the least little bit liberal was willing to say no to the dreamers for fear it would be political suicide.

So the country chugged along with Stanton being able to enact a good three-fourths of his agenda. With the mid-term elections just two months away, President Stanton's approval rating, which was hovering in the mid 30% range a year earlier, was now 49%, just a tick above the percent of popular vote he had amassed upon his election.

This fact was not lost on the Republican members of the House as they all welcomed his support in the upcoming November election. By all accounts, the Republicans were projected to hold their large majority in the House, and even perhaps pick up an additional Senate seat or two.

Stanton was already gearing up his organization for his re-election bid in 2020. Meanwhile, the Democrats were scrambling to narrow the field and focus in on a handful of its best and brightest candidates to face off with the President just two years hence.

Chapter 23 – Washington, D.C.
October 10, 2018

Victoria Cheshire, the senior Democratic Senator from Massachusetts was gearing herself for a run, and was thus torn by the fact that Massachusetts had managed to get the necessary signatures to put the secession question on the November ballot.

At age 52, her political career was quickly coming to a crossroad. She was nearing the end of her second term in the U.S. Senate, and with her progressive social views, and no nonsense fiscal views and antipathy for Wall Street and big corporations; she was popular among the Democratic voters of the Commonwealth. She was a virtual lock for re-election in four weeks, leading her Republican challenger in the polls by 22 points. Massachusetts in 2018 America was staunchly Democratic. Sure there were the occasional Republican anomalies like Mitt Romney or Scott Brown but as a rule, Massachusetts the home of the Kennedy dynasty, was as liberal Democratic as they came.

Cheshire had been a practicing attorney until 2006 when she was caught up in a whirlwind election that landed her in the U.S. Senate. She had run on a whim at the prompting of then Senator Ted Kennedy, who had decided not to run for re-election after over 40 years in the Senate. Kennedy's health was failing and he had met Victoria at a fundraiser and looked favorably upon the young lawyer who was building a successful career as a civil rights attorney in Boston.

Kennedy convinced her to run in late 2005, and with his endorsement, which was akin to Moses coming down from Mount Horeb after speaking with God, the Massachusetts voters swept her into office.

She was a devoted wife to husband Paul, and mother of two teenage daughters.

She quickly distinguished herself in the Senate with seats on both the Judiciary and Finance Committees, as she took on the big banks that engaged in predatory lending practices during the housing bubble of 2008. She was a major supporter of Dodd-Frank and quickly gained a reputation as a champion of the little guy.

On this day she was in her Senate office reviewing legislation brought forth by the Republicans to water down the Dodd-Frank law when her intercom signaled a call. It was Marcus Pilfery calling.

"Hello Senator Pilfery, to what do I owe the pleasure of your call today?" She said with overt, yet unnecessary formality.

"Hello Victoria. How are you today?" Marcus pleasantly responded.

"I'm not good Marcus. Have you read this bill? It's a travesty. No way this thing gets 60 votes. Not if I have anything to say about it."

"No I've not read it yet, although from what my staff tells me, its going to need an undertaker because that piece of crap is dead on arrival."

Cheshire snickered as she dropped her pen and sat back in her high-back leather chair. "So what's up Marcus?"

Pilfery geared up for the seriousness of the subject matter. "Word on the street is that you're thinking about 2020. Any truth to that rumor?"

Victoria had been anticipating the call from the Minority Leader and now secessionist proponent. She briefly hesitated, but then spoke. "Yes, Marcus I'm strongly considering it."

Pilfery was actually relieved to hear her say she was considering a run for President in 2020. Many Democrats, including Pilfery, believed she had the best chance of defeating Stanton. She was liberal, but not too liberal so as to turn off moderate voters, but liberal enough that she was assured the majority of the millennial, minority, and women's vote. She was a hard-working, self-made, American success story who didn't come from privilege and didn't feel like the Presidency was owed to her. She was likable and pleasant, and not the least bit snarky when it came to her political beliefs. So voters listened to her and valued what she had to say. Plus she looked Presidential, which in these times of mass media and image was a big plus. Some said she resembled a younger version of Diane Keaton. She was confident, smart, sassy, but above all capable.

"Well, I'm glad to hear that. I think you could give Stanton a real run for his money. I would support you."

"Thanks Marcus. That means a lot to me, but I would plan to do more than just give the President a run for his money. I would plan to win."

Pilfery had been around politics long enough to know the power of the incumbency. Defeating a sitting President hadn't been done since 1992, and now Stanton's approval ratings were on the rise, by virtue of keeping most of his campaign promises and enacting the majority of his agenda. Although it was two years off, it was difficult to imagine that anyone the Democrats had to offer would be able to unseat Stanton. Nevertheless, he continued his adoration toward Victoria. "I know that's what you would plan to do. I wouldn't expect anything less. But there is another issue."

"Oh, and what is that?" Victoria asked knowing full well what that other issue was.

"The secession vote on the Massachusetts ballot this November."

No shit Marcus, Victoria thought to herself. It was the 700- pound elephant in the room, no Republican pun intended. "Yes, what about it?"

"Well you haven't exactly been vocal on the idea. Have you thought about what a yes vote might mean to your campaign? You'd potentially be running for the highest office of the country your voters would be looking to break away from. How would you square that?"

"I don't have to necessarily share the same view as the Massachusetts voters no matter what the outcome of that vote is. I hold office in the Senate, not the *people's* house. And I'd be running for national office, national office of the United States of America. Secession is a long shot at best, and besides, I don't happen to agree with the secessionist movement. I for one think this country is salvageable from Stanton, and worth it. I'm not prepared to take my ball and go home just because I don't like the way the game is being played right now." Cheshire's feistiness was never more on display than right at this moment. Pilfery was a bit surprised but retreated.

"I'm a little surprised to hear that. After the repeal of the ACA, I thought you were all on board with secession. What happened to change your thinking?"

"That was simply an emotional reaction at the time Marcus. When I had time to calm down and reflect, I realized I love this country and could never leave it, or see it broken apart."

"I hear you Victoria. And I understand your feelings. I'm just saying you have to be prepared for the question if the Massachusetts people vote for secession, that's all."

Pilfery's tone was somewhat condescending and Victoria didn't like it, but she chose not to show it. No need to antagonize the Senate Minority Leader, not with an election coming up, and certainly not if she wanted his endorsement in 2020. "I will be ready for the question Marcus. Thank you for the heads up."

"You're welcome Victoria," Pilfery said earnestly trying to smooth over any ill will between the two long-time colleagues.

Victoria's views on secession had turned 180 degrees since the repeal and replacement of the health care law nearly a year-and-a-half earlier. Initially, her disappointment and anger over the repeal of the previous administration's most significant achievement had wet her appetite for a breakaway Republic. But it was a visceral reaction. It was one that emanated from her heart, not her head. When the sting of that defeat had worn off, she realized that secession was not the answer. So to preserve her standing within the party, she promised herself she would be publicly neutral, although she was personally opposed to the idea.

Victoria quickly changed the subject so as to put this contentious one behind them. "Hey about dinner tonight? I'm meeting Julia Novak and Ben Goodwin at the Capital Grille at 8." Novak was the first term Democratic Senator from Ohio who Victoria had taken under her wing, having been elected in 2016. Ben Goodwin, was the Republican Senator from Kansas who was also newly elected in 2016

"Goodwin? He's a Republican," Pilfery said with puzzlement. What's that all about?"

"Hey Republicans are people too you know. Just call it a bi-partisan working session," she joked.

"Thank you, but I have plans. You guys go ahead and enjoy. I'll see you on the floor tomorrow. I still have to read that bill."

"Ok Marcus, you do that," she said laughing, knowing that the bill as written wouldn't garner a single Democratic vote. "And Marcus, thanks for your support on the 2020 issue."

"Alright lady, you got it," he said with half-hearted sincerity.

Victoria returned to the bill. It was going on 6 pm, and she had about another hour to read the drivel in front of her.

When she wrapped up at about 7:10, she called Julia and confirmed they were still meeting for dinner. As she made her way out of the Senate office building she was alone in her thoughts.

Would she become the next President of the existing United States of America? Or, in the event of a loss to Stanton, would she have to choose between the nation she loved, or help form the kind of new nation she so desperately wanted.

Chapter 24 – Washington, D.C.
October 10, 2018

When Victoria arrived at the Capital Grille at 8:15, Senators Novak and Goodwin were already seated and had ordered drinks. Julia had ordered a large bottle of Pellegrino that she offered to share with Victoria. Ben Goodwin went with a Sam Adams lager.

"Oh, that lager sounds good. I'll have a Sam Adams also," Victoria said to the waiter, who had accompanied her to the table.

"Hi Tori, how are you?" Julia said greeting Victoria with a smile. To her colleagues in the Senate she was Victoria or Senator Cheshire, but to her family and close friends she was Tori. The nickname suited her. It was casual but unusual and not the least bit pretentious, instead rather girl-next-doorish.

"Hi Julia, fine, sorry I'm a bit late," she said apologetically. "Good evening Ben," acknowledging Senator Goodwin.

"Good evening Victoria," Goodwin stood as she arrived. Alas, chivalry was not dead, at least not in Kansas. "Get through that finance bill?"

Victoria smiled and rolled her eyes, indicating the bill did not meet with her approval. "It needs a lot of work Ben."

Goodwin knew the bill was very partisan and would likely not garner a single Democratic vote. "Its an opening bid," he said almost apologetically. "Let's see where everyone stands on it." Goodwin, along with Cheshire sat on the Senate Finance Committee.

150

This bill had just come out of the Republican dominated House, where it passed strictly across party lines. These days, that was enough in the House, but not nearly enough in the Senate.

Much of what Stanton had accomplished thus far was through the reconciliation process where only a simple majority was required in the Senate. Or, in the case of the infrastructure bill, a number of moderate Democrats had voted to shore up the country's crumbling infrastructure. This was no more evident than in the so-called rust belt states of Michigan, Pennsylvania, and Julia Novak's home state of Ohio. She had gone along with the President's infrastructure bill and the tax bill in the hopes of raising the employment prospects for her constituents, who had also surprisingly voted for Stanton.

"Well, we'll see this week when it comes up for vote," Cheshire submitted.

After the usual political banter around the typical topics on which Republicans and Democrats rarely saw eye-to-eye, such as immigration reform, education, and defense, the three ordered dinner. Goodwin and Novak went with the New York Strip steaks, while Victoria ordered Salmon.

"Salmon in a steakhouse?" Julia kidded her fast friend from Massachusetts.

"Hey, don't knock Salmon. Its very healthy," Victoria fought back playfully.

"Yes, but not much fun," Julia retorted as Ben looked on smiling and enjoying the culinary battle between fellow Democrats.

When dinner arrived, the three quietly dug into their meals and enjoyed the respite from their busy days fighting with colleagues over the legislative issues of the day. After about ten minutes of small talk about sports, stocks, and food, Goodwin took the discussion to the upcoming mid-term elections.

"Do either of you foresee any gains in the House?" Goodwin offered up as the icebreaker.

The two women looked blankly at each other as they considered the question, which was at best rhetorical and at worst sobering. They both knew that the Republicans had a solid grasp on the House and the mood in the country was such that it was not likely to change anytime soon. Stanton was on the rise and the people across the country were generally okay with what he had accomplished so far. There would likely be no change in the balance of power in the House. The situation in the Senate was similar, although the Republican advantage was much smaller and was likely to remain that way.

Goodwin knew all this but was hoping for a reaction on the public question of secession that was now on the ballot in nine additional states.

Since the passage of the public question in California, Washington, Oregon, and Colorado, there had been a flurry of secession activity in Vermont, Rhode Island, Illinois, Connecticut, New Jersey, Maryland, and Delaware. In addition, Marcus Pilfery's support had led to the issue being up for public vote in New York. Massachusetts, long a bastion of progressive thinking, was not to be left behind, and despite Victoria Cheshire's lack of support for the question, Massachusetts voters would be addressing the issue in less than a month.

Victoria looked up from her plate and chose her words carefully. "I fear there is a sentiment in certain parts of the country right now that favors secession. It's a sentiment that's reactionary, emotional, and not well thought out. It's grounded in a belief that certain Democrats feel disappointed in their party for letting Stanton move forward with his agenda and basically throw away the work of the previous eight years. They can't bear the thought. I can understand this. I can't bear the thought either. But secession is not the answer. It's no answer. It's a quitter's answer. But I fear we seem to be heading in that direction and I feel powerless to stop it."

Novak was silent, and looked down at her plate. Goodwin was transfixed on Cheshire. He was following her every word and looked at her in wonderment.

He too was opposed to the secession movement and unlike Cheshire, he had been very public about it, in fact, he was outspoken about it. But he couldn't grasp why she hadn't spoken out on the issue publicly. He hadn't yet come to grips with the notion of getting re-elected and doing everything necessary to position yourself for that objective. He was too new, too innocent, and some would say too naïve. He was too naïve to know that a politician like Victoria Cheshire would likely do or say anything to get re-elected. Or not say something that would jeopardize the possibility of being re-elected. They both shared the same belief. But his belief would protect him with his party. Her belief would instead be risky with certain elements of her party and prevent her from winning re-election. The dichotomy was striking.

Chapter 25 – Washington, D.C.
November 7, 2018

"There are now 13," the CNN morning host Thomas Monroe was emphatic, if not melodramatic. "There are now 13 states that have approved a measure that could lead to their secession from the United States."

The drama continued and seemed to ooze out of every pore of his body, as he, and many members of the left leaning media seemed to be enjoying the move on in the country that they believed had been brought on by the Stanton administration's divisive policies and unwillingness to compromise with correct-thinking Democrats. And now Stanton and the Republicans would be held responsible for the disenchantment of the voters in those states, who the day before, had voted in favor of eventual secession.

Monroe was egged on by his co-anchor, Wilson Adderley, who appeared to be restraining his enjoyment of this public indictment of the Stanton presidency.

"Wilson, one has to wonder where this groundswell of support in traditionally blue states for secession will end. Will the secession fever that has apparently taken hold in 25% of the country continue to accelerate and ultimately lead to a fracturing of the Republic."

"Yes Tom," Adderley chimed in. "And one has to wonder what the founding fathers would be saying if they were here to witness the ever growing divide in the country they formed over 241 years ago," he added sternly.

Marcus Pilfery sipped a cup of coffee as he watched intently as the previous night's vote results played out on cable television. He was simultaneously tuned to two other stations in the bank of T.V. monitors that were perpetually on in his Senate office. One was tuned to MSNBC, while the other was tuned to Fox News. Senate colleagues often wondered why he watched Fox, and he always replied: "You have to always know what your opponents are up to."

The groundwork had been laid. Over the past year Seth Dudley had run a highly skilled advertising campaign that seemed to fan the flames of secession fever like no other public relations campaign in history.

It had consisted largely of negative ads centered around Stanton's political and public speaking mis-steps. Many of the ads showed Stanton speaking at various rallies and fundraisers saying and supporting one thing, but then showed him contradicting himself or doing something completely different.

There were contradictory ads relating to climate change, gun violence, hurricane relief, white supremacists, and of course, Stanton's almost non-stop Achilles heal, the Russian hacking of the 2016 election.

For his expertise and efforts Seth Dudley had been paid $100,000 for each of the 13 states that had gotten the public question on the ballot, plus an additional $250,000 for each state that successfully passed the public question. All told, that amounted to nearly $4.7 million for little more than a year's efforts. It would've taken Seth over 10 years in his previous position to earn that kind of money. Regardless of the outcome, he had cemented his reputation amongst the Democratic power brokers in Washington as a highly skilled and influential operative. He would be able to write his own ticket on future political campaigns.

Although nothing had been proven in terms of Stanton or any of his surrogates colluding with the Russians to influence his election, the media, particularly CNN and MSNBC, had absolutely refused to let go of the story. Their viewers, in searching for a reason why their candidate had lost, we're absolutely convinced that Stanton had stolen the election and wanted that narrative perpetuated. And the networks, hungry to satisfy their viewers, were unrelenting in their pursuit of the story. It had become to Stanton what Benghazi had been to Elizabeth Morley. Scarcely a news cycle would go by without one of those networks spending a significant amount of time harping on the Russia theme. It was good for their ratings as it fed the anger of their progressive viewers who were hell bent on making every day of Stanton's administration pure agony for the billionaire businessman turned politician.

So now for the next year the objective of Pilfery and Dudley would be to line up political support both in Washington and at the state level for secession. The hard work had been done. The populace had been won over. Now it was time to go to work on the politicians.

That part would be easier because both Pilfery and
Dudley knew that the way to the hearts of sitting
politicians would be through their re-election.
Especially since the just completed mid-term elections
had resulted in further losses of congressional seats for
the Democrats.

Chapter 26 – Washington, D.C.
November 7, 2018

The mid-term elections proved to be yet another setback for the beleaguered Democrats. The Republicans picked up another 12 seats in the House of Representatives giving them now a 242 to 193 advantage. But more significant than that was the fact that the Republicans had won four more Senate seats giving them now a 56 to 44 advantage. It was still not enough of an advantage to overturn filibuster attempts by the Democrats, but it was enough of a majority that if there ever were votes, on which the ever-fracturing Republicans were divided, there'd likely still be enough Republicans to achieve a majority.

In addition to infuriating the Democrats with his policy decisions, as well as his abrasive demeanor, President Stanton had also managed to alienate members of his own party by criticizing them in the media on a regular basis. His hit back harder, take no prisoners mentality was a constant source of irritation for certain Republicans, as the President continually fed his base voters the anti-Washington rhetoric they so much enjoyed.

Nevertheless, with commanding majorities in both houses of Congress, Stanton was sure to be able to drive his agenda forward for the next two years of his term. That advantage would also be critical in his pursuit of re-election. And it would be that re-election that would most likely drive Marcus Pilfery and his

allies to push the issue of secession and create a new
and distinctly different United States of America.

Chapter 27 – Washington, D.C.
March 22, 2020

"The ayes are 62 and the nays are 38. The bill passes," said the acting President of the Senate, Harlen Prescott, Senator from North Carolina.

This was yet another setback for the Democrats on a true lightning rod political issue—immigration reform.

This bill achieved what hadn't been achieved in the last 30 years. It established a new system for the orderly immigration into the country of those who wished to become U.S. citizens. The law, that was yet another of Stanton's campaign promises provided a path to citizenship for the estimated 12 million undocumented immigrants currently residing in the U.S.

It was a true compromise law that rankled both Democrats and Republicans alike. On the one hand, it required that those who were to be granted citizenship had to register with the government, be issued a conditional social security card, obtain and keep employment for a period of two years, pay taxes, and if they were unable to find and keep employment, they would be required to essentially "work for welfare". In fact, President Stanton had managed six months earlier to get a bill through Congress that required that all able bodied citizens who were to receive public assistance had to essentially "work for welfare". There were actually similar laws in many red states and some of the blue states, like New Jersey for example. It was a tough sell to the Democrats, but Stanton insisted it be a condition to a comprehensive immigration reform bill.

The extreme left yelled loud and long, but the moderate Democrats saw it as the only way to achieve immigration reform once and for all.

The Republicans complained that it essentially rewarded undocumented immigrants who had broken the law by entering the country. But they caved under pressure from President Stanton who threatened to not only extend the DACA provisions, (Deferred Action for Childhood Arrivals), to so-called "dreamers", but also proposed to extend the DACA provisions to all 12 million undocumented immigrants through executive order. He essentially was going to "out-DACA" his predecessor in order to get what he wanted. And what he wanted was to be the one person who would be remembered for reforming the immigration system.

His action wasn't totally noble though. Stanton was hoping that a good number of those 12 million would realize what he had done for them and would reward him with their votes in 2020. It was a gamble Stanton was willing to take. He was counting on at least everyone who voted for him in 2016. If he could add only a fraction of the 12 million to his vote count, it would give him the popular vote win also, which he was unable to secure in 2016. That fact had stuck in his craw for nearly four years and his massive ego would not tolerate another popular vote loss. So he rolled the dice. Worse case, he'd lose the election and he'd have to go back to being a billionaire. It could be worse, he reasoned.

So after months of wrangling and arm-twisting the President got the 60 votes he needed plus a couple more for good measure. He actually got 52 Republican votes and, amazingly, 10 Democratic Senators from states like Minnesota, Iowa, Nevada, and Pennsylvania who were desperate for a way to make their undocumented populations legal and most importantly tax paying citizens.

Meanwhile, the extreme leftwing of the Democratic party, especially the now so-called "secessionist" states, were steadfastly opposed to the immigration bill, partly because they secretly thought it would actually endear Stanton to some of those who would benefit from coming out of the shadows. Like Stanton, the Democrat's primary aim was not to promote the well being of the 12 million, but rather to turn them into citizens who would become part of their voting block. Furthermore, any success by Stanton, especially on such a troublesome issue as immigration reform, would be an enormous political victory that would help further Stanton's re-election hopes. Just like the strategy the Republicans had adopted after President Prentice had been elected in 2008, the Democrats primary strategy was to obstruct Stanton at every turn to make him and their Republican opponents appear weak and ineffectual. So far, this strategy was not working. The Democrats had not counted on Stanton reaching across the aisle and actually compromising to get things done. It would prove to be a fatal mistake for the Democrats, come 2020.

Chapter 28 – Seattle, Washington
July 23, 2020

Victoria Cheshire waited backstage with husband Paul as former President William A. Prentice was onstage addressing the delegates at the Democratic National Convention. It is Thursday night. The night the party's nominee takes the stage to rally the delegates for the impending general election campaign. Cheshire is excited, anxious, and cautious. She breezed through primary season as she systematically dispensed with her challengers one by one.

There was the usual rabble of political challengers dipping their toes in the water to see if they could capture the imagination of the Democratic electorate. There was former Vice-President, Jim Boxer, who had served under President Prentice, and who four years earlier had ceded to run to the then heir apparent, Elizabeth Morley. He had been filled with regret ever since, especially when Morley had been soundly beaten by Stanton. He was now re-surfacing for his last hurrah. That turned out to be a mistake as he was soundly drubbed in the debates by Cheshire. He had been regarded as one of the elder statesmen of the party, but was long past his political prime. He was indeed a sad, if not loveable holdover from an administration whose legislation had largely been dismantled by Stanton over the past four years. The party needed to move on and without Jim Boxer.

There was Leonard Stokely, the Senator from
Vermont who was unsuccessful in 2016 against
Morley. The knock on Stokely was that he was simply
too liberal to be elected. In fact he was a self declared
socialist, and with all the turmoil in Europe
surrounding terrorism, security, and out of control
social spending resulting in huge budgetary problems,
Stokely's socialist, nanny state shtick just wasn't going
to cut it in 2020 America. He wound up exiting the
race in mid-May.

And finally there was the Junior Senator from
New Jersey, Cameron Clarke, who was regarded as
part of the new breed of young, vibrant, progressive
Democrats who were the new hope of the party. He
was brilliant, affable, handsome, and black. Had it not
been for the Democrats so badly wanting to elect the
first woman president, the nomination surely would
have been Clarke's. But after the loss by Morley in
2016, the desire for the first woman president to be a
Democrat was stronger than ever. If it ever came to
pass that a Republican woman were first elected to the
White House, the Democrats would view that as an
indelible stain on their party for all time. So 2020 had
to be the year of Victoria Cheshire. And just to
reinforce the Democrats' message of inclusiveness and
diversity, Cameron Clarke was nominated to be her
running mate.

As Cheshire and Clarke emerged from the
stage wings of the Seattle Convention Center to
thunderous applause, the table was being set for the
2020 Presidential campaign. Next month in

Milwaukee, in a mere formality, President Stanton would be nominated for a second term. The Republican primary season turned out to be a non-event as it is for most incumbent presidents. This one in particular was non-existent as no one had the money or the influence to have any hope in unseating the President.

So the Democratic tour de force of Cheshire and Clarke, accompanied by their spouses, smiled and waved to their throngs of supporters, as they were ready to march into history as the first ever major political party ticket to not contain a white male. Even more unusual was the fact that both were from states that two years earlier had approved a public question to secede from the United States of America. Neither realized that no matter the outcome of the November election both, as representatives from secessionist states, would become profound focal points in the history of American politics.

Chapter 29 – Brooklyn, New York
October 10, 2020

"Thanks for meeting me today Seth," Marcus Pilfery said earnestly to his long-time friend, Seth Dudley. The two were meeting at Di Fara's, one of Pilfery's go-to places whenever he was home from D.C. It's located in the Midwood section of Brooklyn and boasts some of the best pizza in New York.

"Hey, I never miss a chance to eat pizza in Brooklyn, especially when you're paying!" Dudley cracked as the steaming hot pie arrived at their table.

While the two friends ate, Pilfery gushed over the New York Yankees first round playoff win over their archrival, the Boston Red Sox. "Aaron Judge was a one man wrecking crew in that series. He owned the Boston pitching staff. So now it's bring on Cleveland," the long-time Yankees fan said with confidence. Dudley was unimpressed. He wasn't much of a baseball fan. Football was his sport of choice, and his favorite team, the New York Giants, had been struggling as of late, so he had little to gloat over.

After the two had gotten their fill of pizza, the conversation drifted into, what else, politics. "Looks like Cheshire isn't going to make it, Marcus," Dudley lamented pointing out the obvious.

Pilfery was calm and pensive. He was always thinking ahead, planning, calculating. Post election was already on his mind. After all, Stanton was leading Cheshire in the national polls by a margin of 53% to 42% with the usual fringe candidates such as the Libertarian, Socialist, and Green Party splitting 3%, and the undecided making up the balance. Any of the Libertarian defectors would likely go to Stanton while the Socialists would break for Cheshire. Marcus knew at this point that, lacking a major scandal affecting Stanton, the election would soon be lost. However, he was not at all dismayed.

Stanton and Cheshire had debated three times. And three times the consensus was Cheshire, at best, had just come out even in the debates. Stanton had dominated the discussions around economy and jobs as expected. Unemployment was at a 12 year low, and furthermore, wage growth had steadily climbed over the past two years. And with the tax legislation that Stanton had managed to get through Congress, the economy was growing at steadily higher rates. The last three fiscal quarters had each grown in excess of 3.2%, and many experts were predicting 3.5% to 4.0% was on the horizon.

And while Cheshire did well on social issues like education, women's rights, and pushing for tougher gun laws, it hadn't been enough to stop Stanton's momentum on the economy. At the end of the day, jobs and security, were first and foremost in people's minds. Many of the pundits felt Stanton sealed his re-election when he got comprehensive immigration reform through Congress and into law.

It didn't matter much to people that Stanton lacked social grace and most times didn't "act Presidential". People were working, making a decent wage and felt safer than they did four years earlier.

Stanton even managed to score some Democratic voters along the way, by pushing for, and getting an increase in the federal minimum wage to $12.50 an hour. This infuriated the extreme right, but he didn't care much, because it delighted many in his base who were blue collar types working in economically challenged communities all throughout the Midwest and deep South. The tax reform he had gotten passed had jump started the economy and resulted in less resistance by small businesses on raising wages.

Stanton was truly a populist drawing upon both Republican and Democratic principles to move the country ahead. He cared no more about what Rush Limbaugh said than he did about what Rachel Maddow said. He seemingly only cared about his voting base, which by all accounts had expanded over the previous two years.

Pilfery had been planning for this eventuality all along. This was precisely why he had hired Seth Dudley three and a half years earlier. It was beginning to look more and more like plan B would have to be invoked. Secession was now the strategy. Pilfery knew it and Dudley knew it. It wasn't so much about the fundamental disagreements he and other progressive Democrats had with the President. It was more about a loss of political power. Stanton had sucked power away from Republicans and Democrats alike. But the Republicans seemed to care less because at the end of the day Stanton was still a Republican and had more in common with the Republicans than he did with the Democrats. And besides, a Stanton endorsement would always be helpful to any Republican running for re-election.

Although Stanton was unpolished and at times boorish, he managed to get things done which most Republicans agreed with. And for the things they didn't agree with, they could live with them for another four years if meant holding onto their jobs. In 2024, things would get back to "normal" with likely a more establishment type Republican in office and that suited the Republican power base just fine. After all, there was only one Oliver Stanton. He was the worst kind of narcissist they had ever seen. There would probably never be another one like him, or at least that's what the establishment Republicans hoped.

Pilfery on the other hand saw no end in sight to the misery. Stanton had succeeded in making political party affiliation less significant than ever. That was a serious problem for those in the minority, namely the Democrats. Pilfery, and other like-minded progressives, who were at the one end of the political spectrum had difficulty imagining an America where those at either end of that spectrum would ever dominate politics in the foreseeable future. This obviously didn't sit well with those on the fringes. Politics and establishment of political power had seemingly changed forever. Marcus Pilfery was an endangered species and he looked to resolve that in a most extreme way. The move toward secession would begin in November—after Election Day.

"Mr. President, I am calling you to congratulate you on your victory this evening. You ran a good campaign and the voters have spoken. I wish you well over the next four years," Victoria Cheshire said in almost robotic like fashion into the phone. It pained her to utter these words, but she had always been gracious to her political opponents, and this evening was no exception.

"Thank you very much Senator Cheshire. I appreciate that and I appreciate the very positive campaign you ran. I look forward to working with you over the next four years as you return to the Senate. You're a class act."

Cheshire was buoyed momentarily, but brought back to reality with the notion that she was indeed going back to the Senate. Her dream of being President would have to be put on hold for at least another four years, and it was a deflating thought.

Stanton had won in pretty much a landslide. He had captured 342 electoral votes to 196 for Cheshire. He managed to win once again win the traditionally blue states of Pennsylvania, Ohio, Michigan, and Wisconsin. But this time he also carried Virginia, which he had narrowly lost in 2016, and also held onto Florida, another key battleground state.

Even more impressive was the President had won the popular vote, which was something he had not done in 2016, and was a nagging source of irritation for Stanton. The preliminary vote count showed him at 52% versus 46% for Cheshire, or a margin of close to five million popular votes. The Democratic Party leadership was absolutely incredulous over this and almost instantly began questioning its political vision for the future. Cheshire had been a staunch progressive for years and came into the campaign with little or no baggage. Clearly the mood of the country was such that the voters were inclined to allow Stanton another four years. Many felt he had broken the gridlock in Congress by reaching out to moderate Democrats when the situation called for it and had enacted more significant legislation than his last two predecessors combined.

And finally, in what Stanton would regard as the icing on the cake, the Republicans had captured four more Senate seats in the election and now had a 60-vote majority. Along with 248 out of 435 House seats, the Republicans now had the keys to the kingdom. They could essentially enact any law they wished while the Democrats would be forced to sit idly by. While many in the close circle of secessionists viewed Stanton's second term as the triggering event for secession, the 60-vote majority in the Senate was the last straw. That fact alone would provide further impetus for those Democrats who were opposed to secession.

Clearly, the Democrats would need to adopt a new tact for 2024. As it would turn out, they would not have to wait that long.

Chapter 31 – Washington, D.C.
December 7, 2021

Nearly a month had passed since President Stanton's re-election. The message had been overwhelming. A clear majority of the country's voters had endorsed the Stanton agenda and had clearly rejected the progressive Democratic policy direction.

Most establishment Democrats, including many of the Senators from the thirteen states that had approved the question of secession and formation of a new Progressive Democratic United States of America, were absolutely inconsolable over the thought of another four years of President Oliver Stanton. Something had to be done. Something extreme and something decisive was called for. It couldn't simply be business as usual with the "resist" moniker that had been in vogue after Stanton's initial election in 2016. That time was over.

The resist battle cry had resulted in the passage of a new health care law that watered down the work of the previous administration while doing very little to reduce the overall cost of health care. Resist had resulted in tax reform that favored corporations, and lower and middle class taxpayers, but amazingly, also wealthier Americans, which was completely unpalatable to the Democrats since it did nothing to solve their issue of income inequality in America. It had also resulted in an Immigration reform law that was far more onerous in terms of work requirements, personal accountability, and border security than any progressive Democrat would ever be satisfied with. Some good, in the opinion of Democrats, was accomplished, such as an infrastructure-spending bill, that would rebuild America's roads, bridges, tunnels, and utility grids, but those types of gains were few and far between.

Now with Stanton firmly in office for another four years, the Democrats were fearful of what his next move would be.

A group of Democratic Senators was now gathered in one of the capital's local watering holes frequented by members of Congress, called the Lantern. The group included Michael Simmons of Washington, Angela Gutierrez of Colorado, Diane Mitchell of Illinois, Peter Bollinger of Connecticut, Leonard Stokely of Vermont, and of course Marcus Pilfery, Senate Minority Leader from New York.

The Senate had adjourned for the day an hour earlier at 8 pm and the group was unwinding from the last few days of voting on some of the Republicans' new initiatives for Stanton's second term.

Since the Republican sponsored budget for fiscal 2021 had just been approved two months earlier, under budget reconciliation rules, the Republicans were now coming back around to the issue of federal funding of President Stanton's border wall with Mexico. The wall construction had begun in 2020 but funding, as part of the compromise bill agreed to by 10 Democratic Senators had been limited to the point where roughly only 30% of the construction had been accomplished. Now it was being re-surfaced as a standalone issue as part of a budget reconciliation measure that would require but a simple majority to pass.

Many of those 10 Democratic Senators, including Peter Bollinger, felt duped by the President who insisted he would have Mexico pay for the wall and no further U.S. funding would be required. Now, with Mexico digging in it's heals on funding the wall, the President and the Republicans were looking for the remaining funding. The President had insisted all along that even if Mexico didn't agree to pay for the border wall, he would impose a duty on the import of Mexican goods to pay for it. But that position became untenable when Stanton, two years earlier had re-negotiated NAFTA, and imposed a 5 year moratorium on Mexican duties in exchange for a better trade deal for the U.S. The President got the trade deal he wanted, but he forfeited a mechanism to force Mexico to pay for the wall.

Stanton was used to give and take in such deals, so when he acquiesced on the duty issue, he figured he'd go back to the Congress for the money. Since his voting base wanted the wall with all their heart, Stanton would pressure those Republicans who disagreed with funding the wall to give in, or they would be challenged publicly and potentially "primaried out" in 2022. Essentially, the President would cause a sitting Republican Senator up for re-election trouble by endorsing another Republican during the primary election season. It was a favored tactic of the politically ruthless, and Stanton had no hesitation to use it when he needed to.

So now with a clear Republican majority, Stanton would get his wall funding and fulfill one of his most important campaign promises. Better late than never, he would say afterward.

"That vote today was brutal," Senator Bollinger said with disgust. "I counted no less than five Republicans who were clearly uncomfortable with their yes vote."

"Just business as usual in the Stanton administration," quipped Senator Gutierrez from Colorado.

Senator Stokely from Vermont chimed in. "Yes, but this is clearly a harbinger of bad things yet to come over the next four years. Now that he's got another term, he's gong to get more ruthless. Now he doesn't have to worry about re-election and he doesn't give a shit what he does to the Republican Party or the next Republican nominee."

Marcus Pilfery was sitting back sipping a glass of Cabernet taking it all in. When Stokely finished his diatribe he leaned forward and seized upon the moment. "So, let him do it. He'll just ruin his party. What should we care?"

"We have to care, Marcus. He's got four more years. We can't put up with this crap," Diane Mitchell of Illinois offered.

"We don't have to put up with his crap. We can control our own destiny," Pilfery insisted.

"Yes I know," Diane shot back. "Secession, right?"

Pilfery paused and smiled. "Yes, we knew this day was coming. We knew it back in October after the debates. Its time to act."

"Having voters approve a public question and actually pulling the trigger on a campaign of actual secession are two different things," Senator Simmons of Washington reasoned.

"Why should it be? The voters want it. We simply need to have the political will and courage to give it to them," Pilfery responded.

"Yes, yes. But public questions like this are largely symbolic. Remember Texas after President Prentice was elected?" Simmons countered.

"That was a one off, Michael. We've got thirteen states that want a real change. That's a lot of people, close to a hundred million I would guess," Pilfery insisted.

"That's a very strong argument," Stokely added. "Not to mention the GDP those thirteen states bring to the table. I ran the numbers after those states approved the question. 42 percent, let me say that again, 42 percent is the GDP contributed by those thirteen states. That will get a lot of attention. Hell, California by itself would be one of the top ten economies in the world. The thirteen would probably be top five."

The group was silent for a moment as it chewed on the notion.

Pilfery spoke next. "Of course, it would be complicated, a lot of issues and details to work out. Things like national defense of the new Republic, splitting up the Social Security trust, the Medicare trust, and so on. That is assuming we went all the way and got it through the Congress, the President, and the State Legislatures."

"Yes, but I can envision how it could work. We'd need a defense treaty. We'd essentially just become a new member of NATO. That could work," Stokely added.

"And perhaps we divide the social program trust funds based on per capita or percentage of historical contribution," Diane offered.

Now they were getting it Pilfery thought to himself. It's a good time to reveal the study undertaken by Seth he further thought. "I want to share with you all a study I had undertaken two years ago after the approval of the public question by the thirteen states. I was anticipating this day, so my office in conjunction with the Soros organization funded a study to determine how exactly the United States might be divided into two nations."

Pilfery reached into his briefcase and emerged with a half dozen bound reports, which were about two inches thick each and bound in a plain black binder. On the cover, the name read simply:

"Resolve"

Around the block at another Washington bar called the Beacon, Ben Goodwin was dining with his Republican colleague and House Majority Leader, Brent Locker of Wisconsin. A most unusual dinner guest, Victoria Cheshire, accompanied them.

Over the past four years Senator Goodwin, the Senator from Kansas had become good friends with Senator Cheshire from Massachusetts. They frequently met for dinner to engage in friendly, but spirited debate about the legislative issues of the day.

And over the years, their families had gotten together once a year in August during the Congressional summer recess for vacation. Each year they would alternate. One year they'd vacation in Branson, Missouri, near Ben's home state of Kansas. The next year they'd meet in Massachusetts on Cape Cod.

Ben and Victoria were contemporaries. Ben was now 57 and Victoria had just turned 53. They each had two teenage girls between the ages of 16 and 20. Ben's wife, Jennifer was a nurse, and Victoria's husband Paul was an Anesthesiologist. So the two families had a lot in common.

What they didn't have in common was their political ideology. In fact, they couldn't be more opposite. Ben's family was Midwestern, conservative, Baptist, while Victoria's family was northeastern, liberal, Episcopalian. But somehow their differences made them more interesting to each other, and it certainly made for some curious discussions around the dinner table at night.

No matter. They were those rare kinds of people who could put their politics aside and just be good friends when they weren't slugging it out on the Senate floor.

"Ben, does the President really think he can finish the wall? Eight billion dollars more is a big chunk of change to keep people out of the U.S. when we now have immigration laws that make it easier for people to enter and obtain citizenship. You guys pushed for a merit system, and you got it. You pushed for more border guards and you got them. You pushed for welfare for work and you got that. People aren't coming here anymore to be on the public dole. Why finish the wall?"

Goodwin squirmed a bit, knowing that Victoria was making a lot of good points. "Hey, you sound like you're still running for President," Ben teased. "Look Tori, I know what you're saying. You make some good arguments. But you're all too familiar with the politics of it. This is one of the President's last unfulfilled campaign promises. His legacy will be incomplete without it. Eight billion in the grand scheme of things is not a huge price to pay for what honestly is a valid component of border security. There is always going to be the criminal element to deal with; the gangs bringing drugs across and the like. It means a lot to the President's constituency in Texas and Arizona. Besides, with budget reconciliation, your side should pick another battle to fight because you can't win this one. Plus, if we can't do it budget neutral, we'll just wait until inauguration day when we'll have 60 Republican Senators. If I were on your team, I'd be more focused on women's health. That's where the President wants to go next. Planned Parenthood funding for late term and partial birth abortion still sticks in his craw. He wants to cut off that funding."

"Well, I don't agree with partial birth either but when it comes to the life of the mother, where do we draw the line on late term? It's a slippery slope on the way to partial repeal of Roe v. Wade."

Ben knew they were in that no man's land on yet another "third rail issue". Neither side was ever going to see the other side's viewpoint. And besides Roe v. Wade was the settled law of the land. He decided to drop the debate. "I'm just saying there are more important things you could focus on besides eight billion for a wall."

"Can't disagree with that Ben, but I still don't like it."

"You don't have to like it. You just have to live with it," Goodwin said half-heartedly. "I've learned to."

"Hey you two, we're supposed to be out to dinner relaxing, not debating," Speaker Locker said as he tried to focus his two colleagues on the menu. "If we're going to debate anything, it ought to be about something that's of greater importance to the country than walls."

"Like what?" Cheshire inquired.

"Like the rumblings I hear coming from across the aisle in the House having to do with secession," The Speaker said bluntly.

The word instantly cast a pall on the conversation as the mood darkened.

Victoria looked down avoiding eye contact with the Speaker. "You know where I stand on that issue. I won't support it."

"Neither will I for obvious reasons. Preserve the Union. That's what Lincoln said and *did*," Goodwin stated emphatically.

"Well there seems to be a real appetite for it by some of the House Democrats ever since Election Day," Locker continued. "These things have a way of taking on a life of their own and gathering momentum. I think it's more of a danger than ever. Some of my Republican colleagues are already saying, good, let them go, and don't let the door hit you in the ass on the way out. It's a dangerous notion and an emotional one too, not grounded in any clear or sober thinking."

The thought chilled the group, in particular Victoria, who represented one of the thirteen states. She had known all along that her election loss to the President might drive Marcus Pilfery and his ilk in that direction. As she blankly stared at the menu, she knew her worst fears were being realized.

Ben Goodwin also knew that there were elements in his party, including, some said the President, who were all too willing to let the secessionists go and be done with them forever.

Goodwin and Cheshire's eyes met, sadly.

Forty-five minutes had passed with none of the Democratic Senators at the Lantern having said as much as a word. Their heads were buried in the document Marcus Pilfery had given to each of them earlier. They even ignored the server when he stopped by to see if anyone needed a refill on their drinks.

Finally, Leonard Stokely looked up from the binder and spoke. "This was obviously well thought out. I'm astonished at how thorough it is. Who did this and how?"

A consultant I hired by the name of Seth Dudley. He's brilliant. He also ran the P.R. campaign for the public question in all thirteen states including your own Senator Stokely."

Stokely was dumbfounded as he stared at Pilfery who never blinked.

Stokely looked down at the document and just sat silently thinking further about what he had just read.

"Any other reactions?" Pilfery asked pointedly.

The group shifted nervously in their seats. All struggled to process what they had just read. It was like some Orwellian novel or worse, something like science fiction author Ray Bradbury would have written.

The document seemingly covered everything. There were sections on the formation of the new government right down to the composition of a new congress, executive branch, and judiciary, with rules for requirements, nomination, election, and term limits. There were sections dealing with national defense, intelligence gathering, infrastructure management, social programs including social security, Medicare, Medicaid, national healthcare for everyone else, education, treasury function, labor laws, commerce laws, housing laws, food and drug administration, and revenue generation through taxation and enforcement. Any area that was part of a federal pool, such as social security, contained several methodologies for proposed division of those funds between the two countries, old and new. There was even provision for the physical location of a new federal government with the site being either San Francisco or Boston.

It was effectively, a blueprint for establishing a new country within the current borders of the United States of America, and it was a sobering experience for the group to read.

"I like it," said Diane Mitchell of Illinois. "How do you move forward from here?"

"Me too, I want to know more," said Michael Simmons of Washington.

The others nodded their agreement.

This group would come to be known as the "Gang of Six".

They would regard themselves as modern day patriots. Not revolutionaries, because that term implied rebellion. This was not a rebellion. This was a recapture of lost liberty. Liberty lost to a man who

behaved like a king, and his party, who they believed
had taken them backwards. They likened themselves
to Jefferson, Adams, Franklin, Hancock, and
Washington. They believed their cause to be righteous
and noble, and they would take pride in forming a
new nation, as they believed the original founding
fathers would have intended.

The storm had begun.

Chapter 34 – Washington, D.C.
January 20, 2021

"…and will to the best of my ability, preserve, protect and defend the Constitution of the United State, so help me God," President Stanton states with confidence, chin raised, with a look of resolve on his face.

There it was. At just past noon President Oliver Stanton had taken the oath of office for a second time and was about to embark on his second term. The Democratic Congressional members who were in the audience could scarcely believe what they were witnessing. It was like the same bad dream from four years earlier repeating itself. Their tone was reserved, if not somber; as if they were attending a funeral, not the swearing in of the President of the greatest Democracy the world had ever known.

As the band regaled the President with Hail to the Chief, he smiled and waved to the crowd assembled on the Capitol steps and beyond into the mall area. The crowd was a bit smaller than four years earlier; a fact the President's Press Secretary would attribute to the less than ideal weather on this inauguration day. No matter to Stanton. In his mind he had redeemed himself from four years earlier when he had won the electoral vote but failed to capture the popular vote. Not this time. Now he would dare the mainstream media to report that fact, and call them out when they failed to do so.

His ego had been satisfied--for the time being.

As he and the first family, after the obligatory handshakes and well wishes from the largely partisan gathering of supporters, left the Capitol, another man on a mission also left the Capitol steps.

Congressman and House Minority Leader, Horace Dettinger of California headed to the office of Marcus Pilfery. Congressman, Brian Bridger of Maryland, the House Minority Whip accompanied Dettinger. It was the job of the Whip to survey and keep record of the voting intentions of all the members of the Whip's party. In this case, Bridger had spent the previous three days speaking with the 187 House Democrats to see where they stood on the issue of secession. Bridger had that information with him, which he and Dettinger would shortly share with Marcus Pilfery.

When they arrived at Pilfery's office, Pilfery's assistant waved them into the Senator's office immediately. "He's been expecting you," she said motioning them into the office.

Pilfery was standing at the U.S. map with Seth Dudley. The two men were examining the map and discussing additional states that they were hoping would come on board with the thirteen.

When Dettinger and Bridger entered, Pilfery approached them and introduced them to Dudley.

"So you're the man who led all those successful secession campaigns. It's a pleasure to finally meet you," Dettinger said smiling and offering his hand to Dudley.

"It's an honor Congressman," Dudley responded respectfully.

"And Seth, this is Congressman Brian Bridger, our House Whip. You two are going to be working very closely," Pilfery stated succinctly, with emphasis on the *closely*.

It's a pleasure Congressman. I look forward to working with you," Seth offered. Bridger looked a bit confused and Pilfery took note.

"Now Brian, Seth is an excellent negotiator, and very persuasive. I'd like him to help you whip the vote for H.R. 71. I think he'll prove invaluable in helping convince some of our more reluctant members," Pilfery stated pleasantly.

Bridger seemed a bit cautious as he looked to Dettinger for help. "Its o.k. Brian. We're going to need some special help on this bill, and I agreed with Senator Pilfery to have Mr. Dudley be of assistance."

Bridger relaxed and smiled as he exchange nods with Dudley who was smiling.

Pilfery gathered the group around his meeting table where he took a seat at the head of the table. "Please, everyone sit down, be comfortable."

The men took seats and Pilfery asked, "How was the inauguration? A bit chilly and gray out there today, huh?"

"Very chilly," Dettinger said sternly. "And indeed, gray." Dettinger was no fan of the President. He had opposed him and his policies at every turn over the past four years. From health care, to taxes, to immigration, Dettinger was constantly at odds with the administration and made no secret of it. The most recent disagreement between the two men occurred when Stanton stripped certain elements of federal spending from Dettinger's home state of California because the Governor there, who was a close friend of Dettinger declared his entire state a sanctuary for undocumented aliens who were still not registering under the newly passed immigration bill. The President's action had cost California dearly, and secession fever was at an all time high in the golden state.

"Yes, well, sorry I was unable to make it. Seth and I were discussing the likelihood of any more states joining us in the secession movement," Pilfery stated as he pointed to the map on the wall. "Long story short, only two additional states, Maine and Hawaii, have been circulating the petition, and our reports tell us that the signatures just aren't there. Those states rely an awful lot on tourism to fuel their economies and the citizenry just don't seem like they want to do anything that may jeopardize the inflow of dollars into their states. And other than a similarly weak campaign in Nevada, there doesn't appear to be any more interest at this point. So we'll be focused on our thirteen going forward."

Dettinger responded. "That's fine Senator, I think we have a viable path forward with the thirteen. Interest among the citizens there remains high, and with the Republicans picking up those additional four seats to give them 60, well that may the push we need to get this thing over the finish line."

Pilfery seized on Dettinger's comment. "So where are we with the House? What does the support look like?"

"Brian, why don't you take us through the latest numbers," Dettinger looked over at Bridger, who was reaching into his briefcase.

"As of 8 pm last evening, out of our 187 members, we've got 89 who are fully in favor, 44 who are opposed, and 54 non committal. In order to pass the resolution and move toward a constitutional amendment we need 2/3, which is 125. So we need 36 more." Bridger quickly clarified. "Ah, that assumes of course that 2/3 of the Republicans are in favor, but I think that's a virtual certainty in the House. Most of the House Republicans are so extreme, they want us the hell out."

Pilfery took note. "Aha, better than I expected at this stage. 36 eh?"

"Yes, 36. Ah, assuming we hold onto the 44," Bridger added.

"And how are we doing in the thirteen?" Pilfery pressed.

"Very well, we have a clear majority in each of those states, very few dissenters. And unanimous in California," Bridger noted.

"Naturally," Pilfery noted with a wry smile, that wasn't lost on Dettinger. "I wouldn't have expected less from your home Horace."

Dettinger dismissed Pilfery's editorial comment on the political climate in California.

Dudley, who had been intently listening and making notes immediately went for a deeper dive. "Of the 54 non committal, how many of them are from states that Stanton carried in 2020?" Dudley was obviously zeroing in on Democrats who might be vulnerable to a Republican challenger and who, therefore might need additional Democratic support or funding for re-election in 2022, or worse, who could be threatened by being "primaried out".

Bridger was getting it. "20."

Dudley nodded. "Ok, there's roughly half of our 36."

Dudley went on. "The same for the 44 who are opposed. How many from red states?"

Bridger scanned his list. "I'd say about 24, give or take a few."

"Ok, more than enough to get us to 36, but we need a better handle on that number. I've got to know precisely who we're going to target," Dudley said coldly.

Dettinger's eyebrows went up as he looked over at Pilfery. "My oh my. I like this fella." Pilfery nodded and smiled while Dettinger turned to Dudley and asked "Son, you ever think of running for Congress?"

Dudley and Pilfery exchanged knowing smiles.

Chapter 35 – Washington, D.C.
February 17, 2021

The normal daily press briefing by the White House Press Secretary, Suzanne McLaughlin had just begun. As was her normal protocol, McLaughlin called on the Fox News reporter, John Chambers, first.

"Suzanne, we've heard many reports coming out of the House the last few weeks around a bill being sponsored by Congresswoman, Anita Saunders of Illinois, seeking to eventually amend the Constitution to allow any state to secede from the United States subject to Congressional, Executive, and State Legislature approval. First, are you aware of this proposed bill, and second, what is the President's view on this proposal by the Congresswoman?"

McLaughlin was obviously well prepared for this question. The White House had known for quite some time about the rumblings in the House about moving toward a 28th amendment to the Constitution. One that would allow a state to secede subject to approval by 2/3 of both the House and the Senate, and then subject to the approval of three-quarters of the states, 38 at a minimum.

She took a deep breath before answering. "The President is aware of discussions in the House relating to passage of a 28th amendment that would allow state secession. The President is extremely disturbed by the notion of such an amendment, and in no way would he support or endorse the passage of such an amendment. He believes with all his heart and might in the United States of America in its present form and is saddened by the idea of secession. There is absolutely no problem or difference of opinion between political parties than cannot be solved in a forthright and satisfactory manner in order to preserve the union. Preservation of the union is his firm belief and he will do everything in his power to defend it. He took a solemn oath to defend the Constitution and he intends to do so no matter what."

The reporter from NBC news was next and was all over McLaughlin's response.

"Suzanne, if the Constitution were to be amended through an act of Congress, would the President veto the amending bill, knowing that in all likelihood, that Congress could in turn override the veto with a subsequent 2/3 vote? And secondly, what would the President do if his veto were overridden?"

"The President doesn't believe such a bill would gain the support of 2/3 of both houses of Congress, so it's a bit speculative to say at this stage what he would do. This is especially speculative in light of the fact that the issue would also go to the state legislatures where 38 states would also have to ratify the amendment. But having said all that, the President would be opposed to such an amendment."

The NBC reporter pushed the issue. "But Suzanne, what would the President do in a case where such an amendment is passed and ratified?"

McLaughlin paused. She knew there was no way out of the question. The reality was if such an amendment were to be passed and ratified, there would be little any sitting President could or would do. In essence, an overwhelming majority of the country would have voted for the right of any state to secede. How could the President oppose the will of the people in such a case. But she held her ground, and refused to give in to the obvious. "Let's see where this matter goes. The sponsors of this legislation have a lot of hurdles to get over before we get to that point."

The reporter from CNN was next and was not going to let this hot potato go. "Would the President consider any legal action, up to and including the Supreme Court, to overturn the passage of any such Constitutional amendment?"

Suzanne cut off the tail end of the reporter's question and was obviously becoming irritated with being boxed in on this question. "Again, such a scenario is highly speculative, and I don't believe it makes senses to speculate further on legislation that is not even close to being passed."

The media persisted. They were enjoying seeing McLaughlin squirm and they would press it until she forced them to the next topic with the words all Press Secretaries dreaded.

"Would the President consider enacting any of his Executive powers to set aside such an amendment, and what might those powers look like," the reporter from CBS news persisted.

An exasperated McLaughlin responded. "I'm not going to comment any further on this topic. I believe I've addressed what the President's position is, so let's move on."

There, the press had gotten what they wanted. McLaughlin had retreated and was saying, no more. The press loved when this happened because it sent the signal that the Press Secretary was unable to resolve the question to the satisfaction of the media. The networks would be sure to bring that fact to the attention of the American people on the evening news.

In addition, with the matter not having been resolved in this press conference, it meant that the media would be poised to bring it up again and again in future press conferences making it appear that the White House was on the defensive.

Oliver Stanton sat watching on CNN in the Oval office, and fumed at the idea of being the President under who secession was even being discussed. He'd have to address this himself, directly — and soon.

Chapter 36 – The Oval Office
February 18, 2021

The White House had requested, and was granted one hour on all the broadcast networks, for the next night at 9 pm eastern time.

All day long, the President's speechwriters had labored over the speech the President would deliver that evening to the American people on the issue of secession.

Chief of Staff Latimor had spent the better part of the last 36 hours trying to calm the President down. He even managed to convince the President that he could turn this "crisis" into a positive by espousing phrases like: "the will of the people", "spirit of democracy", "the founding fathers intended for the people to have the right to self-determination", and so on.

The President would take the high ground in the speech and not snipe at the Democratic demagogues who were behind this movement. He would be humble and respectful of the democratic process, and above all else, Article 5 of the Constitution, that allowed for such Amendments. He'd key on groundbreaking amendments such as the 13th, which abolished slavery, the 15th which gave the right to vote to all men regardless of race, and of course, the 19th, which gave women the right to vote.

He was determined to not come off as cantankerous, or insulted that secession had surfaced as an issue during his Presidency. Latimor counseled him to put aside any personal animosity and be a "statesman".

Now that he was calm and resolved, he began.

"My fellow Americans, I speak to you tonight from the Oval Office on a matter of the utmost importance to the future of our country; a matter that strikes at the very heart of our democratic republic that the founding fathers established nearly 245 years ago.

I speak to you tonight about the issue of secession. Over the past four years there has been an ongoing dialogue amongst the people of our great nation. That dialogue has at its core, a theme centered around the American people and their right to liberty and self-determination. These rights have been in place since the founding of our nation and are guaranteed by the very foundation of our nation, namely, the U.S. Constitution.

Our constitution, as drafted by the founding fathers, is a living document. It is a document that has evolved over the history of our nation. In fact, our Constitution has been amended on 27 separate occasions. The founding fathers, who were true patriots, knew in their hearts and in their heads, that the document they originally enacted in 1787 was not perfect. They knew, in their ultimate wisdom, that other patriots would follow them, and see the need to modify or add to that great set of laws as our country grew and advanced. They anticipated, and in fact, they expected that the Constitution would need to evolve as the country evolved.

As you all know, the people of thirteen of our United States have expressed their desire, if they so choose to secede from our great union and exercise their right to self-determine their future.

There is now a movement in Congress to amend the Constitution and secure that right to secede. If enacted by Congress and then ratified by a ¾ majority of our state legislatures, the Constitution will then grant them that right to self-determination. This is not something to be undertaken lightly or frivolously. It is something to be done soberly and thoughtfully, because once done, it is something that will impact many, many Americans. It will change our very existence and will touch the lives of every citizen of the United States for generations to come.

There have been times in our history when amendments to our constitution have been so profound and so obvious that they were absolutely necessary to ensure we remained on a course of liberty and justice for all. Amendments such as the 13th that abolished the heinous institution of slavery, were so necessary and so righteous that Abraham Lincoln fought a great civil war to ensure that all people, regardless of race, would live as free people in the United States. It was, in the view of President Lincoln, worth the blood of men, so that all men would be free.

The 15th amendment followed and gave the right to vote to all men, regardless of race, color, or previous condition of servitude. And the 19th amendment, which came 57 years after President Lincoln's emancipation proclamation, gave women the right to vote, ensuring that all citizens of the United States could participate in determining the path forward for our great democracy. These were indeed essential and profound amendments to our Constitution that paved the way for greater freedom and progress amongst all our people.

I speak to you tonight and I say, I do not support or endorse a movement that would result in the dissolution of this great nation. I, speaking as both your President and as a citizen of this great union, believe there is no disagreement or issue that is so large that it would ever warrant or require a disbanding of this great republic. To the contrary, I believe it is our differences and our ability to express them and work through them that truly unites us and gives us the strength and wisdom to act for the benefit of all Americans. It is only through our democratic processes and the sincere goodwill of all of our people that we will work through our differences and make this nation stronger and more united.

Having expressed these beliefs to you this evening, I also say to you that I support and will forever defend that process by which our Constitution may be amended. I say let the will of the people be done through our Congress and our great state legislatures, and if it be the will of the people to form a more perfect union, then let it be done or let the heavens fall.

Thank you for your attention this evening. God bless you all and God bless the United States of America."

"Quite an eloquent speech, I thought," offered Marcus Pilfery. He was speaking to the gang of six gathered around the meeting table in Pilfery's Senate office.

"What else could he say? He can't say that Congress can't pursue the amendment. Article 5 is pretty clear," Diane Mitchell stated matter-of-factly.

"No, he had no choice. Even a blow-hard like Oliver Stanton couldn't possibly buck the constitution," Leonard Stokely added.

"No. But he took the high ground and came off as very statesmen-like. Plus, now he's on the record. And we can use that to our advantage with some of our representatives who need a little push into our camp. This may give it to them," Pilfery said with confidence.

"Not to mention, that it may also help us with the Republicans we need to pass the amendment. Stanton is basically daring them to vote yes and let us secede. But what makes you think they will and let us? I mean they have super majorities in both houses," Michael Simmons asked.

Pilfery glanced over at Seth Dudley, who as usual, was taking it all in and processing the information before speaking. "It's all true what you say, Senator Simmons, but there's another thing that the extremely conservative Republicans are focused on."

"And what would that be Mr. Dudley," Simmons asked curiously.

"Total control. Total power," Dudley stated emphatically.

"Care to elaborate, Mr. Dudley," Simmons countered.

"Certainly. Yes, they've got a super majority right now, which makes things easy for them legislatively. But that kind of thing doesn't last forever. 2022 isn't far off, and there will be 18 Republican Senators up for re-election, with 12 of those being in states that are not hard right. They could go either way. So there's that. Secondly, they are busting your legislative balls so badly right now, is there any doubt that when the political pendulum swings back in the Democrats' favor, and make no mistake it eventually will, that you won't return the favor and make their lives equally miserable? And thirdly, when Stanton's term is up, who do they have waiting in the wings? I'll tell you who; establishment Republicans, that's who. How do you think that's going to go over with Stanton's base? They don't want to refill the swamp with establishment politicians from either party. So 2024 is a complete Presidential crapshoot. Do you think the hard right wants to risk that? I don't."

"Ok, Mr. Dudley, nice analysis. But how do we take advantage of what you're saying. Nothing of what you said is a given. How do we get the right-wingers to see it your way and give us their vote for secession?"

Seth Dudley, if nothing else, had learned in the past four years how to play political hardball. He was prepared to resort to whatever it took to make certain Republicans feel good about voting in favor of the amendment, and in the process, kicking the Democrats right out the door of the country, **their** country. "Mr. Simmons, that's why you hired me isn't it? To get the votes you need for secession. Just leave it to me."

"But what are you planning—" Simmons was cut off before he could get the sentence out.

"Senator Simmons, it's best if we don't know everything Seth has planned. There's something to be said about plausible deniability," Pilfery said stoned-faced. "I think we'll just leave it to Seth."

Chapter 38 – Washington, D.C.
May 13, 2021

And leave it to Seth, they did.

For the three months following President Stanton's address to the nation, and the Gang of Six's meeting in Pilfery's office, Seth Dudley became a one man wrecking crew. He had a lot of help though.

Through influence peddling with lobbyists, and enlisting the aid of democratic political bosses and operatives at the local level, he had managed to swing enough of the House Democrats into the secession camp so that there were more than enough Democratic Congressmen on board for the vote. All told 180 Democrats would vote yes.

Of the 248 House Republicans, there were actually 58 who, right from the start were actually of a mind, to "let those fool Democrats go." They were largely members of the Freedom Caucus. Their view was "give them enough rope to hang themselves". "We'll be better off without them," was what one hard right Republican from Texas said when asked how he'd vote.

That meant to get the 292 votes they'd need for the required 2/3 majority, Seth would need another 54 votes from the Republican ranks.

He got 44 of those through lobbying efforts that resulted in various labor organizations at the grass roots level convincing their members to back off their efforts on pushing for further increases in the Federal minimum wage in exchange for the Congressman's vote on the secession amendment.

He secured 7 more Republican votes by enlisting the aid of local Planned Parenthood organizations, that were located in the thirteen secession states, to agree to a two year moratorium on late-term and partial birth abortions in the Republican Congressmen's home districts in exchange for their yes votes on secession. Dudley assured the Planned Parenthood officials that once secession occurred, the moratorium would quickly end.

And finally Seth dug up enough dirt on three other Republican Congressmen, two involving extra-marital affairs, and one involving a certain Congressman's penchant for Las Vegas call girls, that resulted in three more yes votes.

So when all the votes were tallied the Gang of Six had amassed the 218 House votes needed to pass the constitutional amendment allowing secession.

Seth Dudley was certainly proving his worth to the Gang of Six and they were anxious to see how he would swing the Senate vote in their favor.

Chapter 39 – Brooklyn, New York
August 24, 2021

"How's you summer going Seth?" Marcus
Pilfery said as he greeted his long time friend and now
political operative at the front door of his Brooklyn
brownstone. "Come on in, buddy," Pilfery cheerfully
sad. "Beer?"

"Sure, sounds good."

After grabbing bottles of Sam Adams from the
kitchen, the two headed out on the back deck of
Pilfery's Brooklyn home. It was a warm, humid,
summer afternoon and Pilfery was in the full throws of
the congressional summer recess. He and his wife had
just gotten back from two weeks on the Jersey shore,
Cape May to be more precise, and Pilfery was feeling
relaxed and confident that his plans were moving
ahead as he hoped; in fact better than he had hoped.

They took seats across each other at the small,
round, glass patio table. There was a dull hum of city
traffic coming from the surrounding street that was
partly drowned out by the sound of children playing
in the adjoining backyards.

"I've had a good summer Marcus. Which
means you've had a good summer," Dudley said with
confidence.

The inference was clear to Pilfery. "So what's
the tally look like?" This was an obvious reference to
the status of the Senate vote on secession.

"Ok. We need 67 right for 2/3? All but two of
the Democrats are on board."

"Oh?" Marcus seemed a little surprised. "Which two?"

"Joe Kovacs from Virginia."

"Yeah, I like Joe. He's a straight arrow, a man of real principle. Any chance we can sway him?"

"I doubt it. He's vehemently opposed to secession; would never support it. His Dad came from Croatia. He worked two jobs to put his son through law school. He still lives in the house he grew up in near Roanoke. Loves this country and would never do anything to break it up. He told me himself. Plus he's clean, no vices, no baggage. He just got re-elected last November. He can't be influenced."

Pilfery thought for a moment. "Hmm. Do we have anything he wants?"

"Nope. I checked that. He's pretty moderate. Likes much of what the President has done, health care, tax cuts, immigration reform."

"Who's the other?" Pilfery pressed.

"Hold on to your hat. Victoria Cheshire."

"Oh shit. You got to be kidding me. She's still hanging on for hope?"

"Yup. Practically threw me out of her office when I tried to bargain with her. You're not going to get her vote," Dudley lamented.

Pilfery paused. "Ok. You leave her to me. How about on the Republican side?"

"Ok. So with 38 Democrats, we need 29 Republicans. The first 24 were pretty easy. Conservatives, hard right guys for the most part. You know guys like Carlson from Texas and Prescott from

North Carolina. They are a yes all the way. They can't stand you or what you stand for. You can't get the hell out fast enough as far as they're concerned," Dudley editorialized for effect.

Pilfery chuckled. "And the remaining 5? Who do you think they could be?"

"I pretty much know who we should be targeting. There's Brookings from Montana, Jennings from Nebraska, Gleason from Pennsylvania, Prescott from South Carolina, and Salinas from Florida."

Pilfery was making notes as Dudley spoke. "What makes them likely to go our way?"

"Brookings, Jennings, and Prescott are staunch right-to-lifers. If Stanton chooses to go down that road in his second term and take a hard line, those three might want the thirteen out of the picture. It'll make it much easier to water-down Roe v. Wade. Gleason has a real hard-on for fossil fuels. The western Pennsylvania miners almost single-handedly got him re-elected in 2018. He's a climate change denier and he wouldn't mind having the thirteen take their alternative energy crusade elsewhere. Then there's Salinas. He's the son of a Cuban immigrant. He hates the Castro regime and wants nothing to do with normalized relations with Cuba until human rights are improved there. I think he'd be happy if the thirteen weren't around to screw up future votes for sanctions on Cuba. But he's a real patriot. He'd fight to the end to preserve the union, just like Stanton."

"Anyone else? How about that first-termer from Kansas? Ah, what's his name, Goodwin? Ben

Goodwin. How about him? Kansas is conservative," Pilfery reasoned.

"Not a chance. He's a real boy scout. Did you know the word on him is he's not planning a second-term run? He's one of those term-limit nuts. Says everyone should serve only one term and get out. No running for re-election, says it doesn't serve the voters. What a pain-in-the ass, huh?"

"Hmm. Ok, well you work on those five. I'll work on Cheshire. We need five out of those six. I'd like to get this to a vote by the end of October."

Chapter 40 – Washington, D.C.
October 19, 2021

Seth spent September working his contacts and those who had influence with the five Republican Senators.

Brookings, Jennings, and Prescott, the right-to-lifers, as it turned out were fairly easy to turn. All three cared deeply about protecting the unborn. So after a reasonable amount of cajoling from various religious groups that Dudley had managed to "put in contact" with each of the three conservative Senators, the groups were able to lobby and obtain their votes to amend the constitution and allow those thirteen "god forsaken bastions of abortion" to leave the union forever. Truth be known, the three Senators were teetering on the edge of a yes vote, and this was just the impetus they needed to come down on the side of a yes vote to the amendment.

Thomas Gleason, the Republican from Pennsylvania, who's main constituency was working men and women from the western part of the state, at the end of the day, was happy to give his yes vote if it meant pleasing his voter base. Somehow, Gleason's base had become aware of the Senator's indecision on the vote and staged a march on his office in Washington to help the Senator make up his mind. Oh, that Seth could be quite industrious when it came to securing a vote that he really needed.

Ironically, the vast majority of the Senate Republicans who were ready to vote yes on the amendment were doing so to appease their base in what they thought would be simply a symbolic vote. They scarcely believed that secession would ever really occur. It was almost like their failed 30 or so votes to repeal the Affordable Care Act over the eight years of the Prentice administration. They never expected it would lead to anything. It would prove to be yet another serious miscalculation by Senate Republicans.

Chapter 41 – Miami, Florida
October 22, 2021

Seth Dudley stepped off the elevator at the offices of Florida Republican Senator Enrique Salinas. As he entered the Senator's outer office area he was pleasantly greeted by the receptionist, a smartly dressed, trim, woman in her early fifties, who looked like every professional secretary you ever saw on T.V. or in the movies.

After the usual niceties and small talk, she showed Dudley into the Senator's office. The Senator was finishing up a phone call and gestured for Dudley to take a seat in front of the Senator's desk.

As Seth waited, he scanned the room and noted the usual office décor complimented with family pictures scattered around the room. Opposite the floor to ceiling windows, that faced east toward the Atlantic Ocean in the distance, was the Senator's "ego wall". It contained his college diploma from Florida State, as well as his law degree from Yale. Amongst the diplomas were a series of various federal, state, and community awards, many of which were related to youth services and work performed in the Hispanic community.

Being the son of a Cuban exile, Salinas was a proud American and an ardent Republican. At 39 years old, he was just beginning his second term in the Senate, and was one of the youngest serving Senators. He was regarded as an up and coming star in the Republican party and he was already being considered

213

a future Presidential hopeful, not in 2024, but beyond. He was fiercely proud of his heritage and was not in favor of normalizing relations with Cuba until that government significantly improved its posture with regards to human rights on the communist island nation.

The Senator finished up his call and rose to greet Seth. "Mr. Dudley, Enrique Salinas, pleasure to meet you."

"Thank you Senator. My pleasure. I appreciate you seeing me today."

"Yes," Salinas said curiously as he re-took his seat. "I'm not quite sure of the purpose of our meeting today. I know you are one of Senator Pilfery's supporters and organizers of the secession movement."

"Yes, Senator. I am. I actually head up the media campaign supporting the movement."

"I see," said Salinas cautiously. "So what is your purpose here today?" Salinas had made it a point not to ask Dudley what he could do for him. He had already decided he was not intending to do anything for a man who was making his living promoting the dissolution of his country. Yet he never turned down an opportunity to meet with an adversary in the hopes of gathering some useful information.

Seth smiled, as he tried to put Salinas at ease, but the Senator remained stoic. "My purpose is to better understand your position on H.R. 71 and why you oppose it so ardently."

Salinas sighed and paused as he counted to five to himself in order to keep his temper. Then he spoke. "Mr. Dudley, I oppose any legislation that attempts to undermine the existence and progress forward of the United States. Surely you can understand why most fair-minded people, who have thought this issue through, would oppose such an amendment to the Constitution."

"Well Senator I would say that millions of people in thirteen different states are not opposed to the legislation. They simply want the right of self-determination. Would you say those people are not fair-minded?"

Salinas knew better than to take the bait on that kind of question from Dudley. He would never criticize, either publicly or privately, the electorate of any state as not being fair-minded. "No, Mr. Dudley I would not say those voters were not fair-minded. I would simply say they had not adequately thought the issue through, and were perhaps being misled by their leaders."

Dudley was very impressed with the Senator's response and the great care he had taken in choosing his words.

"Furthermore Mr. Dudley, I would say the kind of government and country contained in the promises of Senator Pilfery and others who hold his beliefs, are hollow and unsustainable. Does Senator Pilfery and his backers really believe that a government that offers free health care, free child care, free college tuition, and a host of other giveaways can be sustained without chasing away the tax base that would be necessary to pay for all that?"

Seth dug in his heals. "Senator, those things you just described are basic human rights, and most progressive Democrats believe that and the people in those thirteen states believe that. We're talking about establishing a society that supports that idea."

"It's a noble idea Mr. Dudley, but that "experiment" had been tried in places like the Soviet Union, Venezuela, and even in Scandinavian Europe, and its either failed or is failing. And where it is not failing, it is only because those countries don't bear the full cost of their own defense, and in fact rely on the United States for that defense. Do you think that comes at no cost to the U.S.?"

Seth had feared this. The meeting had deteriorated into an ideological debate that he couldn't possibly win. The Senator was an ideologue, just as was Marcus Pilfery. They just happened to be on opposite sides of the same argument.

"Senator, respectfully, I didn't come here today to debate you. I merely wanted to understand better where you stood on the amendment, and what it would take to convince you to let the American people determine for themselves what kind of country they want to live in."

"Mr. Dudley, the American people have that right today. This is the greatest democracy in the history of the world, and when people vote for their representatives, they can make that choice. The answer is not to simply to take your ball and go home.

Too many men and women have fought and died to give them that right to pick the kind of government they want. The people have voted and this is the government they have chosen, and to change it the way you propose, it will take more than a simple majority. It will take an overwhelming majority, as the framers of the Constitution had decided. That is my position, and that is why I will not vote in favor of your amendment."

That was that, Seth thought. "Very well, Senator, I admire your principles, and I respect your position. Thank you for your time today." Seth rose and extended his hand to the Senator, who took it with a bit of suspicion about this man's motives in coming to see him today.

"Good day, Mr. Dudley."

"Good day, Senator Salinas."

Chapter 42 – Boston, Massachusetts
October 22, 2021

Fifteen hundred miles away, Marcus Pilfery was finishing up a similar meeting with Senator Victoria Cheshire. Pilfery was having the same difficulty with Cheshire that Dudley had had with Salinas. But this was a bit different. Cheshire was a member of his own party. The Democrats were usually locked-step on most issues, but not this one, and not today.

"Victoria, I think you're being unfair to the people who voted to see this amendment through to the end. For God's sake, the people in your own state want this."

"Marcus, we've been over this ground before on several occasions. My views have not changed. I believe in this country, as it exists. While I obviously have problems with many of the President's and the Republicans' policies, I simply don't see the value in throwing away everything we've accomplished as a nation, and splitting in two because of ideology. It is not beyond repair. It is not irredeemable." Cheshire looked Pilfery dead in the eye. "You do not get my vote on this, ever."

Pilfery restrained his anger. "Well Senator, you just threw away your political career. What are you going to do when the thirteen secede, oh and make no mistake about it, we will find a way, and they will secede. And then they'll recall you, and you'll be out of a job. You'll be the former Senator of Massachusetts, a state that will now be a part of a new and more hopeful country. Where will you go? What will you do?"

Cheshire sighed. "Oh Marcus, I feel sorry for you."

Pilfery looked puzzled. "Whatever do you mean Victoria?"

"I feel sorry for you because you define yourself by the job you hold, not by the person you are and what you believe in. You're terrified to remain as part of this country because you can't stand the thought of not being the one in control and not having the power. You're not willing to work to get it back. And you don't have the courage to get it back. You'd rather just run away instead of working within the greatest system in the world to improve it. You're a quitter and I won't stand with a quitter."

Pilfery was silent. He was resigned. All he could do was leave. But before he did, he turned back to Cheshire. "You should know, that if we don't pass the amendment, we'll primary you out. Count on that Senator. That's probably the last time I'll call you that."

As Pilfery reached for the door, Cheshire stopped him. "Senator, you better hope the amendment passes, because if it doesn't, it'll just prove to the people of New York how ineffective you are. And this will be the last time I call you Senator."

Pilfery slammed the door as he exited.

Chapter 43 – Washington, D.C.
October 29, 2021

Peter Bollinger, Senator from Connecticut, Minority Whip, and Gang of Six member shook his head as he looked down at the latest Senate vote count.

"One vote. One *single* vote."

He was seated across from Marcus Pilfery and Seth Dudley in Pilfery's Senate office. It was late. It was going on midnight, and the group was stumped. They lacked the final vote to secure 67 and a 2/3 Senate majority to pass the 28th amendment to the constitution and establish the right of states to secede. Of course, they'd still need 38 state legislatures to approve the secession, but first things first.

How would they get one more Senate vote?

They knew Salinas was probably a long shot, but they hadn't counted on Victoria Cheshire being so obstinate.

"I don't think any more of the Republicans are in play," Bollinger commented. "So we have to look at the remaining Democrats. And since Cheshire is out, that leaves Joe Kovacs."

"I've taken a run at him already, early on," Dudley offered. "He is a no go."

Pilfery thought long and hard. Have you gone into his past, his background?"

"Yes, I went all the way back to his Senate run and forward. Nothing. He's clean; a model citizen," Dudley assured Pilfery.

Pilfery thought for minute. "What about earlier? Wasn't Kovacs a Congressman before he became Senator?"

"Yes. Yes, he was," Bollinger chimed in. "Tenth congressional district of Virginia."

"Did you go back that far Seth?" Pilfery asked.

"Ah. No, I didn't. I didn't realize he was a congressman before the Senate role," Dudley admitted hesitantly.

"Well, let's do a little more digging on him. Maybe there's something from back then we could use to persuade him to vote for the amendment," Pilfery directed Dudley. "We've got to pull out all the stops at this point."

Chapter 44 – The Oval Office
November 5, 2021

Election day 2021 came and went rather inconspicuously.

Being an odd year, there were no House elections, no Senate elections, and just a handful of Governor's races, where the Republican and Democratic incumbents managed to secure re-election. As far as election seasons went, it was a real yawner.

So much so that CNN and MSNBC focused most of their attention on doing a one-year retrospective on President Stanton's second term. There were the usual potshots taken by the usual group of political pundits, most of whom were former Prentice administration staffers or Democratic has-beens like Elizabeth Morley.

The most critical thing the talking heads could say about the President was that he hadn't come out strong enough against the secession movement. In fact, many speculated that probably, secretly Stanton wanted the secession amendment to pass. He had often referred to the Democrats as obstructionists, and was particularly critical of the leadership in Congress from the thirteen states, often referring to them as crybabies. CNN in particular seemed to take great joy in showing some of Stanton's less gracious sound bites from the past year with the post script: "Stanton bullying continues".

President Stanton watched the MSNBC panel, as he often did, with great interest. He never ceased trying to understand why they hated him so, or at least appeared to, in his opinion.

While it didn't matter what the media reported, he reasoned to himself, he had his record, now a fairly decent five-year record to fall back on.

Unemployment was low at 3.8%. Job creation continued, and GDP growth was still hovering around 3% each quarter. ISIS' influence and reach seemed to be waning, and North Korea had finally come to the bargaining table due largely to Stanton's bluster and unwillingness to bend to their intimidation. An ever increasingly harsh level of economic sanctions against the hermit kingdom hadn't hurt the effort either.

As he watched his former opponent Elizabeth Morley on MSNBC, he couldn't help but feel sorry for her. Here was this once great hope for President, a former Secretary of State, and former Senator now reduced to sitting on a panel with Democratic partisans passing themselves off as objective. It was at best humbling, and at worst downright shameful.

But for the grace of God, Morley might instead be sitting in the Oval Office today watching the equally partisan talking heads on Fox News trash her, while Stanton was out running his multi-billion dollar company. Stanton smiled to himself.

But Morley had one last hope. Marcus Pilfery, in exchange for her efforts to help drive the secession vote, had assured Elizabeth that she would be in line for the Presidency of the new nation.

Since they had initially spoken about it, Marcus assured her on many occasions that she was indeed the logical choice. So she endured and worked and campaigned for secession. And although she garnered a lot of attention and publicity for her efforts, few ever gave the idea of secession much of a chance at succeeding. So she was largely dismissed as a desperate politician in the twilight of a failed career. Her popularity began to wane, even while the secession plan gained momentum.

So she still desperately clung to the hope of leading a nation. It was all she had left.

Chapter 45 – Brooklyn, New York
November 6, 2021

Eileen Pilfery arose late on this Saturday morning in New York City. Marcus had once again remained in Washington for the weekend claiming that the push to get the 67th vote in the Senate to pass the 28th amendment would keep him occupied all weekend long.

This was the third weekend in a row that Marcus had not come back to Brooklyn. Their daughter Lauren was at a sleepover at a friends house so Eileen was alone again for the weekend. Her only companion, yet another bottle of 2019 Rombauer Chardonnay and some Chinese take out food.

She was feeling depressed. Marcus had become consumed with the passage of the amendment, and even when he was at home, hours were spent on the phone wrangling for votes. He was also looking ahead to the passage of the amendment and was already making contact with the various Democratic State Governors to see where their legislatures stood on the issue of secession.

She felt as if there was no end in sight. Even when the amendment passed, there'd be the unending canvassing of the various state legislatures to secure the 38 votes they would need to ratify the amendment. That would take months. And even when that was done, there'd be the issue of the secession itself and the formation of a new country. That could take years. Years that Eileen Pilfery had not signed up for. Now that her only daughter would be attending college soon, Eileen was looking to enjoy her newly found freedom with Marcus. She wanted to travel, and experience new things with Marcus at her side, but feared that type of life was slipping from her fingers.

She had to do something. She was only 49, three years older than Marcus, yet she felt like her life was ending.

Chapter 46 – Washington, D.C.
November 16, 2021

Seth Dudley had done well. He had come through once again for Marcus Pilfery. They had gotten their 67th vote in the person of Democrat Joe Kovacs, Senator from Virginia.

It took weeks of digging by two different private investigation firms, but Seth found what he needed to convince Kovacs to cast his vote in favor of the 28th amendment.

It seems that 15 years earlier during Joe Kovacs second term in the House of Representatives, his wife Colleen, had had an auto accident. It was late on a Friday night and Joe had been held over in Washington on an important vote that went on into the weekend. Colleen had gone out with a few of her girlfriends for drinks and dinner.

On the ride home it had started to rain and the roads were slick. Colleen lost control of her SUV and hit head on into a Toyota Corolla that was being driven by a young mother who's two year old was in the back seat. Both the mother and the child were killed instantly.

As it turned out, Colleen had pulled a .12% blood alcohol, 50% over the legal limit. She was looking at two counts of involuntary manslaughter. That is until Congressman Joe Kovacs stepped in.

Joe was a local guy, whose father was also a local workingman in rural Virginia. The Kovacs family was well liked, and highly regarded.

Joe was able to convince the local district attorney, an old high school buddy, to bury the breathalyzer-test, and get the accident knocked down to reckless driving. Also, in exchange for his efforts, Joe assured the D.A. that funding for a new county jail made sure to surface onto the Congressional legislative agenda. The county got it's funding, and Colleen was given a fine and lost her license for three months, but wound up with no criminal record and no jail time.

This was critical since, Colleen was a member of the city council in the small town outside Roanoke in which she and Joe lived.

While the breathalyzer-test was buried, it was still on file with the police although the records from the incident were sealed.

Seth's investigators had combed the last 20 years of local newspapers looking for every article related to Joe and his family. When they came upon the article related to the accident, the investigators dug deeper until they were able to bribe a records clerk to give them access to the breathalyzer-test records, and bingo, there were Colleen Kovacs' test results.

Once Seth had the results in hand, it was just a matter of meeting with Joe who was now more than happy to see that the democratic process be allowed to play out. He agreed to his vote in favor of the 28th amendment.

For the first time since he had known him, Marcus Pilfery was learning to actually fear Seth Dudley and of what he was capable.

The Senate vote would be the next day.

Chapter 47 – Washington, D.C.
November 17, 2021

"The ayes are 67. The nays are 33. The bill passes."

The Senate Clerk's words seemed to hang in the air like a foul stench. It was an odor that could be sensed throughout the nation.

Improbably and amazingly, Congress had passed a bill that created the 28th amendment to the United States Constitution.

The bill was rather simple. It stated quite clearly that any state(s) could, at its (their) choosing and by approval of a majority of it's voters, and ¾ of all state legislatures, deem itself to be independent from the United States of America. Such independence would allow such state(s) to select a form of government of its choosing.

Of course, the bill, before it became law, would have to be ratified by ¾, or 38 of the 50 U.S. state legislatures. The Executive Branch does not have a say in amendments to the Constitution, so even Oliver Stanton was powerless to stop what, over a period of carefully orchestrated years, had become a run away train. There was no stopping it now.

The Drake Hotel is a beautiful little boutique hotel nestled on a quiet little street in Georgetown, right off of Wisconsin Avenue. It caters to an upper class clientele with spacious rooms and luxurious bathrooms that would befit any upscale home and garden magazine.

Its location is far from the hustle and bustle of Capitol Hill, and it is rarely, frequented by politicians, or other Washington power players like lobbyists or diplomats. In fact, the Washington metro subway system stops short of Georgetown at the Foggy Bottom station, so the Drake isn't even considered a convenient location for tourists or others who have business in D.C.

It is truly a unique, and beautiful, but out of the way place for tourists and Washington politicians.

That is what makes it such a perfect location for Marcus Pilfery this weekend. He called Eileen earlier in the day to break the news that he would, yet again, not be home this weekend. Now that the secession bill had passed Congress, Marcus and the Gang of Six, were anxious to get the ball rolling on securing the ratification of the 38 state legislatures it would need to turn the bill into the 28th amendment to the U.S. Constitution.

Eileen's reaction was almost one of numbness. She scarcely cared at this point. She was drinking too much these days to care about anything that Marcus did anymore. As the weather was turning cooler, she'd dig in on this Friday night with a good bottle of wine and perhaps a little brandy afterwards. Anything to soothe her bruised feelings and deflated ego.

Night had long fallen on Washington and the Drake's rooftop bar was coming alive with returning dinner goers who were catching a nightcap. The propane heaters were cranking and the bar was crowded.

Pilfery raised his glass to toast to the good fortune of he and his companion for the evening. "To a new nation."

"To a new nation, and to us."

"And to us," Pilfery added, smiling at Diane Mitchell, Senator from Illinois and Gang of Six Member.

Chapter 49 – Brooklyn, New York
November 18, 2021

Eileen Pilfery was halfway through her bottle of Paul Hobbs Carneros Pinot Noir when the front doorbell rang.

Who could that be, she wondered. Daughter Lauren was out of town for the weekend on Church retreat, and since Marcus started staying weekends in Washington the past couple of months, their social calendar had dried up.

"Good evening Eileen," the man at the door cheerfully said. It was Seth Dudley.

"Seth. Oh, hi. What are you doing here? I thought you'd be in Washington with Marcus."

"Oh. He sprung me for the weekend. Said I earned a break. You know, with the bill passing and all. So I thought I'd check in on you. I know he's been spending a lot of time in Washington so I thought I'd see how you were doing. Maybe catch a late supper or something?"

Eileen was dumbfounded, but nonetheless pleased to see Seth. In fact she was pleased to see anyone. Yet she was a little bit caught off guard with her husband's best friend standing at the front door.

There was an awkward pause, and then she caught herself. "Oh, where are my manners. Please come in. Can I get you a drink?"

"Sure, that would be nice. Whatever you're having would be fine."

"Pinot?"

"Sounds great," he cheerfully responded as she took his coat.

Chapter 50 – Washington, D.C.
November 18, 2021

Senators Pilfery and Mitchell are no sooner inside the door to room 24 at the Drake, when they begin to furiously undress each other while locked in a passionate kiss. The bottle of wine they shared at dinner followed by the Bourbon they each had at the rooftop bar, has had the desired effect of removing all of their inhibitions.

Leaving a trail of garments on the way to the bed, the two fall to the bed and are almost immediately locked together in a tangle of arms and legs.

Diane Mitchell, at 42, is four years younger than Pilfery and has the body of an athlete. She is a runner and her muscles are toned and her aerobic fitness is that of a 20 year old. Her skin tone is a medium brown and her eyes dark brown.

She has long been attracted to Marcus Pilfery. Even at age 50, Pilfery is in almost as good a shape as he was back in his twenties. Plenty of time in the Congressional gym has assured that.

His confidence and grasp of the political scene in Washington is intoxicating to the first-term Senator from suburban Chicago. His prowess in bed is just as formidable as his presence on the Senate floor. And she is enjoying this moment to its fullest.

Diane had been planning to bed Marcus for months. Ever since the Gang of Six had been formed, Diane was intent on becoming indispensable to

Marcus. This evening she had taken her game to a new level.

Afterwards, they lay silently in the dark, enjoying the feel and scent of each other's skin. Diane broke the silence.

"Are you ok with this?"

Marcus turned his head toward Diane as if to indicate he didn't understand the question.

She saw his consternation. "I mean do you regret tonight, or are you ok with it?"

"I'm more than ok with it. I don't want it to end."

She breathed a sigh, and smiled softly as sleep followed.

Chapter 51 – Brooklyn, New York
November 18, 2021

Eileen Pilfery lay quietly in Seth Dudley's arms. It was late, almost 1 am, and the neighborhood was still. There were the sounds of an occasional passing car followed by lights that cast a brief shadow on the bedroom ceiling of the massive brownstone.

The evening had started out innocently enough with the two friends discussing their families. Seth was now divorced after his wife had just decided one day that she didn't love him any more. "Just a mistake of my youth," she would later tell him. They had a son, Justin, who was now 14, and who Seth's wife, Gretchen, now had custody of and was living with in Philadelphia.

Seth didn't see his son much, just on holidays. Sometimes Gretchen would say to Justin, people just fall out of love. That was how she felt about Seth, and they parted on decent terms.

They talked about where their plans had gone astray, and soon after Eileen opened another bottle of wine. Eileen wound up crying to Seth about how she felt that she had lost Marcus and would never share with him the kind of life she had hoped for.

Before long, Seth was holding her and comforting her, when they kissed. He hadn't planned to go to bed with the wife of his best friend but she was so vulnerable at that moment and so attractive, that he gave in to his own loneliness.

Now the two were dozing and holding each other and for the first time in a long time, Seth Dudley truly cared about another human being. What a mess he had gotten himself into.

Chapter 52 – Wichita, Kansas
November 26, 2021

Congress was in recess for Thanksgiving and Ben Goodwin was home for the extended holiday. The Senate would reconvene on December 8th for two weeks before the Christmas break would arrive.

Goodwin and his family had enjoyed a wonderful Thanksgiving dinner the day before with the immediate family as well as with wife Jennifer's brother and his family. There was no talk of politics, particularly the recently passed secession related legislation. It was truly a chance for Goodwin to decompress and enjoy his family. The past several months had been tense in Washington as the media speculated about what would happen with the proposed bill. Now that it had passed, they moved on to discuss the likelihood of the new law being ratified by ¾ of the states.

It was an interesting dynamic in the media. The right leaning Fox News channel was confident and hopeful that the states would never go for it. The Fox News view was one of clear patriotism and of wanting to preserve the union at all costs.

CNN tried to remain objective, but was somewhat slanted toward secession as they tended to be sympathetic with the secessionists referring to them as "new age patriots", and simply flexing their democratic muscles in order to see their way clear to a new republic. And besides, CNN regarded it as an absolute ratings boon. They would no doubt spend countless hours discussing and analyzing the issue inside and out.

MSNBC, as anticipated, took every opportunity to exploit the secession story as yet another failing of the Stanton administration. Their reporters were simply aghast that the potential dissolution of the United States was happening right under the nose of the President and he was powerless to stop it.

They would ask questions like: Why wouldn't the President sit down with Democrats and the secession movement leaders and hash out a deal to avoid secession? Why wouldn't a President, who was so prone to using executive orders to get what he wanted, use them to avoid secession? And where were the courts in all of this? Why hadn't Stanton take this issue up with the federal courts, up to and including the Supreme Court.

And while raising these very legitimate, yet antagonistic swipes at Stanton, MSNBC anchors and executives were secretly rooting for secession and the formation of a country where they could become the dominant news voice of the people and its socialist government. It always came down to money, and MSNBC executives saw this as a chance to reinforce their hold on progressive thought and generate a ratings bonanza as effectively the "state run media" of the new nation.

As Ben Goodwin tuned in to both Fox and MSNBC this morning, which he often did, figuring the truth lie somewhere in between the reporting of the two news outlets, he dialed his friend and colleague, Victoria Cheshire.

"Tori, how's it going? How was your Thanksgiving?"

"Very nice Ben, and yours?"

"Relaxing. I needed it."

"Didn't we all."

"Tori, I just wanted to say I admire your stand on the bill. It took a lot of guts to go against Pilfery and your party's leadership."

"Thanks Ben, but that was not *my* party voting for this amendment. The Democratic party I've been a member of my entire career wouldn't run from a fight the way Pilfery and his ilk did. They'd have stood on principal and continued to fight for their beliefs."

"Yes, well, there's still a few of your colleagues who feel as you do," Goodwin said trying to reassure his friend.

"The operative word there is *few*," Cheshire lamented.

It was true. In the final vote counts, there were only seven Democratic House members who didn't vote for the amendment, and Cheshire, after Joe Kovacs caved at the end, was the lone Democratic dissenter in the Senate.

"Well I'd say those few are better patriots than those from my party who didn't mind helping push the Democrats out the door. Those folks aren't any better than the Pilfery gang," Goodwin said with obvious disdain for his Republican colleagues who voted for the amendment.

That was also true. A total of 112 House Republicans, and 38 of the 60 Republican Senators, had voted for the measure. Goodwin was equally ashamed of those people.

"What's your take on what the States will do?" Cheshire asked, hoping the State Legislators would think twice and not ratify.

"What I'm hearing is not good. There are three schools of thought. First there are the states that are vehemently opposed to a secession amendment; states like Maine, Michigan, Ohio, Wisconsin, Iowa, and Kansas; Middle America for the most part. Those folks believe in this country and would never give up on it. Then there are states that are all in and are sympathetic to secession. They think this is simply democracy in action and they say let the states decide their own fate. That would obviously be the thirteen, but then places like Texas, Hawaii, Nevada, Utah, Montana, Idaho, Alaska, the Dakotas, parts of the deep south.

And then there are the fence sitters, or everyone else. They could go either way. They'll try to gauge the sentiment of the country as a whole, and they'll tend to follow the lead of their constituents; Florida, Virginia, the Carolinas, Georgia, Arizona, New Hampshire, to name a few. Many of them have voted red or blue over the years. It's less about party loyalty and more about what's consistent with their principles. It would be difficult to predict where they'll net out."

"I can see you've put some serious thought into this Ben," Victoria said sounding impressed with her colleague's analysis.

"I saw a report the other day in the New York Times that had conducted an informal poll. It suggested that 27 states were likely to vote yes, and 23 were a no vote. But who knows?"

"It's going to be hard to get a handle on this. There are hundreds of legislators obviously, but the thing is no one really knows who they all are. So it's hard to predict what they'll do," Goodwin added.

"You're right. It's a total unknown."

"Tori, have you thought about what you'll do?" Goodwin paused to choose his words carefully. "I mean what you'll do in the event this happens and Massachusetts secedes?"

The words were like a sledgehammer to the forehead to Cheshire. It was the first time someone had ever uttered them out loud, and they left her cold.

"I've thought about it a long time; ever since the Massachusetts petition was signed. While it will kill me, I won't stay here if we secede. I'll serve out my term that ends in 2022, but Massachusetts will no longer be my home. I couldn't bear the thought of not being a citizen of the United States."

Goodwin was both heartened and saddened by this. Heartened because like himself, Victoria had a deep love of this country and would do anything to see it preserved. Saddened because Massachusetts had been her life long home, and under secession it would no longer be a part of the U.S. It would wind up as part of some bastardized version of the U.S.; the Democratic Socialist United States of America was the name that some of the secessionists had floated for consideration. Appalling, thought Goodwin.

"Where would you go," Ben asked her.

"I don't know. It depends on what kind of work I want to do."

Like many in Congress, Cheshire was an attorney by trade. "Maybe I'll teach somewhere. Or maybe I'll just go somewhere and hang out shingle; become a small town lawyer. It'll also depend on Paul, although he's agreed we'll leave Massachusetts. He wants to continue to live in the United States. He can practice Anesthesiology anywhere. He's board certified so any hospital would love to have him." Cheshire thought for a minute. "Hell, maybe we'll become Kansans! Is that what you call yourselves?"

Ben chuckled. "Yes, Tori that's right; or Jayhawks, but not if you went to Kansas State. They're the Wildcats," Ben remarked trying to lift the mood of the conversation.

"You went to Kansas, right Ben?"

"Yes Tori. I did," he replied softly.

"Ok, then it's settled. I would be a Jayhawk!"

Goodwin laughed again. "All right, but let's hope it doesn't come to that."

Cheshire paused. "Yes, let's hope," she said soberly.

President Oliver Stanton was back at his desk after an extended vacation during the holidays. The dust had settled around the passage of the House and Senate bills allowing for a Constitutional amendment that enable states to secede from the U.S. Since that passage, the liberal media had spent nearly 100% of its time reporting on the story and the vast majority of that time was focused on the President's shortcomings in allowing this unprecedented crisis to occur.

Never mind that the process was run strictly in accordance with the very Constitution that Stanton swore to uphold. He had come out and explicitly denounced the movement, and was now allowing the process to proceed according to the Constitution. Since the President does not have a role in the Constitutional Amendment Process, he was effectively powerless to do anything. He was at least on the record as having opposed it, and all he cared was that history would show that.

There were calls for him to issue executive orders to delay the process or get the Supreme Court involved in staying the bill, but he had been roundly criticized all throughout his first term for executive overreach. He was not about to overstep his bounds on a matter as significant as this. He was counseled by Latimor and others to, "let the will of the people be done". He was only too happy to let the process play out all the way. Besides, there was still another hurdle for the secessionists to clear, namely ratification by 38 states. He would always have the option later to step in should the states indeed ratify the amendment. If they did not, he would say: "See, we just needed to have faith that the system put in place by the framers of the Constitution would yield the right answer."

He was torn. On the one hand, he didn't relish going down in history as the only President to allow a successful secession of states. He knew that historians would not be kind. All the good work he had done would always be overshadowed by the specter of secession and he knew it. On the other hand, a small part of him, the vindictive part, was anxious to see the secessionists fail and create a holy mess of a new country. He wanted nothing more than to have them come crawling back at some point begging for re-admission to the United States. And he would do it, he reasoned to himself, to show everyone that he could be both compassionate and conciliatory. That would indeed be a very nice chapter in his legacy. It might even make for a great made for T.V. movie in which he would star, he joked with Latimor.

So President Oliver Stanton would wait and bide his time while the country was to be torn apart. That part he didn't fully appreciate or understand, nor would he ever.

With the Christmas recess long behind them and Congress back in session, the Gang of Six was now focused on the States and how their legislatures would vote on the amendment. The Gang of Six needed 38 States to ratify the 28th amendment, and if they did so, it would pave the way for states to secede and become independent of the United States as it existed.

When the Senate bill had passed with its veto proof majority that became the trigger for the next step.

Constitutional amendments had historically been ratified by the states under two different methods. It was either done by straight up vote by each state legislature or by a special state *convention*. The use of a special state convention had ever only occurred once in the history of the United States. That was in 1933 when the 21st amendment repealing prohibition was enacted. It was the only amendment ever enacted to repeal an earlier amendment, that being the 18th amendment, which had been ratified 14 years earlier.

The current Congress had, believing that secession was of such gargantuan and profound impact to the Republic, stipulated that ratification was to be done by special state convention in each state.

But Congress also believed that such a historically significant amendment was potentially so impactful, it stipulated that statewide elections were to be held for the delegates to the conventions. Each state would elect a number of delegates equal to the number of Congressional districts contained in that state. Those elections were to be held within 90 days of passage of the bill by the Senate. Once the delegates were elected they would then be assembled for a straight up vote on ratifying the amendment. That vote was to be taken within 30 days of the election of the delegates.

Since the Senate had passed the bill on November 17, 2021, the ratification vote by each state convention had to occur by no later than March 17, 2022.

It was at that point that the amendment would become a fully functioning part of the United States Constitution. It was only fitting that that date nearly coincided with the arrival of Spring.

Today had been the final day for the States to conduct their special election of delegates to each of the State's conventions for the purpose of ratifying the 28th amendment, which was now entitled, quite simply, "Secession of States".

All but three states had managed to conduct their elections before this last day before the deadline would pass. Those states were California, Alaska, and New Jersey.

California had run into some voting machine issues in some of its outlying areas that hadn't been resolved until two days before the election. Alaska had been hit with some severe mid-winter storms two weeks earlier that would have affected voter turnout. So the Governor had postponed the election until today. And New Jersey took it down to the wire, because, well, things always seemed to take longer in New Jersey. It had taken the state over 20 years to fight through ordinances and complete a 10 mile stretch of interstate highway, and three years to add a couple of traffic lanes to a two mile stretch on another.

But now the elections were concluded and the special electors would be meeting in one month's time.

While this went on, Pilfery and the Gang of Six had commissioned the Gallup organization to conduct nationwide polls by state to see what the sentiment of the citizens of each state were.

The special electors in each state had established mechanisms such as hot lines and websites to constantly monitor the sentiment of the citizens of their state so that they would vote based truly on the public's wishes. It was an extraordinary demonstration of public awareness and good faith by the special electors, who were taking their responsibility very seriously.

The Gallup polling was indicating that 30 states were favoring approval of the amendment, well outside the poll's margin of error; 10 were opposed to the amendment, again well outside the margin of error and 8 states were simply too close to call, with 4 favoring the amendment, and 4 being opposed. It was going to be close, and the Gang of Six was at their wits end trying to envision a scenario that resulted in ratification.

Marcus Pilfery had assembled the "gang" in his office and they were referring to the poll data that Seth Dudley had obtained from their Gallup consultant.

"Let's start out by focusing on the 8 states where the polling is less certain. First, the states leaning to yes, and where we think the sentiment is today," he nodded to Seth.

"The states leaning yes, but within the margin of error are: Mississippi, Minnesota, Nebraska, and Alaska."

Michael Simmons of Washington was first to react. "That's quite a collection of states in terms of where they fall on the ideological spectrum. Minnesota being blue is kind of the oddball in there."

"Yes, unlike the obvious conservatism of the other three, Minnesota is the outlier. On the one hand, the large urban centers tend to be more liberal and sympathetic to our cause, but the rural areas are extremely patriotic and believe in a strong unified nation, hence the split," Dudley described succinctly.

"Why do you suppose the other three aren't more heavily leaning toward "kicking us out" the way Texas is?" Angela Gutierrez, from Colorado," asked.

"My guess is that while those states are fairly conservative, they are hesitant to see the union dissolved easily. So the citizens there are torn, plus the urban areas seem to lean toward secession, while the rural areas favor remaining. Other than that, it's hard to say," Dudley reasoned.

"Let's move on to the states that are leaning no, but not clearly so," Pilfery said trying to the keep the group focused.

Dudley continued. "So the states that are leaning no, but not overwhelmingly so are: Michigan, Maine, Missouri, and Indiana. That's a mix of Democrat and Republican states, some Middle America, some industrial. They are very similar to Minnesota in sentiment but just going the other way, leaning toward remaining in the union. Maine always seems to be hard to read. They always have a divided legislature, and the Senators and Governors tend to be moderate or even Independent. I'm surprised by Michigan. I thought they'd be with us because many thought that they would think they could get more sympathy for their economic plight from the

Democrats. You know, like perhaps a bailout for some of their struggling cities like Detroit. But I think what we're seeing there is the Stanton effect. Namely, Michigan went decisively to Stanton both times. They believe in his economic plan in bringing jobs back to America and they're willing to see it through to the end of his second term. So far, Stanton is giving them what he promised them."

"Seth, anybody on the definite no side, that we might have a chance to swing over to our side?" Pilfery asked hopefully.

"Perhaps. Maybe there's a chance with Georgia. There are some large urban centers there, like Atlanta that tend to go Democratic, and the hard right leaning folks might just be convinced to let the liberals go and say good riddance. But so far, pride in traditional American values is keeping them on the no side.

We might also have a shot at Wisconsin, Virginia, or North Carolina. Those states have large urban centers there that aren't doing particularly well at the present time. They might want to move in a different direction."

"And what about the strong yes states, any chance we could lose any of them?" Pilfery asked.

Dudley recoiled. "Not really. The definite yes votes are a combination of our thirteen, plus sympathetic blue states like Nevada and New Mexico, and the very conservative states that wouldn't mind seeing us walk out the door because they just view us as a pain in the ass anyway."

Diane Mitchell sneered at this last comment. "They think *we're* a pain in the ass. The nerve of those Fascists," she said indignantly.

Pilfery cringed as the words came out of her mouth. "Please Senator Mitchell, let's keep this on a higher level."

"Senator, there is one thing I should mention about the thirteen," Seth said cautiously.

"Oh. What is that?" Pilfery looked up at Seth from the data.

"Massachusetts seems to be trending toward *no*," Dudley said looking concerned.

"What the hell is that about?" Stokely of Vermont blurted out.

Pilfery shook his head and formed a wry smile. "Cheshire," he said plainly. "Cheshire."

The "Gang" was clearly becoming agitated.

"That bitch!" Angela Gutierrez shouted.

"I knew she was going to be trouble," Bollinger of Connecticut offered, as he seethed.

"She is fierce when it comes to this topic. I am not the least bit surprised. She has been canvassing the state speaking with small town halls about reconsidering secession." Pilfery weighed the groups options for a moment, then turned to Dudley. "Seth, anything we can do about Senator Cheshire?"

The inference in his question was obvious. He was looking for a way to discredit Victoria Cheshire. And he was looking to his chief henchman, Seth Dudley to do the deed.

"I'll look into it, Senator Pilfery," Dudley quickly responded.

"Good. Leave no stone unturned."

Dudley wrapped up. "So that's where we are. We need 8 more states to get us to 38. 10 would be better because it would give us a cushion for the unexpected."

"Ok. Let's reconvene in a week and see where we are. Meanwhile, Seth let's crank up our T.V. ads in the 8 states that are within the margin of error."

"And funding for those?" Dudley inquired.

"No problem. I'll speak to some of our PACs. We'll get the money," Pilfery said to close the meeting.

Chapter 56 – Washington, D.C.
February 24, 2022

The Gang of Six was back at it. Seth Dudley
had assembled a new batch of Gallup data that
morning and the group was now studying it as Dudley
prepared to speak.

"We've made some progress in the last week.
Maine and Missouri are trending from no toward yes,
and Minnesota, Mississippi, and Alaska are now
trending toward definite yes. And Georgia, Wisconsin,
and Virginia are now moving toward yes," Dudley
reported proudly.

"That's excellent Seth," Pilfery said now sitting
up taller in his chair.

"But there's more," Dudley said excitedly.
"Massachusetts is now trending more favorably
toward yes. We may have dodged a bullet."

"Good," Angela Gutierrez said smugly. "I
guess she's not as persuasive as she thought."

Pilfery ignored the comment. "And Seth, how
are we holding with all of our other yes states?"

"Holding steady. It looks like people have
largely expressed their opinions to their State
Legislators. I think the obvious yes and no votes are
probably going to hold. It's going to come down to the
eight undecided and those three that are no votes
trending toward yes. It's going to be close, but I like
the way the data is trending. We'll keep the T.V. ads
running. We've also started phone banks in all 11 of

those states to encourage people to contact their legislators."

"Great job Seth," Pilfery said with confidence. "And Seth, keep digging on Senator Cheshire. We can't be too careful."

Chapter 57 – Washington, D.C.
February 25, 2022

Marcus Pilfery let the hot water run down his back. It was just shy of too hot. Diane Mitchell was at the sink touching up her hair and makeup. This had gone well beyond a one-time thing. The Senate colleagues were now involved in a full-fledged affair. She stood in front of the oversized mirror in the bathroom of room 24, their favorite room in the Graham Hotel in Georgetown.

She was admiring her reflection, wearing only a towel, and daydreaming about what it would be like to be Vice-President in what was likely to become a new country. She decided to test the waters with Marcus.

"Do you really believe Elizabeth Morley would be the right choice for President of the new country? Does she have the necessary vision and will people rally behind her?

Pilfery thought for a moment. His answer surprised Diane.

"No, no, and no," he stated simply

"Oh. Why is that?" she pressed.

"Don't get me wrong. I like Elizabeth. I think she is charismatic, experienced, is well liked by her base, and presidential. I just don't see her taking on the role of leading a new country. This Presidency is going to be unlike any other before it. It's going to take a certain, I don't know call it intuition. It will take an intuition to know exactly what direction to go in and at what pace. It's not going to be business as usual. It will take vision. And above all it will take energy. It will call for energy to lead people who will be experiencing a great deal of anxiety. The kind of anxiety people will be experiencing when they have doubts and are looking to be led and reassured that everything will be all right. I have been thinking about it, and I just don't see her doing that."

She processed that for a few seconds and probed Pilfery a bit more. "So who do you think would be the right person?" she carefully asked.

"Well, I'm thinking the best person, at least initially, might be me as a matter of fact," Pilfery stated as he stepped out of the shower and reached for a robe. "I've been in this thing from the beginning, I can sense the uneasiness people are having with this, even our Gang of Six. There is trepidation, yet I don't feel it. This feels right to me. It's almost as if I spent my entire life preparing for this moment."

"You know I was wondering when you were going to realize what I already knew," Diane stated as she moved closer and put her arms around Pilfery's waist. "I've watched you these past few months; your decisiveness, your confidence, your instincts. They are spot on. It should be you." Diane decided to go for it. Now was the time. And what about Vice-President?" she asked as she held back anticipatory exuberance.

Pilfery had been thinking about this as well. He decided to have a little fun with Diane, more than he had already had the past couple of hours. "Hmm. Let me think for a minute. It would have to be someone who I could trust, supported my policies, was decisive, intelligent, and could step into the top spot if it were necessary," he said while drying his thick, dark hair. "Who could that be?" He teased.

Diane tilted her head, smiled, and played along with Marcus. She let her towel fall to the floor. "Yes, I wonder who that could be?" She playfully asked as she leaned back and pressed her waist in closer to Pilfery.

"Yes. That's it, of course. You Diane!"

"Wise choice, Marcus. Wise choice," she said as she wrapped her arms around his neck as they kissed.

Chapter 58 – Washington, D.C.
March 10, 2022

One week to go. One week until the states were due to convene their special Constitutional conventions and vote to ratify the amendment. Barring the reporting of an unanticipated catastrophe by Seth Dudley, this would be the last meeting of the Gang of Six before the delegates cast their votes.

"Ok Seth, where are we?"

Dudley had an air of confidence surrounding him that the "Gang" had yet to see. "As you can see from the polling data, I believe we are now a lock on Minnesota, Mississippi, and Alaska. And Maine and Missouri are now solidly yes and are outside the margin of error. In addition, the states of Wisconsin, Virginia, and Georgia that were clearly a no and were trending toward yes, are now yes, and are almost beyond the margin of error. If the trend holds, I think we are there."

The look on the faces of the Senators around the table was one of excitement, as well as nervousness. Was this really about to happen, they wondered? As someone once said: "Be careful what you wish for, you might actually get it."

Marcus Pilfery and Diane Mitchell exchanged a quick glance of satisfaction, as the other Senators began busily discussing the polling results, scarcely believing what they saw. It was almost as if they were having difficulty processing the words Dudley had just spoken.

Leonard Stokely was expressionless. He had served in the Congress for 28 years, both as a Congressman and Senator. In between, he served two terms as Vermont's Governor. He truly loved his state and his country, and above all else, he loved the people of the United States. He was probably one of the most highly principled politicians serving in the Congress, and he had dedicated his life to serving his country. He just happened to espouse a political philosophy that was so out of the mainstream, that he was unable to convince a majority of Americans that his policies would not be ruinous to the U.S. economy.

Now sitting here, right now in this office, he, for the first time since this movement had begun, was afraid. He was afraid for his country and what this would do to it. Was this the right path? Would it not have been better to continue to work for what he and his constituency believed in and press forward for change? He was suddenly realizing that it perhaps was too late for that to be an option. He sat quietly looking at the data while his colleagues excitedly discussed it.

Marcus Pilfery, to the contrary, was upbeat, excited, and looking ahead to perhaps future greatness. He knew this was neither the time, nor place to discuss his aspirations to become President of the new nation. That would have been too self-serving and would have detracted from the grandeur of the moment for the other five Senators.

However, Diane Mitchell was also silently and excitedly thinking of what lie ahead. She was

inwardly exuberant. She would be at Marcus's side
and she would be in line for the Presidency eight years
down the road. She was absolutely busting, but
contained herself. And Marcus looked at her and
began to have doubts about her for the Vice-
Presidency.

Chapter 59 – The Oval Office
March 18, 2022

It was an odd night for a Presidential address. It was Friday. Not the typical night to go on national television and capture the attention of the American people. Most people were either out to their favorite watering hole after a tough workweek, or were having a casual dinner, probably take-out of some sort, at home with family.

Aside from Saturday night, Friday was probably the worst night of T.V. viewership in America. Plus, March Madness, namely the NCAA men's college basketball tournament was in full swing, so when CBS cut away from the Louisville/Wichita State game to go to the Oval Office for an address from President Stanton, there was probably a collective moan in bars across the country.

As far as speeches went, it wasn't a particularly long one, and it was a bit anti-climactic. The news had come across the wires that afternoon that a total of 39 states had voted to ratify the 28th amendment, giving states the constitutional right to secede from the United States if indeed a majority of its citizens voted to do so. The speech itself lasted only about three minutes during which President Stanton acknowledged the vote and ratification and had called the vote unlike any other ever undertaken in the history of the country. He had said that the people had spoken and that now it was in the hands of the 13 states to decide for themselves if they would carry-through on their intention to secede. He assured all Americans that the remaining United States of America would do everything in its power to ensure that a thoughtful and careful secession would ensue if that should be the will of the people. He closed by saying that all Americans, regardless of whether or not they came down on the side of secession would always be united by a common purpose and desire, and that was to practice and defend liberty and justice for all.

When the television cameras switched off and the lights went down, Stanton looked down at his desk and was visibly shaken that it had come to this. His Presidency, and legacy would forever be marred by the passage of the 28th amendment. He spoke to no one as he left the Oval Office and retreated to the residency.

Chapter 60 – The Ritz-Carlton Georgetown
March 18, 2022

It was yet another weekend for Marcus Pilfery in Washington. Trips home to Eileen had practically ceased since the Christmas break. She was long past caring, and at this point, she was relieved when Marcus called her on Friday mornings to say he would be staying in Washington for the weekend. It was always about this committee meeting or that special meeting of the Gang of Six, and she had come to expect it.

With her father's absence and mother's indifference, Lauren Pilfery had drifted away from her parents and had gotten in the habit of spending weekends with friends. She had opted for early decision at Duke University and that fall she would be going off to Durham, but in her mind she was as good as gone at this point. She had felt abandoned by her parents and was embarking on her new life sooner than anyone had expected.

And each time Marcus called Eileen to break the news about not coming home that weekend, she feigned disappointment, but played the role of the understanding spouse. And each time she hung up the call with Marcus, she was no sooner placing a call to Seth.

After their first encounter last November, which admittedly had been risky as it occurred right under the neighbor's noses in the Pilfery's Brooklyn brownstone, the two had spent every weekend together that Seth wasn't needed by Marcus in

Washington. They usually met at a mid-town hotel like the Marriott Marquis or Hilton and maintained a low profile dining in out of the way places in the Hell's Kitchen neighborhood of mid-town west Manhattan.

Eileen was vulnerable that first night, and was guilty afterward, as was Seth. But the guilt quickly subsided as Eileen Pilfery realized she owed Marcus nothing. He had used and manipulated her for years and trained her to be the good politician's wife. And she had little to show for it. She had never been cut out for motherhood and so she wasn't particularly close to Lauren; and now with Lauren going off to college, they would be even less connected. Marcus was never around, and was hell bent on the secession movement, so Eileen had felt emotionally abandoned.

Seth was fun to be with, unattached since his divorce, and a skilled and considerate lover. She enjoyed their time together, in and out of bed. She knew she didn't love him, and she doubted he loved her, but they gave each other what they needed, namely time and attention.

So now Marcus Pilfery had chosen a different hotel for this weekend's rendezvous, Georgetown's posh Ritz-Carlton. This was unusual. Marcus Pilfery was a creature of habit, but this weekend his habits had changed suddenly.

He was sitting on the bed removing his shoes when his companion called from the bathroom. "Hey Marcus, this shower is awesome. We should have them installed in the "new" White House, or whatever you're going to call your new home."

He chuckled to himself, "I'll look into it," he called, smiling. "Meanwhile enjoy yourself."

"I would enjoy it a lot more with some company," the voice came from the bathroom, over the sound of the running shower.

Pilfery finished undressing and walked to the bathroom. He stood outside the shower door as his companion let the steaming water cascade over her long black hair as she closed her eyes and enjoyed the warmth. He stood there admiring the sights; the delicate curves, the olive skin, when the woman slowly opened her eyes and upon seeing him, smiled.

"Hello, Mr. President. Or is it premature to call you that?" she giggled.

"Hmmm, maybe. Hello Madame Vice-President. Or is it premature to call *you* that?"

"Perhaps," she coyly said. "Care to join me Senator Pilfery?"

"Would love to, Senator Gutierrez," he replied.

It was the junior Senator from Colorado, and Gang of Six member, Angela Gutierrez.

Pilfery stepped into the shower, and the two anxiously kissed as they embraced.

Part III

DELUGE

Chapter 61 – Washington, D.C.
April 18, 2022

It would end up being a mere formality. Each of the thirteen states, by virtue of their approval of the public question, and whose special electors had ratified the 28th amendment to the constitution, held special elections to give the voters one last chance to reconsider their decision.

The vote counts were overwhelming. In all but one state, 70% of the votes had been in favor of secession. The one exception was Massachusetts, where the yes vote was 63%, still a clear and unambiguous affirmation of the electorate. Senator Cheshire had been on a statewide campaign to have Massachusetts remain in the Union. But the sentiment was clear and the momentum was unstoppable. Massachusetts joined its 12 other sister states and officially declared itself the Democratic Socialist United States of America.

The Marcus Pilfery playbook was about to be put to use, and the first order of business was obviously to establish a new government. Pilfery's draft constitution called for elections, quickly, within 60 days. There was no time to waste. There were many details to work out and much governing to do.

Any resident of the new country could toss his hat into the ring for political office, but it would require a petition containing the signature of 200,000

registered voters. Enough that any old crackpot
wouldn't have the necessary support to be included on
a ballot, but yet not enough that the process would be
bogged down for months.

There, of course, would be elections for
President and Vice-President, and two Senators from
each of the thirteen states, as well as congressman from
each state based on the previously established
congressional districts carried over from the United
States. So for example California had 53 districts
while, New York had 27, and Illinois had 18, and so on,
right down to Rhode Island with 2 and Delaware and
Vermont with one each; a total of 154 congressmen. It
was an even number, that was ordinarily not good for
breaking tie votes, but no one expected there would
ever be ties.

The Republicans in the new nation, while many
regarded themselves as moderate, were clearly
outnumbered and were not expecting to mount
sufficient opposition to anything the Democrats
wanted to do. Some Republicans viewed themselves
at best, as voices of conscience and reason, while others
viewed themselves, at worst, as prisoners within their
own state and country. Those "prisoners", in the view
of many including themselves, would not be long for
this new nation. It was inevitable that they would be
replaced with either Democrats or Republicans who
were RINOs (Republican in name only).

This new nation had been founded on a certain
group think ideology and many of its soon to be
leaders publicly stated they invited discourse and

dissent, but privately they were not in favor of divisive
debates. It was those exact types of sentiments that
had led to secession in the first place, and while they
wanted democracy, they were ashamed to admit to
themselves that they welcomed no such disagreements
in this new order.

There would be no room for conservative
thinking or values. There would only be liberal,
progressive thought, at least in their version of this
soon to be utopian land. It might take time, but
eventually all would come around to a new way of
thinking that was their way, the right way, the only
way.

Chapter 62 – Boston, Massachusetts
April 19, 2022

It would only take Pilfery three days to secure the necessary signatures on the ballot petition and he would become the first official candidate for President of the SDUSA, as it was now being referred to.

Meanwhile there was the matter of dealing with Elizabeth Morley. The failed Democratic Presidential candidate of 2016 was now Medicare eligible and as far as Pilfery was concerned, she was no longer useful to the Democrats or the new nation. She was 65, tired, and irrelevant. She had been waiting around for years, biding her time, writing books, making speeches, and appearing on late night talk shows, all the while thinking she was still the darling of the Democratic Party. She had been loyal to the party and had done what Marcus, former President Prentice, and the other party bosses had asked her to do. She had rallied the vote for secession and kept herself in line waiting for her next chance. It would never come.

"Madame Secretary, please come in," Marcus Pilfery said greeting her with a smile as she entered what would soon become, at least temporarily, the President's office of the SDUSA, the office she had aspired to these last several years. Pilfery was still in the habit of calling her Madame Secretary, a throwback to her role in the Prentice administration, now almost six years ago. It was supposed to be a term of respect and honor, but Pilfery used it like a club to remind her of the last politically significant thing she had done. The vitriol of the term didn't register with her.

"Hello Marcus. It's so good to see you. Congratulations on the ratification. I haven't seen you since the big day. You did a wonderful job leading the cause." Morley said with obvious false praise. She detested Pilfery and everything he stood for. He was needlessly haughty, especially coming from a blue-collar background, self-righteous, and cocky; just like the men she had campaigned against on the way up the political ladder. She felt he wasn't particularly smart or creative, having only achieved a bachelor's degree. She, after all, was a brilliant lawyer, and came from a family of brilliant lawyers, and was extremely intelligent, analytical, and at the same time empathetic towards the common voter, well at least in her own mind.

"And Congratulations to you too, Madame Secretary. We could not have done it without you," Pilfery was laying it on thick now, and Morley was eating it up with a spoon.

"Well, I'm very hopeful that I'll be able to soon discard that moniker and add Madame President," she said with hopeful enthusiasm. Pilfery ignored the reference.

"Please Elizabeth, sit down. Let's talk about the future," Pilfery said plainly.

"Yes, Marcus, the future," she said smiling humbly.

"Elizabeth. I've been in conference with President Prentice, the Gang of Six, and the DNC. We

are all in agreement, that while you did us a
tremendous service helping to get us to this point, it
might be time to take the leadership in a different
direction."

Morley swallowed hard and frowned. "Oh?
What exactly does that mean?" She said sternly fearing
this "direction".

"We see a different role for you; a significant
role; but one of, well, more of an advisory role. Sort of
a special counsel to the President; where you could
have more of an impact behind the scenes, rather than
out front in the public eye. It would be kind of like
what you did for us on secession. You'd be making
policy, setting the tone, sensing the electorate, making
an impact."

Morley was deflated. Her demeanor changed.
She turned inward; withdrew. "I see." Of course she
didn't. Pilfery had played her. Now that he had what
he wanted, she was being kicked to the curb. "And
President Prenctice? He's ok with this? This advisory
role?"

"Yes, of course. He's very ok with it." Pilfery
was embellishing. Truth was President Prentice never
really liked Elizabeth Morley, but she was popular and
having her on the team helped with his re-election.
But now that she was of no use to him, he didn't care
what happened to her. It was her loss in 2016 that led
to Stanton dismantling all that Prentice had
accomplished in eight years. He would always hold
that against Morley, so he was willing to go along with
Pilfery's plan to push her off to the side. Pilfery and

the President were both actually hoping Morley would just take her ball and go home. She was about to.

Morley steeled herself, sat straight up, and unloaded. "Marcus, this is extremely disappointing and very disingenuous of you."

"Madame Secretary---" he tried to speak, but she cut him off.

"Cut the Madame Secretary, bullshit, would you, Marcus? For just once in your life can you just be honest and stop trying to sell me?" She was furious, and Pilfery knew, and had feared it. Elizabeth Morley had a famously bad temper and it was about to come out.

"You used me. You used me all along to get what you want. And now that you have it, you think you can just cast me aside. Well let me tell you something, you're going to regret this. You've underestimated me and what I'm capable of and you will regret this. And I'll tell you another thing, when this experiment of yours starts to go sour, you're going to need me. And I'll be ready to step in and pick up the pieces. This isn't the end of this. I want you to know that," Morley was winding down now, and was saving the best for last. "And who is your running mate going to be Marcus? Is it maybe that little whore from Illinois? Or perhaps that other little opportunist from Colorado?"

Pilfery's eyes were wide with surprise, and the color had drained from his face.

"Yes, that's right. You thought I didn't know about either of them, huh? You must think I'm pretty

stupid. I've been watching you like a hawk for years.
It's been full time work keeping tabs on you. Have
you told Miss Illinois yet that she's out of the contest?"
Morley asked as venom dripped from her fangs. "Oh!
I think you better! She's not going to like it! Maybe I'll
save you the trouble!"

Morley stood up and headed for the door. For
the first time in his political life, Marcus Pilfery was
speechless. As Elizabeth Morley's political opponents
used to say, Marcus Pilfery had been "Morley-fied".

Chapter 63 – Boston, Massachusetts
April 19, 2022

While Marcus Pilfery calmed himself and his composure returned, Morley had reminded him that he still needed to deal with the issue of who his running mate for Vice-President would be.

Initially, he had assured Diane Mitchell that she would be the Vice-President. But then Angela Gutierrez had come into the picture.

Angela was the first-term Senator from Colorado and had been elected in 2016. She was widely considered an up and coming star of the Democratic party and during her first term she had made her mark on a couple of highly visible committees, namely Finance and the Foreign Relations committee. She had a bachelor's degree in Finance and an MBA from Stanford in International Business.

She grew up in Boulder, Colorado, the daughter of Colombian immigrants, who had come to the U.S. prior to Angela being born, and who had become naturalized citizens in 1977. Her father Carlos, was a civil engineer for the State of Colorado, and her mother Anita was a high school math teacher. They worked hard to give every advantage they could to Angela and her younger brother Ricky.

Angela had excelled in Finance at Colorado State and earned a full ride scholarship to Stanford and became the first in her family to graduate college.

Out of college, she went to work for Fidelity Investments as a financial advisor and advanced quickly through the firm to become Director of the firm's Denver office by the time she was 33. Through her contacts at Fidelity she became involved in Colorado politics and at age 35 ran for and was elected to the U.S. House of Representatives. She had a keen financial mind and an excellent grasp of international issues, both financial as well as political. At 38, she ran for Senate and was elected to her current office.

She was up for re-election in November of 2022, and was the odds on favorite. Her name had been mentioned, along with ironically, Diane Mitchell, as a possible Presidential hopeful for 2024. And like her colleague Diane from Illinois, she was ambitious and had set her sites on being Marcus Pilfery's running mate for the Presidency of the new nation; a goal she shared with Pilfery on several occasions.

She was bright, capable, and very attractive.

And with Marcus Pilfery being the master manipulator that he had become, he took full advantage of his ever-increasing power within the secession movement. It was power that allowed him to bed both Diane and Angela at his whim, while dangling the Vice-Presidency in front of both of them.

Ultimately, he had decided it was to be Angela. He believed Angela to be more capable and could see her in the Presidency more easily than Diane.

Diane was a confident, young, African-American woman. Who better than her to have on the ticket of a new progressive nation?

Angela was equally confident, a bit more mature, and very savvy when it came to political relationships. She also possessed better leadership traits like recognizing talent, and developing that talent, along with a humble demeanor. She was also a Hispanic woman. And while there was no doubt that Diane would appeal to the black voters across the new country, he believed more strongly that it was time for a Hispanic to be at the top of the ticket.

Hispanics now made up nearly 30% of the population in the new country and the percentage was projected to grow steadily, especially in anticipation of the new country granting full-out amnesty to the millions of undocumented aliens, with no strings attached, who would now become full-fledged voting citizens of the S.D.U.S.A.

Marcus's decision was no doubt made a little easier by the fact that he enjoyed his off-hour romps with Angela a bit more than those with Diane; not that that should matter, he rationalized to himself.

But it was a fact that he saw himself being more compatible with Angela both politically and emotionally.

So the only thing left to do was how to let Diane down, gently. She would be hurt and probably angry, but unlike Morley, who had savaged Pilfery, she was young and the better years of her political career were ahead of her. She wouldn't risk that career just because she was passed over for a position that she knew in her own heart, she wasn't quite ready for yet.

Pilfery would sell her on a cabinet position, like Energy, Transportation, or Education, which would play to her strengths and let her continue to develop.

He'd paint a picture of eight years in the future, a Democratic ticket with Angela Gutierrez at the top and Diane Mitchell as the Vice-President. It would be the ultimate woman's ticket packed full of diversity and progressive thought. And eight years after that when Diane was only 58, and with over 16 years of cabinet and VP experience, she would be the anointed one.

Yes, Marcus thought to himself, I can sell that. He only hoped that Diane was buying.

Diane Mitchell was not only happy to hear of Marcus' plan for her regarding her political future, but she was downright relieved.

She knew she would be in way over her head as a Vice-Presidential candidate, and she welcomed the opportunity to serve in Pilfery's cabinet. She liked the idea of Secretary of Energy. She was a huge proponent of clean energy, and the environment, and relished the idea of leading the Administration's charge on the global climate change initiative. She believed she could have an impact and gain much needed notoriety by being on the world stage on this important issue.

She liked the idea of being at the table with other important world leaders when decisions were being made with the S.D.U.S.A. supplanting the U.S.A. as the global leader on combatting climate change. It would provide her leadership experience and play well with the voters in eight years when she would join Angela Gutierrez on the most progressive and diverse ticket in political history. Not bad for a poor kid from the south side of Chicago by way of Illinois State.

It didn't hurt either that Marcus suggested that there would be the occasional late night one-on-one meetings with the newly elected President to discuss Energy strategy.

Chapter 65 – Boston, Massachusetts
May 10, 2022

Only two other candidates stepped forward in the days leading up to the election that would be held on June 7th.

The first was Horace Dettinger, the Congressman from California, who had been a supporter of secession, like Pilfery, from the early days of the movement.

Dettinger was an old political warhorse with over 26 years as a Congressman. He was a progressive thought leader, but tended to moderate his positions to get things done with his Republican counterparts. Many of the younger liberals in the party felt he was not as committed to progressive thought as was necessary, especially in what would now be a Socialist country. The fear was that he would talk a good game about things like free college tuition, a single-payer health care system, and cracking down on big corporations with higher taxes to pay for it all, but when it came time to enacting it, he would moderate and not follow through.

So, the political pundits didn't give him much of a chance. Chris Matthews of MSNBC likened him to an old-school George McGovern progressive who was a nice guy, but just didn't have the vision for modern day progressive thought.

The only other serious contender was none other than Elizabeth Morley. This was going to be Morley's last hurrah. It was definitely a political Hail

Mary if there ever was one. She espoused a message of progressive social programs, but with a hint of fiscal conservatism. She argued that Pilfery's programs would bankrupt the new nation and put undo stress on corporations and the wealthy, whose money the new country needed to finance its ambitious social agenda.

She talked a good game of equal opportunity for everyone and a chance to thrive in a new country that put people ahead of profits and humanity ahead of corporations. The message was muddled and didn't resonate with the electorate. Voters were not clear on where she stood with corporate and high earner income tax rates, and she waffled on single-payer health care, pledging a return to rationality and the days of Prentice's Affordable Care Act, and she would not commit to amnesty for undocumented aliens, but frequently talked of a pathway to citizenship that was never well defined.

But the voters had moved on from all of that. They wanted free health care and lower taxes, and green energy initiatives, and an open border culture that promoted immigration instead of controlling it. And above all they wanted it now. Otherwise, why did they go through the trouble and risk of secession if they weren't going to see a new and different paradigm?

Marcus Pilfery gave them what they wanted; all of it. He felt the emotion of the electorate and he played to it. He too reasoned that it was indeed time for a new direction. That people were to be given things like health care, education, a living wage, clean energy, and affordable housing as basic human rights; not merely the opportunity to have access to those things, but in fact, *those things.*

He promised all those things and more, and assured everyone that the wealthy and the corporations that were swimming in record profits and records stock prices would pay for it. He said there would be no cause for concern about bankrupting the country. He cited states like California and New York that were economic powerhouses and huge producers of GDP would lead the way to economic prosperity for all. And the voters rallied behind this refreshing new politician who would finally give them what they needed and wanted.

By the time, the three candidates had secured their places on the ballot for the upcoming election and the first national news polls had been taken, Pilfery was leading in the polls with 57% to 38% for Morley with 5% for the Dettinger.

By the time Election Day would come it would be all over, but the shouting.

In the run up to Election Day, the sitting members of Congress from the 13 states met to plan the transition from the existing U.S. to the soon to be formed S.D.U.S.A.

As one might imagine there were a million details to be worked out with regards to forming a new nation, albeit one that would nevertheless, be closely aligned with the existing U.S.

First and foremost was national defense. The new Congress would propose that the existing U.S. military bases be maintained exactly as is in their present locations, and that the new nation would continue to enjoy the protection of the full-fledged U.S. military.

This, however, would come at a price. The existing U.S. military budget has an annual price tag of $600 billion. Surely, to continue enjoying the benefits and protection of the best military on Earth, there would be a cost to be borne by the new nation.

After some debate, it was decided that the simplest way to apportion the cost to the new nation would be to share the cost based on population. For ease, it was decided that the proportion of House Congressional Representatives that the new nation made up relative to the total of 435 Representatives in the former U.S. would be the percentage that would be used to apportion military and other use based services.

The new nation had 154 House Representative, or 35.4% of the former 435 total U.S. House Representatives. Therefore, the S.D.U.S.A. would be charged approximately $212 billion for its national defense to be provided by the U.S.

The two exceptions to this approach to the military involved the FBI and the CIA. Pilfery and his planners had decided that they would need direct control over some portion of those agencies to deal with both domestic issues and foreign threats that were beyond the scope of city, county, or state issues. So Pilfery appointed an FBI Director, a National Intelligence Director, and a CIA Director. Proportionate staffs were then established with reciprocal agreements for defense of the two nations.

A similar formula was used to allocate costs for the National Highway system, transportation, and other U.S. maintained infrastructure.

However, for the vast majority of social program spending under the caption of "Mandatory Spending", the cost sharing was to be done on an actual use basis, until such time as the various trust funds could be teased apart and in effect "given" to the S.D.U.S.A. So in the case of Social Security, which represented a total cost of $895 billion annually, the new nation would bear the actual cost for recipients who were citizens of the thirteen states. In this case, that cost would be $340 billion, or 38%. California, New York, New Jersey, and Illinois, and their disproportionately higher wage bases more than offset the high cost attributed to the large number of retirees in places like Florida, Arizona, and Nevada, so the cost burden was higher for new nation.

Such was the case for Medicare and Health spending which was a $1 trillion cost per year. Again, the higher cost of health care in the 13 secession states threw the percentages out of whack, so that those states wound up with 41% of the health care costs yet only encompassed 35% of the population.

This had been a major sticking point between the old and new congresses, but at the end of the day, the new nation had no choice but to accept the formula as the U.S.A. controlled the treasury and therefore the funding of the health care institutions in the 13 states.

Besides, Senators Marcus Pilfery of New York and Leonard Stokely of Vermont assured their colleagues: "When we go to single-payer healthcare for our states, we will have better care at less cost for all our citizens."

The same would be the case for Welfare and Food Assistance programs, but there the cost for the 13 states was actually less than the population statistics would dictate. This was due to the higher unemployment, and swollen welfare ranks in poorer states throughout the Deep South, the Midwest rust-belt states, and parts of Appalachia. So the new nation only picked up 33% of the $100 billion annual cost.

It was all very tedious and contentious to divide up a $4 trillion annual spend in an equitable way, but both sides made concessions where they felt they could to get a workable plan.

Both sides wanted it resolved. The S.D.U.S.A. was anxious to get on with building their new nation and believed the disproportionately higher GDP of their 13 states would eradicate any future problems. Plus, they would soon form their own social systems, funded with their own revenues, and would be free of U.S. cost and inefficiency. The U.S.A. just wanted the revolutionaries to go away, so they didn't sweat the details. They were anxious to shed the high cost of social security and health care in the 13 secession states.

So on and on they worked day and night to tease apart the budgets of what would soon be two United States of Americas, one grounded in capitalism, the other in socialism.

They would also eventually tease apart the revenues that poured into the U.S. treasury each day in the form of income taxes, both corporate and individual, along with duties and excise taxes.

Later on, they would agree on a plan to break apart the existing trust funds for Social Security, Medicare, and various taxes. It would be this last step that would allow the S.D.U.S.A. to be, with the exception of their defense through the U.S. military, completely free and independent of the U.S.A.

Lastly, there would be the issue of the National Debt, a whopping $20 trillion. That too, would have to be divided in two under some agreed upon formula.

The new nation would then form and fund their own treasury, levy and collect taxes, and pay for the programs that would benefit its citizens. By the

time this would be fully resolved it would be April of
2023, nearly a year later.

Tomorrow would be Election Day. The citizens of the newly forming Social Democratic United States of America would go to their polls and elect their first President and Vice-President.

The U.S. Congress was in recess to allow for the election of the thirteen states' Congressmen and Senators who would now cease to be Congressional members of the U.S., so Senator Ben Goodwin was at home for the week. He was spending his time traveling around the state hosting town hall meetings with his constituents, and trying to alleviate any fears or tensions the citizens of Kansas may have been experiencing over the impending dissolution of the United States. He had held events in Topeka, Kansas City, Overland Park, and Manhattan, Kansas. Earlier today he had spent time in his hometown of Wichita.

Now he was relaxing at home with his wife, Jennifer, and their good friends Senator Victoria Cheshire from Massachusetts and her husband Paul. Cheshire had been vehemently opposed to the idea of secession from the very beginning and had chosen not to spend Election Day in her home state. She had voted via absentee ballot the week before and in an ironic form of protest, she had written in the name of Oliver Stanton on her ballot. It marked the first time in her entire life that she had ever voted for a Republican for President.

Although she was opposed to virtually every one of Stanton's policy positions, she nonetheless could not bring herself to vote for Marcus Pilfery or any other candidate that would become the leader of the newly formed secessionist country.

The two couples had just finished dinner at the Goodwin home and were now enjoying coffee.

Goodwin had purposely avoided the topic of the election and secession all throughout dinner, instead choosing to keep the conversation light. They discussed baseball and engaged Victoria in a heated debate over whether the Kansas City Royals' pitching staff was superior to that of the Boston Red Sox. They discussed favorite restaurants, vacation spots, books and musical groups. It seems Ben favored the Rolling Stones while Victoria was a die-hard Beatles fan.

Finally, no longer being able to ignore the elephant in the room, Victoria brought up tomorrow's election.

"It looks like it's going to be a landslide for Pilfery. The Massachusetts polling is showing him up by double digits," Cheshire stated with a tinge of melancholy in her voice.

Goodwin hated to see his long-time friend and colleague like this. Cheshire had already decided that she would, immediately upon formation of the new nation, resign from her Senate position. Election Day was to be followed within 30 days with the signing of a working constitution that in many ways would mirror the constitution of the U.S. but with a few major differences, the most significant of which would be the immediate banning of the personal ownership of handguns. Hunters would still be allowed to own rifles and shotguns, but not semi or completely automatic, but handgun ownership would be strictly forbidden.

There'd be a proposed amnesty program, where the states would buy back people's handguns for the first 60 days. Thereafter, any citizen possessing a handgun would be in violation of the law.

The other exception to the U.S. constitution called for the abolishment of the Electoral College. Presidential elections were to be conducted strictly through use of the citizens' popular vote. This had been a sore subject for the Democrats since 2016 when Oliver Stanton had captured enough of the popular vote in states like Pennsylvania, Ohio, Michigan, and Wisconsin to win the electoral votes in those states, yet he had lost the national popular vote by over 3 million votes. He won re-election in 2020 and this time had won the popular vote as well as the electoral vote, but that was of no consequence to the Democrats. Had it not been for 2016 and Stanton securing the Presidency through the Electoral College, the Democrats would not have been in the situation they now found themselves in, in 2022.

"Any thoughts as to who Governor Winchell will appoint when you resign?" Goodwin asked, knowing that the sitting Governor of a state has the authority to appoint Senate replacements upon resignation or recall of a sitting Senator.

"It's probably going to the leader of the State Legislature, Murphy," Cheshire speculated.

"I know Patrick Murphy," Goodwin offered. "He's a good man. He'll do the right thing."

"I hope so," Victoria worried. "He'll be under a lot of pressure from the voters, since his appointment will only be good until my Senate seat comes up for election in November. He'll only have a few months to establish trust and confidence. Plus if he doesn't play ball with Pilfery and his minions, he might have the shortest tenure of any U.S. Senator in history." Realizing her mistake, Cheshire corrected herself. "Shortest tenure of any *S.D.U.S.A* Senator," she laughed realizing that by the time Election Day 2022 would arrive, the S.D.U.S.A. would be scarcely 4 months old.

"Have you decided to leave Massachusetts?" Goodwin asked.

Victoria looked at Paul, who nodded as if to say go ahead. "Yes. We'll be renting a house in Philadelphia, in Germantown. I'm considering an offer to teach Law at Penn. Paul has an offer from Temple University Medical Center. We like Philly. It reminds us a lot of Boston with its colonial heritage and history. It just feels right to us, for the time being," she said trying to convince herself it was indeed the right move.

Goodwin was supportive. "That sounds real nice Tori. Philly is great. I think you'll like it there."

Cheshire was now resigned to her fate. Through an absolutely stunning sequence of events

beginning with the election of Oliver Stanton, she had
been forced to abdicate her Senate role and abandon
her lifelong home state of Massachusetts. How had it
come to this she would always wonder? When had the
world spun out of control? She feared that this would
now be the fate of the country she loved dearly. Her
country had indeed become divisible.

Chapter 68 - Boston, Massachusetts
July 4, 2022

Marcus Pilfery had insisted on this date. The newly elected President of the S.D.U.S.A. had won election a month earlier in what had been a landslide. Pilfery had won 72% of the popular vote to Dettinger's 22%, and Elizabeth Morley's 6%.

He had his mandate from the people and Angela Gutierrez became his Vice-President.

Dettinger had been badly beaten, but had been re-elected to his role in the House. His message of moderation with the electorate simply didn't resonate, so he returned to his House seat in California, where in two years hence, he'd be, no doubt challenged for re-election by some young progressive upstart. His time was clearly past, and the new nation wanted new thinking and much more in the way of progressive policy.

As for Morley, she was now officially and finally out of the national political picture. She would return to her New York home and write her memoirs and try to stay relevant, but clearly her best days were now behind her and she would fade into obscurity.

Even the late night talk shows had stopped calling for her to appear. She was no longer interesting or amusing. In fact, she had become a sad and pathetic shell of her once great self. The speaking engagements ceased and the phone calls ended—abruptly.

Yes. President Pilfery had insisted on July 4th to be both the date of his swearing in as well as the date of the signing of the new nation's constitution.

In a ceremony befitting the first President of a new nation, Pilfery was sworn in, at noon on the steps of the State House in Boston by the Chief Justice of the Massachusetts Supreme Court.

Later that afternoon, the 25 sitting Senators representing the 13 states, and the new Majority Leader of the House of Representatives, Brian Bridger, along with Pilfery and Vice-President Gutierrez would sign the new constitution. Victoria Cheshire was the lone sitting Senator who was not present.

In a matter of weeks, the President would construct a new Supreme Court for the country, and the Senate would hold confirmation hearings and a new court would be sworn in. New district courts would be reconstituted along state lines and the U.S. federal court system would be overhauled to serve two separate countries.

Boston would serve as the Capitol of the new nation, at least temporarily. There were reports that San Francisco was campaigning to be chosen as the new nation's capitol, but Pilfery and the Senators had agreed to go with Boston for the time being as it's proximity to Washington, D.C. made for easier meeting and interaction with the U.S.

The Boston State House would do double duty as both the state capital for Massachusetts as well as the capital of the new country.

How fitting also Pilfery thought, that Boston, the cradle of the Revolution against the British, would now serve as the capital of the S.D.U.S.A. It read almost like a Hollywood movie script, or a cheesy novel.

All afternoon and evening there were celebrations, and gala balls and parties as Pilfery and his first lady, Eileen, appeared at every one of the events. They appeared to be the perfect first couple, as Eileen acquiesced to Marcus' request to, at least give him his moment, before fleeing back to Brooklyn the next morning.

She was the perfect First Lady, and played the role convincingly. A few times throughout the evening she caught glimpses of Seth Dudley who seemed to be following the President from event to event. Seth was careful never to be seen making eye contact with her, and kept his distance from the newly minted President and First Lady.

There would be time enough for being with Eileen once she was back in Brooklyn and away from the spotlight of her estranged husband's Presidency. All the while, Marcus never suspected his long-time friend of carrying on an affair with his wife. And Seth would be sure to never let that fact be known by a man like Marcus Pilfery.

Chapter 69 – The Socialist Democratic
United States of America
Autumn 2022

Life in the new nation was changing rapidly. Bills were being drafted more quickly and new laws were being enacted more rapidly than they ever had been in the U.S. The very first order of business for the new country was to begin raising revenue, and that meant new tax laws. In a matter of six weeks, the new House of Representatives had drafted a new tax code that was very similar to the old U.S. tax code with a few key exceptions.

First, there was the matter of the tax rates. The old U.S. tax rates were progressive meaning that the more you earned, the higher the rate you paid. But even under the old U.S. system, those at the very bottom of the income scale paid a minimum of 10% of their taxable income, with the rates rising gradually over the first several hundred thousand dollars of income, and eventually topping out at 39.6% over about $460,000 of annual taxable income for a married couple.

The new tax law in the SDUSA called for even more dramatic escalation of rates as a taxpayer moved up the economic ladder. After all, the myriad of new social programs and giveaways had to be paid for.

Under the new tax law in the S.D.U.S.A., the tax brackets for a married couple filing-jointly looked like this:

Amount of taxable income	Tax rate
$0 - $40,000	0%
$40,001 - $80,000	10%
$80,001 - $120,000	16%
$120,001 - $160,000	25%
$160,001 - $200,000	30%
$200,001 - $400,000	36%
$400,001 - $600,000	40%
$600,001 - $1,000,000	45%
$1,000,001 - $5,000,000	55%
$5,000,001 and above	66%

Congress considered those earning more than $5 million the ultra-rich, and they would be required to turn over to the government 2/3 of their income earned above $5 million. This encompassed pro-athletes, entertainers, and the very highest earners in the corporate realm, like CEOs, and the upper echelon of the investment-banking world.

This new tax code was projected to *not* raise the new nation's share of the national debt, and was designed to pay for state college tuition for all families who earned less than $120,000 annually. It would also fund a national single payer health care system for all citizens regardless of their income level. And finally, the new projected tax revenue would fund up to three years of free childcare services per child for families earning less than $80,000 annually. There would never again be a financial constraint on working parents obtaining good childcare for all their children.

As far as Corporations were concerned, the Congress was content to, in their words, "modestly raise" the corporate tax rate from 36% to 40% arguing that many corporations, because of their use of offshore tax shelters in places like Ireland and Singapore, were effectively paying much less. Some were paying as little as 18% while most were paying about 27%. Some purely domestic companies like telecommunication concerns that had little or no foreign earnings, were paying at or near the 36% rate.

Many of the most progressive members of Congress remarked that corporations were lucky the rates weren't rates raised even higher as many had been earning record profits for years while barely paying their workers a living wage.

The remaining Republicans in Congress, which frankly numbered less than 20% of the members, were absolutely aghast with the new tax laws. They warned that high earners would flee their home states and move to the U.S., and that corporations would also flee and restructure themselves in such a way as to earn the bulk of their incomes overseas.

Next, the Congress raised the federally mandated minimum wage to $16 an hour, with automatic accelerators that raised the minimum every year based on the consumer price index.

Both President Pilfery and the new Congress's approval ratings continued to soar higher. The citizens had never been happier with their President or their legislators. They were promised free quality health care, free college tuition, free childcare for those who needed it most, and finally a minimum living wage no matter their education or skill level.

But the final, and most dramatic piece of financial legislation came in the form of a series of price controls that were placed on pharmaceutical, biotechnology, and medical device companies. Prices were to be closely monitored and regulated by a new enforcement arm of the FDA that was funded by the tax increases on the wealthy. No longer were companies allowed to set their own prices for live saving drugs. Instead, they had to propose prices to a commission who would have the final say on what prices could be charged for each product. Each company was required to submit to the pricing commission, a detailed multi-year income statement showing their projection of sales, costs, and expenses like research and development to bring the product to market and support it. Profit margins were carefully scrutinized and controlled to prevent profit windfalls at the expense of sick or dying people.

It all sounded very noble and compassionate, but again the Republicans warned that it would kill innovation in a research and development environment it argued was the envy of the world. There would no longer be a profit incentive driving companies to invest billions in new life saving drugs. After years of record corporate profits, the pendulum calling for reform and control had swung in the other direction; and too far, some argued.

By the time mid-October of 2022 had come, the Congress presented President Pilfery with of all things a projected balanced budget. This was something that had not been seen in the U.S. since the second Clinton administration in 1996.

The President and the Congress were euphoric as they now saw a vision for a new America that was even grander than they had imagined.

Chapter 70 – Syntest Corporation
Morristown, New Jersey
February 23, 2023

Jacob Carter looks at the press release describing Syntest Corporation's fiscal 2022 financial results. His eyes move quickly across the page and pause at certain catch phrases that immediately grab his attention: "sales declined by 8% when compared with the prior year", "gross profit margins decreased by 2.4 percentage points when compared with a year ago due to newly enacted government price controls", "net profit declined by 10% versus last year driven largely by price decreases and an increase in the corporate tax rate".

He had known for sometime that this news was coming. The new Pilfery tax laws had been made retroactive to July 4, 2022, so that the new tax rate impacted the entire second half of Syntest Corporation's fiscal 2022. The price controls had taken hold mid-way through Syntest's third quarter, and a government mandated price rollback had been instituted on nearly all of Syntest's new and novel medications that had been launched within the last three years.

Many of those new drugs had been launched during Jake's tenure as the VP of Research and Development for Syntest. The position he eventually had arisen to years after his miracle 2015 discovery of a cure for diabetes.

Now in his first full year as the newly elected President of Syntest Corporation, he sat with his mentor and CEO of Syntest, Dr. Ramesh Nabile, and the Corporate Controller, Michael Perkins.

The three men were reviewing the draft of the press release that would be made public after the financial markets closed later that day. The mood in the room was tense as Syntest's financial results were sure to disappoint investors. And disappointment meant investors were sure to sell their holdings in Syntest stock and the value of Syntest shares would plummet.

This was not what a first year President needed to instill confidence in his Board of Directors and shareholders.

Something would have to be done and it would have to be done expeditiously. The company would have to seek a new direction, a new strategy, a new approach that would overcome the crippling tax and pricing laws the Pilfery administration had enacted in 2022. It couldn't happen overnight, but it would have to happen nonetheless, and as soon as possible.

"Our pricing at the current levels is not sustainable. We cannot support our research and development efforts. Our product pipeline is at risk of drying up, and the tax rate is eating into our profit margins. The shareholders will take their investment dollars elsewhere," Perkins said tersely to the two scientists who were now charged with running the multi-billion dollar pharmaceutical giant that employed 60,000 people worldwide.

Dr. Nabile thought before reacting. Jacob waited for his mentor to speak first. "Michael, these price controls and tax rates, they are affecting all our competitors, are they not?" Dr. Nabile reasoned.

"They are, but only our competitors headquartered in the S.D.U.S.A. Syntest Corporation, as you know, is domiciled in Delaware. Delaware is part of S.D.U.S.A. We pay Delaware tax rates. Many of our competitors are headquartered in places like Texas or Florida or North Carolina and don't have the pricing controls or tax burden that we do. It's that simple," Perkins noted.

"Well the answer is obvious, even to me, and I'm not a financial expert. It seems to me we have to relocate from the S.D.U.S.A to the U.S.A or perhaps even offshore to take advantage of the tax rates that are offered in those locales," Jacob said.

Perkins waited for the words to be fully digested by Dr. Nabile, who had always been a quick study in science as well as other disciplines. "All right Michael. I suggest we commission a study, an analysis of what our options might be. I would like you and Amy to take the lead. Get Alexander Associates involved as well. We'll need expert advice from a firm that's done this before."

Amy was Amy Thompson, Vice-President of Tax and Treasury. Alexander Associates was Syntest's management consulting firm it used for all matters strategic and operational.

"Very good Dr. Nabile, we'll begin immediately," Perkins responded.

"I suggest we craft some wording for the release that will indicate that we intend to explore our organizational structure to mitigate the pricing controls and the tax situation. But we have to be careful how we do it. We cannot come across as greedy or too profit oriented. We have to couch it as protecting shareholder value and sustaining the noble life-saving work of our company," Jake advised.

Dr. Nabile nodded as a look of satisfaction washed across his face. Jacob Carter's judgment and intellect never ceased to amaze him. Dr. Nabile had clearly selected the right person as his successor.

Chapter 71 – Boston, Massachusetts
April 3, 2023

The Wall Street Journal headline leapt from the page and right into President Marcus Pilfery's lap:

"SDUSA corporate earnings plunge, stocks tumble to two year low"

Pilfery was having morning coffee in his Presidential office in the Boston state house with his chief of staff, Carlton Dettwiller. The more he read the more he frowned. Detwiller quietly sipped his coffee waiting for his boss to speak.

Pilfery had selected, Detwiller, a former lobbyist for the mining industry to be his chief of staff. He had never held an elected office, as Chiefs of Staff, sometimes did not. But his connections in Washington were significant as he had spent 18 years with the lobbying firm of Digger and Smute. Prior to that he had worked for one of the large mining firms that had since gone bankrupt. Dettwiller was a Washington insider, but first and foremost he was a deal maker and a survivor. He was precisely what Pilfery, as a new President, needed as Chief of Staff. He was a guy who rarely danced around an issue. He extracted the relevant facts from any situation and always managed to work things to his advantage. He would be the perfect person to control access to Pilfery, and to advise him on policy direction that would benefit those who were in the best position to benefit the Pilfery administration's path forward.

Pilfery had thought about his long-time friend and chief architect of the secession campaign, Seth Dudley. But Dudley was not a Washington guy, and he didn't understand governmental deal making at the ground level. Although Pilfery liked and trusted Dudley, he just wasn't the right guy to both advise and control who got in front of the President.

This, as it turned out, was fine with Dudley. He had earned over $3 million in bonuses for running the secession campaign, including the $1 million bonus that he was paid when secession had actually occurred.

He was weighing his options for his next venture. Pilfery had promised him a position anywhere in the administration that Dudley chose, including ambassadorships to either England or Canada. But Seth was inclined to take his time to figure out exactly what he wanted. He was looking for a position that he'd be good at, but didn't require a lot of long hours or travel. He wanted to position himself to return to the private sector in the future and command a lucrative compensation package.

Meanwhile, he would bide his time and continue to see Eileen Pilfery. He enjoyed sex with her as well as her company, although he was having difficulty imagining being married to her. Still he had something with Eileen that was more than just casual.

Pilfery tossed the Journal on the coffee table in front of him and pouted for a moment before he spoke.

"This doesn't look good Carlton. I don't like where this is going. When the market turns down people will start to become restless. They won't like what happens to their 401K balances, and the elites will moan and groan about their portfolios. They'll look to blame someone and that will surely lead back to me."

Dettwiller, as always, thought carefully before speaking, so as to show his pensive and analytical side to the President.

"Mr. President, we need to reinforce with the citizens all the positive things you have enacted since being elected. Remind them of healthcare, the lower and middle class tax breaks, childcare, the minimum wage. Remind them they are now doing better, and encourage them to live their lives, spend, consume, travel, enjoy their newly found prosperity. That will lead them to stimulate the economy, drive company earnings, and turn the stock market around. It all depends on how the people feel. It's all about consumer sentiment. That's what will stem the tide and get the economy going again."

"Yes, yes, Carlton," President Pilfery said impatiently. "But what about the corporations. I'm already hearing that many of the largest corporations that are headquartered in Delaware, New York, and New Jersey are rumored to be considering leaving their domiciles and either moving to a U.S. state, or even worse, completely offshore. What have you heard about this?"

Detwiller was dreading this direction in the conversation. He had heard more than rumors. He steeled himself. "Well Mr. President, I have it on good authority that Global Computers Corporation, Affiliated Airframe Technologies, and Syntest all incorporated in Delaware were already making plans for exiting to states with more favorable state and federal income tax laws, back in the *U.S*. Not only that, but Marshall Aeronautics, and Digital Industries, both headquartered in Washington, are already moving ahead to relocate to Texas."

"Holy shit! Texas! What the hell is that all about?" Pilfery leapt from his chair, bumping the table and nearly spilling his coffee all over Detwiller. "How can they do that? They're going to turn their backs on the people of Washington after all they've done for those companies? That's how they repay loyalty?"

With the President now royally agitated, Dettwiller tried to remain calm. "It's the hike in the corporate tax rate, sir. It's impacting their profitability and driving down their share price. Texas, which already has Dell, is happy to welcome Digital Industries into their state. The tax laws are more favorable and the workforce there is highly skilled and growing." Dettwiller braced himself for his next revelation to the President. "It seems since the election, there's been a steady stream of tech employees leaving California and re-settling in Texas."

"Shit! What are these people doing? They wanted free health care, free college, and childcare.

We gave it to them! Where are they going?" Pilfery roared as he paced the room.

"Mr. President, many of those leaving are older professional couples, whose children are either out of college or they are younger couples who don't have college aged children yet. Many of them are earning over $200,000 jointly, so they're being taxed at 36%. If they move to Texas, they're taxed at U.S. rates, which are 20%. That's a big difference. Plus, no state income tax in Texas," Lowe added.

"I know there's no state income tax in Texas," Pilfery said with exasperation. "But what about the free health care?"

"They don't need it through the exchanges sir. They get it through their employers. The 9% savings in taxes more than covers their cost, plus there's the state tax savings on top of that."

Dettwiller's argument was irrefutable, at least for the kinds of citizens he was describing. The lower class and lower middle class workers who weren't covered under company health care plans, but did benefit from the free benefit from the government, combined with the rise in the minimum wage, were happy to remain in California. Their skills were less transferable and less in demand elsewhere, so they likely didn't have a choice anyway.

California was quickly becoming a two-class state. There were the lower income, less skilled citizens, who chose to remain in the state and scratch out a living at $16 an hour, plus free healthcare and childcare. And then there were the elites: sports stars, entertainers, those in the arts, who had a vested interest in remaining in the state. They made plenty of money and figured they'd be ok, for a while. They would bide their time and see what happened.

The President was suddenly quiet, and almost resigned to what Dettwiller was describing. He refocused on the companies. He had to do something about the beginning exodus, before it got completely out of hand and touched off an avalanche of departures.

"Carlton, set up a meeting with my Economic council and make sure the Treasury Secretary and the Secretary of Commerce are there as well," Pilfery said decisively. "We've got to do something about this and fast."

Dettwiller nodded. "Right away, sir." He feared it was perhaps too late.

Chapter 72 - Washington, D.C.
April 10, 2023

For as troubling as the economic trends were in the Socialist Democratic United States of America, the trends were quite the opposite in the U.S. Corporate profits for the companies that were based in U.S. states continued to rise to record levels. And along with those record levels, the stock values of those companies were also at all-time highs.

In addition, economic output in the form of GDP was being sustained at a 3.6% level and had been above 3% since Stanton's re-election in 2020. With the lowered corporate tax rate, companies were thriving, generating more income and expanding production and employment. U.S. goods were now more competitively priced around the world and sales of U.S. products overseas increased.

Some companies had even re-located back to the U.S since the tax rates were now more in line with international rates. And as a result, companies were able to reduce their transportation costs for those products coming back into the U.S. so they realized a double benefit, lower taxes, and lower supply chain costs. U.S. unemployment was hovering around 3.5% and wages had begun to rise as demand for more skilled workers continued to rise.

On top of that, many companies headquartered in California, Washington, New York, New Jersey, Massachusetts, and Delaware were beginning to exit those states in favor of states such as Texas, Arizona,

Nevada, Florida, Georgia, and the Carolinas. Those states were more than happy to offer reduced income and property tax deals in exchange for jobs, and the state colleges reaped the benefits of the increase in the tax base through greater state funding. This in turn raised the quality level of the education those institutions offered which then continued the cycle of more companies moving into those states, and the cycle repeated.

While the SDUSA was all about re-distribution of wealth and entitlements, the U.S. focused on growth and opportunity and rewarded creativity and innovation.

As far as Oliver Stanton was concerned, while the secession would forever be a smudge on his political legacy, the economic benefits and increased standard of living for the citizens in the remaining 37 states had never been greater.

He only wished there were a way to bring back the secession states so that history would show how he re-united the country. That would be his crowning achievement. But before that was possible, he reasoned there would probably be more decline in the SDUSA.

The President now sat in the Oval Office with Senator Ben Goodwin from Kansas, and former Senator from Massachusetts, Victoria Cheshire. Stanton had defeated Cheshire for re-election in 2020, yet had always had a very amicable relationship with his Democratic rival. Since leaving the Senate, Cheshire had begun teaching law at the University of

Pennsylvania and was in the Oval Office today at the urging of Senator Goodwin.

Ben Goodwin, upon his election in 2016, had resolved *not* to run for re-election in 2022. However, the residents of Kansas had other ideas. He had been such a popular Senator and his support of Stanton initiatives had brought such benefit to Kansas, that the citizens there literally drafted him into serving a second term. He finally agreed to do so with the understanding that a second term would absolutely be his last term as their Senator. The party bosses supported the notion, the people were happy, and Goodwin ran unopposed and was re-elected in November of 2022.

Since his re-election, Goodwin had become a force in the Senate. He championed bills that promoted clean energy while allowing the oil and coal companies to phase out of fossil fuels. His approach was a phased one that enabled investment in large-scale solar, wind, and geo-thermal power. At the same time, known oil reserves were extracted, refined, and stored as part of the national petroleum reserve, but not burned for energy. This reduced CO_2 emissions, but secured the U.S.'s energy independence from mid-east oil. The sheer scale of solar production lowered the cost of solar and became a job creator in places like West Virginia, Pennsylvania, Oklahoma, Texas, and Louisiana. Wind farms sprung up in places like the Dakotas, Montana, Nebraska, and Goodwin's home state of Kansas. Jobs were created and power generation migrated from fossil fuels to wind and solar.

Goodwin had also sponsored bills that forced stronger and more comprehensive background checks for firearm purchases at both gun shows and through gun stores, and helped push through common sense laws on restricting automatic weapons and high capacity ammunition magazines. In exchange for this extremely unpopular legislation with the far right and the NRA, Goodwin was able to secure a more robust national program of mental health screening, identification, and treatment. It was the ultimate compromise bill and it greatly reduced the number of mass shootings in the U.S. it's first year in law in 2023. All of this was accomplished while preserving the fundamentals of the second amendment.

There was already talk of Goodwin's candidacy for President for 2024. Stanton's Vice-President for his two terms had been, former Army General Henry Morehouse, who had had a distinguished military career spanning over 35 years. Stanton had an affinity for military men and had asked Morehouse to run alongside him in 2016.

The General was not exactly thrilled with the idea, but agreed to be Stanton's running mate in further service to his country. Besides, like many others, Morehouse did not actually expect that Stanton would be elected.

Morehouse was 62 years old at the time and now as he approached 70 and with his health beginning to fail, succeeding Stanton as President was not on his mind. He had made it clear on several occasions in the past year that he would not seek the Presidency. So, the 2024 race would be wide open for the Republicans.

So now Goodwin and Cheshire were seated in the Oval with President Stanton and Chief of Staff Latimor at the President's request.

"Ben I want to thank you for coming today. And Professor Cheshire, I am happy to see you today. May I call you Professor?"

The President asked politely.

Cheshire smiled. "Mr. President, you may call me Victoria if you like."

"All right, Victoria, that's fine," Stanton smiled warmly. "I've asked you here today to discuss the SDUSA. I'm sure you realize they are struggling economically. They are losing companies and high-income earners. I'm also sure by now that President Pilfery is gathering his advisors for advice on what to do. I mean everyday in the news there's talk of this company leaving or that company leaving. I've even heard from reliable sources that Apple of all companies is looking at leaving California. I just don't understand what they did with their tax laws. They're just killing their industries. Pilfery couldn't have thought they'd sit still for that?"

Goodwin and Cheshire looked at each other and the Senator from Kansas spoke first. "Mr. President, I agree with your assessment. They are on a collision course with disaster, but I don't think their Congress realizes what they've gotten themselves into.

Pilfery's approval ratings are very high. The people love him, but the companies and small businesses are fit to be tied. It's just that the people don't know it yet, at least the people who don't own Apple or Microsoft stock directly. Those who own it in their 401Ks won't know it until they look at their next statement. And those who do own those stocks and others, they are fleeing in droves, albeit quietly. But sir, this is an SDUSA domestic matter. What would you propose we do about it? It would be like meeting with the Canadian or Mexican Presidents and advising them on their domestic economic policy. Is that our place?"

Cheshire amplified Goodwin's comments by offering a different but surprisingly uncharacteristic opinion for a Democrat. "Mr. President, SDUSA is a grand experiment undertaken by Marcus Pilfery and a group of extremists who thought it was better to invent a new country with a new system than to work within the one they had and make it better. They lacked the courage and moral fortitude to do what was right for the people of those states. They essentially took the easy way out by bailing out. It was an easy decision, but a difficult process, and one that would produce only one result that they refused to see. And now they are realizing it."

"That's quite a condemnation Victoria, coming from a liberal Democrat," The President commented hands clasped together resting on his chin.

"Deservedly so, Mr. President. Pilfery and his reactionaries hi-jacked my state and a significant part of our country because they didn't get their way. The party platform was not aligned with the wishes of the people, whereas yours was and continues to be. Their pride would not allow them to see that. Mine did, which I why I chose to remain a citizen of the U.S.," Cheshire stated with obvious conviction.

"I'm impressed with your foresight Professor—and your courage. If you were me, what would you do?" The President asked.

Without hesitation Cheshire responded. "Nothing. The first move is theirs. They created the situation. They have to address it. If you reach out at this point, they'll either, resent it and refuse help because they'd look weak to their citizens, or they'll criticize you for meddling in their country's affairs. You won't look good either way. Ultimately, they have to save face. After all, they are politicians. With all due respect, sir, you of all people should know that, having been elected twice."

The President was surprised by such frank commentary coming from someone who was now a private citizen. Goodwin was not. He gave the President a slight nod as Stanton looked to him for a reaction. This was the Victoria Cheshire that Ben Goodwin had known and respected for years.

"Senator Goodwin, your thoughts?" The President said turning toward Ben.

"The Professor makes some good points. It's probably not a good idea to do anything public or overt at this point. Perhaps we can do something through back channel communication. I, and a number of other Senators, speak with our SDUSA counterparts informally from time to time. It may be best to take a less public approach, at least for now."

The President sat and pondered that for a couple of minutes, and turned to Ken Latimor. "Ken?"

"I agree with the Senator's assessment, Mr. President. Let's keep our heads low on this one. No sense getting them shot off. Not with CNN and MSNBC waiting to pounce on us for meddling." As usual, Latimor always worried about the progressive media and how they would control and influence public opinion. This situation could be especially dangerous if the U.S. was portrayed as trying to publicly undermine the government of another country, especially a breakaway republic in its infancy.

"Very good then. No statements to the press and no formal communications with the Pilfery administration. Ben, keep me informed of what goes on in the back channels," Stanton instructed.

The three televisions in President Pilfery's office are tuned to cable news. One is tuned to CNN. Another is tuned to CNBC for the latest business news, and the third is tuned to Fox News.

Pilfery is seated at his desk reading his daily economic briefing. It's been nearly two weeks since he had met with his council of economic advisers to discuss the issue of corporate defections to the U.S. As was typically the case with economic advisers they could scarcely agree on a course of action that the administration should take to stem the tide of companies leaving the SDUSA.

The only thing they could agree on with the President, the Treasury Secretary, and the Secretary of Commerce was that the tax burden on corporations and its impact had been grossly underestimated. "Duh, nice work fellas," was the only reaction the President had for his financial gurus.

So they adjourned their meeting with the direction that the Congress was to immediately begin work on a corporate tax reduction. Chief of Staff Dettwiller was instructed to communicate to the House and Senate leadership the need for a significant tax rate reduction for Corporations. Upon hearing this, Senator Stokely of Vermont and Congressman Bridger of Colorado immediately threw up roadblocks. They cited all of the President's entitlement programs that absolutely depended on that tax funding to operate.

Dettwiller was insistent that a corporate rate reduction was crucial or that there'd be no money at all for the President's programs and, if that were to happen, they'd have to explain to their constituents why suddenly a huge budget deficit would likely occur.

No one was in love with that idea, so the two downtrodden legislators went back to their members to begin work on a proposal.

Pilfery's eyes are moving across the page at high speed as he reads the economic forecasts: Job growth now negative, wages down as jobs dry up, tax revenues shrinking. The President suddenly stops scanning when he gets to the part of the report that describes goings on in the various real estate markets. Homes listed for sale up 24% versus the prior year, prices down 17% in California. Listings are up 21%, prices down 15% in Washington. Listings are up in virtually every one of the 13 states except for Colorado and prices are down in every state by double digits. But the most alarming statistic has to do with foreclosures. Foreclosures are up in six states by 9% from a year ago.

People are fleeing the SDUSA in huge waves. Companies are leaving in droves and taking jobs with them. And the people are following close behind. Pilfery feels a wave of heat cascade across his face as he concludes his review of the report. Then the annoying "Fox News Alert" flashes across the T.V. screen with its unmistakable jet engine and bell ringing sound effect. Pilfery would not normally react to such a news alert because they seemed to happen five times and hour and it usually was some sort of partisan headline that really wasn't breaking news.

But this time, he takes note, because there on the screen behind news reporter, are side-by-side photographs of Seth Dudley and Eileen Pilfery with the caption: "First Lady Love Nest".

Pilfery is stunned and just stares at the screen as the words come out of the reporter's mouth like a tidal wave engulfing the President's office:

"Fox News has learned that SDUSA President Marcus Pilfery's wife, Eileen, was spotted leaving a popular mid-town Manhattan restaurant last evening at 10:30 arm-in-arm with Presidential advisor Seth Dudley. The two were then seen entering the Marriott Marquis hotel in mid-town where they apparently spent the night together. Fox News sources tracked the couple to the hotel where they were seen entering a 9th floor room, from which they emerged this morning at 9:30 am.

Eileen Pilfery, who some reports have indicated has been spending the bulk of her time at the Pilfery residence in Brooklyn, has been seen occasionally dining out with Dudley in Manhattan. This is the first report of the couple being seen entering a Manhattan hotel and apparently spending the night together. Some reports indicate that Eileen Pilfery has been estranged from President Pilfery since before his election.

Dudley, we understand has been divorced from his wife, Gretchen who resides in Philadelphia, for two years. Seth Dudley, who was the architect of the public relations campaign leading to the passage of the 28th amendment that enabled the secession of 13 U.S. states, we have learned keeps an apartment in both Philadelphia and Washington, D.C. More details will follow as they emerge."

Pilfery instinctively reached for the phone and connected with Carlton Detwiller. "Carlton, you better come in here right away."

"I just saw it Mr. President. I'll bring Marie Conti with me."

Chapter 74 – Boston, Massachusetts
April 17, 2023

Marie Conti is the Press Secretary for the Pilfery administration and had no pre-warning of the Fox News story. "They obviously didn't want us getting out in front of this. They just wanted to spring it on us and make you look bad, sir."

"Well, they sure as hell did that!" Pilfery roared as he stomped around the office.

"They didn't want to risk us sharing it with CNN or MSNBC ahead of their report, because they knew both of them would have "soft peddled" it as no big deal.

"Well, those bastards aren't going to get away with this. For Christ sake, they operate in New York! My home state! I'll ban them from the press office, from news conferences. They'll be persona non grata from here on in!"

The President was stomping around the office, mumbling under his breath about slander and other incoherent charges.

"We'll get Marie out in front of the media in an hour with a reaction. We'll simply state that we were not made aware of the report ahead of time, and that this was obviously an attempt, by a clearly partisan news outlet, to embarrass the President with shoddy, ill-advised journalism," Detwiller coolly stated. "Marie, start working on a statement."

"Right away, Carlton."

"Get me Seth Dudley," The President angrily said to Detwiller.

"I'll get him on the phone right away, sir."

"No. I want him here. Now."

Chapter 75 – Philadelphia, Pennsylvania
April 17, 2023

Seth Dudley and Eileen Pilfery had gone their separate ways earlier that morning. Eileen went home to Brooklyn. She had a lunch date with one of her few remaining friends outside the political world, and hadn't seen the Fox News report on she and Seth. But during lunch, she began hearing from family and friends about the report and was left shocked as she tried to enjoy her lunch. She apologized to her girlfriend and hurriedly left the restaurant.

Dudley had taken the 10:30 am Amtrak Acela out of Penn Station which arrived in Philadelphia by 11:20. From there he grabbed a cab to his apartment near the Wharton School at the University of Pennsylvania.

He checked his snail mail, listened to a few voice messages on his mobile, and flipped on CNN at about 1 pm. An hour later, CNN picked up the story from Fox News. Seth sat unabashed as he listened to the CNN reporter spill onto the airwaves the story of he and Eileen from the night before. He had always expected that at some point, they would be found out, but never seemed overly concerned about it. He was divorced and Eileen and Marcus were estranged and had stopped caring for one another a long time ago. Marcus was firmly entrenched as President so the scandal would probably run its course for a few news cycles and then people would forget about it. Dudley was fairly secure financially and really didn't want a position in the Pilfery administration anyway, so he had little to lose. At least, so he figured.

When the call came from Pilfery's office summoning him to Boston, he unhurriedly left his apartment and took a cab back to the train station, where he boarded another Acela, this time heading northeast to Boston. He would arrive by about 5:15 pm where a limo driver with an iPad displaying his name was waiting for him.

On the ride to Pilfery's office in the State House, he thought about what he would say to his long-time friend. He'd apologize for causing Pilfery the embarrassment, but he'd be non-apologetic for having slept with his wife. She was a lost soul and needed someone in her life to validate her worth. He too had been lonely since the divorce from Gretchen and was in need of someone who would value him on an emotional level. He sure as hell wasn't going to get that from working in Washington politics. Eileen had always been a friend, but now she had become more. And it hadn't been until that very moment when he was being driven to meet with the President of his new country, that he realized that he had true feelings for Eileen. He loved her. If Pilfery would let her go, and if Eileen would have him, he decided right then and there that he would marry her.

Chapter 76 – Boston, Massachusetts
April 17, 2023

When Seth Dudley entered Pilfery's office, the President was alone, seated behind his desk. He neither stood to greet Seth nor walked from behind his desk to acknowledge Seth's arrival. He was staring down at some papers, and without looking up, told Seth to take a seat. This was an obvious power move by Pilfery, which neither impressed Dudley nor concerned him. He knew his long-time friend was prone to these types of head games.

Dudley sat and stared at The President who was finishing jotting down some notes on the document he was reviewing. When he finished he removed his glasses and looked up at Dudley.

"Would you care to explain yourself?" Pilfery asked coolly.

Dudley was stone faced. "I love Eileen."

Pilfery was amused. "You love Eileen. Well, isn't that just grand?" The sarcasm was dripping from every word.

"I do Marcus. It didn't start out that way. It just started as two people who were alone and needed someone."

"In deference to the office I hold, you'll address me as Mr. President," Pilfery admonished.

"All right, Mr. President. I love Eileen. And I won't apologize for that. The only apology I owe is to her for embarrassing her. You, Mr. President are entitled to nothing from me. I'm a big part of the reason you're sitting in that chair. Someday, you'll realize that. Did you know that you never even thanked me?"

"Thank you? I thanked you a million times over. I suppose you forgot about all that money I paid you to help put me here?"

"I don't mean money," Dudley said with disdain. "This isn't about money. It's about one person being grateful to another for doing more than just a job. I'm talking about how I compromised my principles and my ethics to get you something you valued. I'm talking about selling my soul so that you could get something you didn't truly earn."

"What the hell are you talking about? Pilfery chided. "I earned this position. I busted my ass to create a vision and bring it to life. You just helped convince those who couldn't see it to open their eyes. It was your tactics, but it was my message. I created this. You were just an enabler."

"You just don't get it do you?" Dudley said shaking his head.

"Get what?"

"All that we did. The dirty tricks, the extortion, and the payoffs we made to get you the votes. It wasn't your message. It was all the shit that I stirred for you for all those years."

"It doesn't matter about that now. I'm here and that's what matters, and now I can build a legacy that will be remembered. And you, you're nothing now. And you'll be nothing because I'm going to see that you never work again in your industry. I'm going to ruin you. Your reputation won't be worth spit when I'm through with you. Who's going to hire the man who split up the President's marriage?"

"It'll be my word against yours."

"Big deal, your word. Your word against the President's"

"And Eileen's word too."

"Eileen," scoffed Pilfery. "She's not going to give up her lifestyle to be with you. How long do think you can keep her in the lifestyle she's become accustomed to with what we paid you. After, you paid all the taxes on that, what do you have left? What do you have, a million and a half, maybe two? She'll burn through that in four or five years. And then what are you going to live on? You're a young man; probably live another 30 years easy. Then what? Ha! She'll listen to reason. She'll stay with me if she knows what's good for her."

"Is the appearance of a stable marriage really that important to you?" Dudley asked.

"For re-election purposes? You bet it is. A stable family man always does better with the voters. Look at what happened to John Edwards when his extramarital affair came to light. It was the end of his political career. How could anyone trust him after that?"

Pilfery got up from his chair and walked to the window and looked out over the Boston Common. "I think we're just about done here."

"Well there is the matter of Senator Kovacs," Dudley left that statement hanging in mid-air for Pilfery to consider.

Pilfery spun on his heel and glared at Dudley. "You'd never go public with that. You were the one who spoke to him directly and extorted that vote out of him. You'd be facing criminal charges."

"Oh, I would do it. I have email records of our discussion of that situation coming right from your account. That was a big mistake Mr. President. You should have never emailed me on that subject. People will see that you authorized it. You'll be complicit. And besides, if you ruin me, I'll have no choice. I won't be able to make a living anyway."

The President was slowly reaching his boiling point. "I'm warning you Seth, you'd better not go public with that information."

"Well then you better not black ball me," Dudley said firmly. "And you better give Eileen a divorce if she wants it," he added.

"You son-of-a-bitch. You can't give me ultimatums. Get the hell out of here!" The President was furious.

Seth remained calm and headed for the door, but he wasn't finished. "Oh, and Mr. President, don't forget to mention to Eileen your affairs with Senator Mitchell and Vice-President Gutierrez."

Pilfery's jaw dropped as he stared at Dudley in disbelief.

"That's right. You didn't think anyone would find out about those, right? Well, Mr. President, I'm a survivor. I didn't get to where I am by not being thorough. I've got hotel records from both the Drake and the Ritz-Carlton as well as surveillance film of you coming and going with your Senate lady friends. Now that would go well beyond just being a problem with Eileen. Think about your constituents. No sir, their not going to like that one bit."

Dudley had the President by the balls, and the President knew it. He didn't even react. He just turned away from Dudley and looked blankly out the window.

"Thank you, Mr. President," Dudley said with mock respect as he closed the door behind him.

President Marcus Pilfery was reeling from his encounter with Seth Dudley. His head was spinning and his mind was going in a million different directions.

He sat at his desk for a while and just stared straight ahead. What can I do to control this situation he thought to himself? No, it calls for more than just control or containment. The situation needed to be eradicated. Dudley must never be allowed to reveal any of the information he threatened the President with today. Pilfery would be ruined if the Kovacs revelation came out, let alone the affairs with the two Senators. Dudley must be stopped.

Pilfery dialed Carlton Detwiller. "Carlton, get me some time tomorrow with the National Intelligence Director." Pilfery paused while Detwiller asked a question. Pilfery responded. "No Carlton, just me, one on one, thank you."

Chapter 78 – Philadelphia, Pennsylvania
April 18, 2023

Gretchen Dudley sits in a Starbucks in downtown Philadelphia less than a half mile from Independence Hall and the Liberty Bell. Seth had phoned her the night before and had asked her to meet him this morning at 9 am.   It was 8:55 am and Seth had not yet arrived.

Gretchen and Seth Dudley had been married for 15 years. The two had met just after college at a Marketing and Advertising conference in New York City. Seth was an entry level advertising executive working on Madison Avenue, and Gretchen was a marketing communications representative for a second-tier ad agency just off of Madison.

It wasn't exactly love at first site. Both were immediately attracted to each other and they sat together at lunch during the first day of the conference at the New York Hilton on 7th avenue.

Seth was a young, confident, high-energy guy and was the quintessential advertising type. Polished, smooth, can-do, and upbeat, easy on the eyes too as far as young Gretchen Jansen was concerned.

Gretchen had grown up in Minnesota, the daughter of Dutch immigrants. Her Dad was a stonemason and her mother worked in a printing shop as a typesetter. Gretchen was a wide-eyed recent graduate of the University of Minnesota, now living in New York City in a 400 square foot walk-up she shared with her roommate, who was a junior auditor at Price Waterhouse Coopers.

Gretchen had decided to move to New York after graduation to build her Marketing career on Madison Avenue. As was usually the case with most new grads, she started out at a small firm that did marketing communications work for companies that were in the bottom half of the Fortune 500. She was a quick study, hardworking, and career oriented. She didn't discourage easily and was more than willing to pay her dues at a small firm just to get the necessary experience to jump to a larger firm at some point.

With dirty blond hair and hazel eyes, she was pretty without being overtly sexy, and Seth was attracted to her girl next-door kind of looks.

The two began dating, and two years later they were married. Two years after that, their son Justin came along, and Gretchen's career was put on hold for few years as Seth rose through the ranks at his firm and was making good money. The couple bought a home in Brooklyn, and soon after Gretchen returned to work and re-started her career.

As they matured, they drifted apart a bit as people sometimes do until one day Gretchen asked Seth for a divorce. She said she simply didn't love him anymore. Seth was devastated, but nevertheless didn't fight the divorce and the two parted ways on amicable terms with Gretchen taking custody of Justin.

Gretchen had landed a promotion in Philadelphia and moved there with her son. Seth remained in Brooklyn as his career continued to flourish. Then one day his old college friend Marcus Pilfery called.

When Seth went to work with Marcus on the secession campaign, he decided to move closer to Justin so he could spend more time with him. So Seth took an apartment in Philadelphia.

Philly was also better proximity to Washington, D.C. for his work with Pilfery. He even hoped that someday maybe he and Gretchen would reconcile, although he didn't hold out much hope for that.

Seth's call to Gretchen the night before had had a serious tone to it, so that when Seth entered the Starbucks and the two saw each other, Seth smiled but Gretchen looked nervous.

"Hi Gretchen, thanks for meeting me," Seth said as he gave her a peck on the cheek.

"Seth is there something wrong, you sounded a bit shaken on the phone last night?"

"No. No, I'm fine. I'm just under a bit of pressure right now. I'm trying to figure out my next career move, so I've got a lot on my mind, that's all."

Gretchen studied Seth's demeanor and body language and knew something was awry. You didn't live with someone for 15 years and not know when something wasn't quite right.

"So what was so urgent that we needed to meet right away?" Gretchen asked as she looked down at the brown manila folder that Seth had brought with him.

"I want you to hold something for me," Seth said as he slid the manila folder over to Gretchen.

"What is it?" she asked curiously looking at the folder.

"It's a hard drive," Seth replied, as Gretchen looked puzzled. "It's a back up of my computer and my phone."

"Why are you giving me a backup of your computer and phone? I don't understand."

Seth swallowed hard and looked around the room, and lowered his voice. "I've done some things that are not good. I'm not proud of them, and they may come back to haunt me." He paused and looked around again before continuing. "If they do, I will need you to get this hard drive to someone."

"What do you mean haunt you?" Gretchen asked. "Are you in some kind of trouble Seth?" She asked lowering her voice.

"Yes, I may be, but I don't know what might happen. But if it does, you'll know it, and then I want you to get this drive to someone."

"Seth, you're scaring me. Are you in danger?" Gretchen asked as her face flushed.

"Honey, I may be. So promise me you'll deliver this package, if something happens to me. You're the only one I can trust," Dudley said quietly but firmly.

"Yes. Of course Seth I will. Who exactly do you want me to give it to?"

Professor Victoria Cheshire at the University of Pennsylvania Law School.

Chapter 79 – SDUSA
May 4, 2023

The Wall Street Journal front page stories screamed like a series of alarm bells:

"SDUSA Unemployment at 9% as Corporate Defections Escalate"

"California, New York, New Jersey Home Prices Tumble in Wake of Citizen Exodus"

"U.S. GDP Growth at 4.1% for 1ˢᵗ Quarter; SDUSA Growth Goes Negative"

There it was in black and white for all-the world to see. The great SDUSA experiment was unraveling, and there was little Marcus Pilfery and his government could do to stop it.

Pilfery's congress was paralyzed. They could not reach agreement on what exactly to do with corporate income tax rates and with each passing day of indecision, more and more companies fled the SDUSA for the business friendly U.S.

Moderate Senators like Simmons from Washington and Bollinger from Connecticut had had enough. They desperately wanted a roll back in the corporate and higher earner tax rates, but the extreme left progressive wing of the congress would not hear of it.

Senator Stokely of Vermont and his progressive caucus had dug their heels in on holding fast on corporate tax rates. He was convinced that the disposable income that had been delivered to the lower and middle classes would result in consumer spending and economic stimulation. It was only logical to him that more money in the pockets of those people would drive the economy and cause companies to produce more goods and services to meet the new demand.

But it didn't. Instead, those people paid down installment debt, student loan debt, and put money away in savings for a rainy day. With the ever-increasing defection of corporations from the SDUSA, people became more nervous and hesitated to spend and became more cautious with their money.

And the less they spent, the more the remaining businesses felt it. People were laid off and jobs were lost as companies tightened their belts to weather the economic downturn.

Wages fell, as unemployment rose and there was a surplus of workers, especially at the minimum wage level.

The economic downturn spiral continued and fed on itself. Stock prices for SDUSA companies plunged and people's 401K balances declined and their retirement savings were put in jeopardy.

The pension funds of groups like teachers, and municipal, county and state workers also took a hit as many of those funds were invested in blue chip SDUSA companies.

Spot shortages of certain consumer goods began to pop up in Illinois, Colorado, and Oregon, as those states began to experience labor shortages in supply chain related professional jobs. Goods were simply not getting to where they were needed. Price inflation began to escalate and touched off panic buying of consumer staples like canned food, over the counter medicines, and baby products.

President Pilfery had reduced information flow to the media by cutting back daily press briefings to twice weekly, citing that the administration was more focused on solving the country's economic crisis rather than answering the same old tired questions from an increasingly hostile press corps.

The President remained holed up in the State House in Boston with his economic advisors as they desperately tried to develop a plan that his now deeply divided congress could support.

And all the while, the threat of Seth Dudley weighed on the President's thoughts and was a serious distraction to clear thought on running the fledging country. He needed to extricate himself from that threat once and for all and decided to act. He arranged for another meeting with the National Intelligence Director to whom the CIA was accountable.

Chapter 80 – Brooklyn, New York
May 7, 2023

A few weeks had passed since Fox News broke the story of the first lady of the SDUSA and her ongoing tryst with Seth Dudley, one of President Pilfery's most trusted advisors. There were the usual cable news panel discussions, most involving Fox News. This was red meat for its mostly conservative U.S. audience. The Fox reporters were positively tickled by the unfortunate circumstances surrounding Eileen Pilfery and the embarrassing impact the affair with Seth Dudley was having on the SDUSA President. They referred to it as immoral and tawdry and used every opportunity available to characterize the affair as typical of the questionable ideology of the so-called rogue nation. It dominated their programming and boosted their ratings into the stratosphere.

However, CNN and MSNBC got into the act also, not because they were enjoying the President's misfortune caused by the affair, but because it was simply great theater and they knew people would tune in to watch. Moreover, the two left leaning networks would present a sympathetic slant on the story citing the poor first lady and how she had become a victim of the vicious political system that was pervasive in both countries and seemed to revel in the agony of others. They also used it as a forum to attack Fox News for its failure to inform The President of the breaking story ahead of time, which was a clear violation of the media's unwritten code of conduct that dictated that you gave the subject of a potentially embarrassing story the courtesy of commenting before the story aired. Fox was portrayed as yellow journalism guilty of perpetrating the worst kind of vitriol outside the bounds of normally accepted reporting standards.

This in turn fed the Fox narrative that both CNN and MSNBC were Pilfery apologists and that, no matter what, he could do no wrong. The sniping and bickering between the networks went on for weeks, until finally a serious news story surfaced involving renewed calls for the dissolution of the European Union in light of recent labor riots in Italy and Greece. President Stanton had thrown gasoline on that already burning fire, by calling for the jailing of the rioters and the networks lost no time jumping into those fertile fields of controversy.

So, now with the constant media attention that had been heaped on Eileen Pilfery and Seth Dudley now receding, Seth had traveled to Brooklyn to see Eileen for the first time since the story broke.

When Seth entered the Pilfery brownstone, Eileen threw her arm around Seth and wept.

"I'm so glad to see you Seth," she sobbed. "The media has been camped outside for weeks. I couldn't go out. I felt like a prisoner in my own home."

"Its ok now Eileen. Take it easy. Relax. Let's be still. Come let's sit down and have a drink."

Dudley put his arm around Eileen and took her to the living room, and sat her down on the sofa, while he poured them both some bourbon on the rocks.

As the two sat quietly sipping their drinks Eileen calmed down. "What did Marcus say to you? Do you know he hasn't been home since? He hasn't even called me. He's freezing me out. It's like I don't even exist to him now." She looked down and just shook her head.

"He was pretty angry. He said he was going to ruin me. Said I'd never work again, that he'd see to it. He also said, he'd never let you go. He'd force you to stay with him."

Eileen suddenly steeled herself, and sat up straight. "He said that? He can't control me. He can't keep me from doing what I want to do. I was planning on leaving him. This just proves my instinct was right."

Seth was buoyed by Eileen's resolve. His instinct was right about Eileen. She was stronger than he had thought. "Eileen, I want us to be together. I think we're good for each other. I know you're good for me. I've needed someone to care for and I care very much for you."

He could see from the look in her eye that she felt the same. "Seth, I've felt the same way about you for months. I just wasn't sure how you felt, and I hesitated to tell you because I was afraid we were going too fast." Seth thought of Pilfery's threats of a few weeks ago and cut her off.

"Eileen, listen. I want us to be together, but before we can do that, you've got to speak with Marcus and tell him how you feel about him and me. Only after that happens and he's forced to realize it will he let you go. Then we can be together. Until then I won't know for sure that I'm free from him."

Eileen knew what she had to do. "I'll go see him tomorrow."

Seth never noticed the black SUV parked outside his apartment. He had spent the night at Eileen's home in Brooklyn, and then took a 6 am train back to Philadelphia. It was Monday morning and Dudley had a 9 am interview with a public relations firm in the downtown area, so he headed back to his apartment to shower and dress for the interview.

It was a little before 8 o'clock and the neighborhood, which largely consisted of small row houses that were occupied mostly by students at nearby Penn, was just coming to life. It was finals week at the university and students busily hurried off to the campus. By all appearances it was a fairly normal Monday morning.

As Seth came into view up the street, a man in a short leather jacket, dark jeans, and ankle length leather boots emerged from the driver's seat of the Suburban. He was also wearing black, latex surgical gloves.

The man in the leather jacket timed his walk perfectly such that as Seth climbed the stairs outside the row house and let himself in the lobby, the man was able to catch the door before the security mechanism engaged. Seth was up the stairs to his apartment in a matter of seconds with the man a mere eight feet behind him.

As Seth inserted his key into the lock of his apartment door and turned the bolt, the man was directly behind him, knife drawn.

As Seth entered the apartment he never realized there was anyone directly behind him. In a matter of a few seconds, the man reached around Seth's head and clamped his hand over Seth's mouth, the hand wielding the knife came around the other side of Seth's head and before Seth could even blink, the man raked the knife across Seth's throat in one fatal motion.

Seth's body went limp immediately as the man guided him all the way into the apartment and lowered Seth's lifeless body slowly to the floor. Seth's eyes were wide open with shock as he stared back at the man crouching over him.

The man closed the door and went to work. He first took Seth's wallet and cell phone from Seth's jacket. He next scanned the room and immediately caught sight of Seth's laptop computer on the desk in the corner of the room.

He grabbed the computer and then rifled through the desk looking for peripherals and storage devices. He found a small external hard-drive, and two thumb drives, which he placed on top of the laptop.

He next checked the rest of the desk for documents and found nothing of obvious interest. There were a few unpaid bills and some mobile phone records, which he left. He checked under the sofa and chair, and under the seat cushions. He felt each seat cushion for any signs of items being stored inside. They were clean.

He made his way to the bedroom and checked the dresser and night table. Nothing. He then pulled open the closet door and scanned the shelves. There were a few boxes of books, mostly novels and a few non-fiction works, but no media or other storage devices.

He pushed aside the clothing and checked the walls of the closet for the presence of a safe. Seeing none he threw back the throw rug at the end of the bed to check for storage compartments in the floor. None. He checked under the bed and the underside of the bedframe, between the mattress and box spring, nothing there. He scanned the room for other possible hiding places. Again, there was nothing. The house was built in the nineteen thirties so it had radiators and no air ducts, which could've been a further hiding place the man certainly would have checked.

The man next checked the kitchen drawers and cabinets, and finally the fridge and the freezer. There was just the usual kitchen gadgets, a loaf of bread, a few eggs, a stick of butter, a few beers, and some leftover Chinese food. He checked under the sink, and behind the fridge. Taped to the back of the fridge he found two more thumb drives and grabbed them, duct tape and all.

This guy was thorough. Though, CIA agents usually were.

The man took one last scan around the kitchen before he went to the bathroom. There he checked under the sink, behind the toilet tank, and inside the toilet tank, nothing there.

All told he had spent about seven minutes searching the apartment. He grabbed a small duffle bag that was on a chair in the living room and loaded it with the wallet, phone, laptop, hard-drive, and USB sticks, zipped it closed and threw it over his shoulder.

He took once last scan around the room before he cracked the door open slightly to be sure there was no one in the corridor or entering the building. He slipped out the door, closed it and left it unlocked. He quietly walked down the stairs, and checked the street for any unusual activity before he exited the building. He calmly walked across the street and slipped into the SUV and sped off.

Chapter 82 – Boston, Massachusetts
May 8, 2023

Eileen Pilfery has been waiting 20 minutes in President Pilfery's reception area as the President finishes up a phone call with the Canadian Prime Minister. She nervously checks her cell phone for emails and texts, particularly from Seth Dudley, but she's received none. She had caught the 11 am Amtrak Acela to Boston and now at nearly 1 pm she waits to speak with her husband, who is in no hurry to accommodate her. Nevertheless, he finishes up his call and asks his secretary to send in Mrs. Pilfery.

She enters the President's office and he greets her with an insincere kiss on the cheek. It's the first time the two have been together, much less spoken, since her affair with Seth Dudley had been revealed on the national news.

"Eileen, so glad to see you," Pilfery says cheerfully.

"Really Marcus. I didn't think you'd be that thrilled. What with all the embarrassment I've caused you and your Presidency. I'm surprised you even agreed to see me at all."

"Oh, Eileen, don't be cross. Of course I'm glad to see you. I have to admit, at first I was hurt and angry to hear of you and Seth, but that was simply a visceral reaction. After I had time to cool down and think rationally, I realized that we had been drifting apart for some time. I know you're not happy and I can't be happy if you're not. So I'm willing to listen to you and hear your thoughts on what you'd like to do about us, I mean our marriage."

Eileen was taken aback. She had not expected a civil conversation with Marcus, much less one in which he cared about what *she* thought. "Marcus, I don't know what to say. I thought you'd be very upset, even angry. Seth is your best friend and he violated your trust. He told me you were very angry and that you intended on ruining him and that you'd never let me go."

Pilfery put up his hands to stop Eileen. "Not at all. Again, that was my deep seeded emotional response, just a reaction, and not a very rational or well considered reaction. I have no intention of, as you say, ruining Seth, and I certainly won't try to keep you in a marriage in which you'd be unhappy. That would be politically unwise of me, and furthermore, it would be a lousy thing to do to two people for whom I care a great deal."

Eileen was downright relieved and she knew Seth would be as well. Now she could get on with her life and be with Seth. She would finally be free of all the political drama, loneliness, and doubt about her future. "Marcus, I can't tell you how happy that makes me to hear you say that. That's really very decent of you, considering the circumstances."

Pilfery smiled and nodded as he returned to his desk. With that his phone buzzed and his secretary came on the intercom. "Mr. President, the FBI director is on line 2."

"Thank you," he said as he reached for the phone. He took the call standing but abruptly sat down as he listened intently to the caller.

"What happened? How? A pause of a few seconds followed. The President's eyes squinted as he tried to process what the FBI Director explained further. "Oh my god! When? Oh my god! No, no! I want all our available resources on this Douglas, all of them. Do the Mayor and Governor know?" Another pause followed. "All right, good. And what about his ex-wife? Ok. Ok. Keep me informed of any developments. Yes, thank you. Goodbye." The President stared at the phone as he hung it up, and looked up at Eileen in astonishment. Eileen's eyes were wide with curiosity.

"Marcus, what is it? What's happened?"

"It's Seth," The President swallowed hard. "He's dead."

Eileen was stunned and struggled to the chair in front of the President's desk. "What? What happened? How?" She was too shocked to cry, but her eyes welled up as the news crushed her. She struggled to catch her breath.

"He was attacked in his apartment a few hours ago. He was robbed. They think the robber killed him," The President stated soberly. "His cleaning lady found him. His throat had been cut."

Eileen Pilfery sobbed as Marcus came from behind the desk and took her in his arms. The President didn't shed a tear.

Chapter 83 – Boston, Massachusetts
May 8, 2023

By mid-afternoon the news of Seth Dudley's murder had broken all over cable and network news. A swarm of reporters was out in front of Dudley's apartment, while a team of both Philadelphia police and FBI was on the scene.

Several of Dudley's neighbors had been interviewed and heard and saw nothing. It had been just a typical Monday morning in a quiet neighborhood on a cool spring day. Business as usual they all maintained. Until Dudley's cleaning lady arrived at about 11 am just as she did every Monday morning expecting to clean Seth's apartment just as she had been doing for the past three years. She had her own key to the apartment since Seth was rarely there while she cleaned. When she arrived she noticed the door was unlocked so she thought he might have been at home. She entered the apartment and saw him lying on the living room floor in a pool of blood and screamed. Two of Seth's neighbors heard the scream and came running. One of them, an off-duty EMT, checked Seth's pulse and found none. He was dead and they noticed the apartment had been searched. They immediately called 911 and awaited the arrival of the police.

In Boston, Marcus Pilfery had his wife driven to his Presidential residence on the other side of the Boston Common, where a member of the President's staff stayed with her while she tried to recover from

353

hearing that the man she was falling in love with had just been murdered.

With the Dudley matter resolved, Pilfery had now taken care of one of his potential problems. Eileen would be no problem. While it would take some time for her to recover from Seth's death, Pilfery had no doubt that she would soldier on and not cause him any issues. She may eventually want a divorce, that he would reluctantly give her solely because of the public relations embarrassment, but he was convinced she'd be no problem in terms of probing into Dudley's murder.

However, such was not the case with Dudley's ex-wife, Gretchen. The CIA had informed Pilfery that she and Seth had met on at least one occasion and that she was observed accepting a manila folder that appeared to contain something a bit more bulky than just documents. This was of concern to Pilfery. So much so that he ordered another operation aimed at getting whatever was in that folder as well as performing a thorough search of Gretchen Dudley's residence. Pilfery made it clear that Gretchen was not to be harmed in any way. Pilfery was godfather to her son Justin, and Pilfery would not make him an orphan.

So President Pilfery was determined to remove all obstacles in the way of moving his new country forward. Even if it meant, committing a number of heinous crimes, not the least of which was using the CIA in a domestic operation. The CIA's role had always been one of foreign investigation and operations. The FBI handled the domestic issues, but were also authorized to assist on international matters as well. But use of the CIA on domestic operations was clearly out of bounds.

With the new nation struggling economically, and the threat of Pilfery's practice of extortion during the secession campaign being exposed, he would seemingly stop at nothing to preserve his control over the SDUSA.

Chapter 84 – Philadelphia, Pennsylvania
May 9, 2023

Gretchen Dudley was terrified. Since hearing of Seth's murder the day before, she had been in shock. She called out sick for work today from the advertising agency she worked for. When the knock came on her Germantown apartment door a few hours after Seth's body had been discovered, she was completely blindsided. She had just gotten home from work, and the appearance of a Philadelphia homicide detective at her door was both curious and unnerving. As the detective, Nick Brockton delivered the news, she sat stunned, devoid of emotions. She could only think of her meeting with Seth several weeks before during which he expressed his concern for his safety. Now the concerns were being realized.

When she learned of the circumstances under which Seth had been killed and how, she completely lost all control.

"Ma'am. Do you have anyone you can call or perhaps anyone you can stay with?" Brockton asked trying to offer Gretchen some comfort and a suggestion on how to deal with the situation.

"No, no one really. It's just my son Justin and I here, in town. My mother is in Minnesota and she's not well, so she can't travel. I have a few friends I can call, but I'm not sure right now. I'm just trying to understand this," she said while crying. "He was robbed? Why would they kill him? Why not just take his stuff? Why did they have to kill him?" She asked, desperately trying to make sense of what had happened.

"Ms. Dudley, do you know of anyone who might want to harm Mr. Dudley?" The detective asked retrieving his smart phone from his pocket to make notes.

Well that was a loaded question. Since his involvement in politics with Marcus Pilfery over five and a half years ago, there had probably been many occasions to make an enemy or two. After all, Seth had been directly involved in the campaign to orchestrate the most stunning political event in the history of the U.S. There were no doubt a lot of people who would hold him responsible and wouldn't mind seeing him dead. But it wasn't until the meeting last month with Seth that that seemed like a real and imminent danger.

She thought for a moment before speaking. "Detective, Seth was a controversial figure, so I'm sure he made some enemies along the way, but he never spoke of anyone specific. So no one comes to mind right away."

"Yes, Ms. Dudley, I'm aware of your ex-husband's role in the secession movement. We'll be interviewing many of his political associates. I was just wondering if he had expressed any concern to you recently."

He sure as hell had. But now, suddenly Gretchen Dudley didn't know who she could trust. This was starting to seem like much more than a robbery, and she didn't know how high up this might reach. The only thing she knew for sure was that Seth

had been afraid and had come to her for help. There
was only one person that Seth had told her to contact,
and she decided right then and there not to tell the
detective about that person.

"No, there was nothing."

"When did you see or speak with your ex-
husband last, Ms. Dudley?"

"Last month. We got together for coffee, and
just to catch up a bit. Our divorce was amicable and
we got together occasionally so I could catch him up
on our son Justin. Seth only really saw him on
birthdays and holidays. He was so busy and all with
politics, plus he was trying to decide to go back into
Advertising or take a position in the Pilfery
administration. He was undecided when we last
spoke."

"Uh huh, I see," said the detective as he tapped
notes into his phone.

"I'm going to leave you my card with my
mobile number," Brockton said reaching into his coat
pocket. "If you think of anything, please call me
anytime, day or night."

"Thank you detective, I will."

Brockton thanked her again for her time and
left.

Gretchen immediately went to the bedroom
closet and retrieved the manila folder Seth had given
her several weeks ago and opened it. It was the first
time she had done so, and saw the hard-drive. It was
wrapped in a single sheet of paper with the name
Victoria Cheshire written on it. There was an office

address at the University of Pennsylvania Law School, and a phone number. Without hesitation she dialed it.

"Professor Cheshire is in class right now, may I take a message?" A very official sounding assistant responded to Gretchen Dudley.

"Yes. This is Gretchen Dudley. I need to speak with the Professor right away."

"Well, I'm afraid her calendar is full today, but she does have office hours tomorrow afternoon. She can see you at 3 pm."

"That will be fine. Thank you."

Gretchen hung up the phone and hid the folder.

Chapter 85 – Philadelphia, Pennsylvania
May 9, 2023

There it was, Gretchen thought to herself. Tomorrow I'll turn the hard drive over to Professor Cheshire and she'll know what to do with it.

Since Seth had given Gretchen the folder weeks ago, Gretchen had done a bit of research on Victoria Cheshire's life outside of politics. Since losing the 2020 election to President Stanton, she had been a staunch opponent of the secession movement and was determined to see the country remain unified. It had not been a surprise to Gretchen that Cheshire stepped aside from politics after the passage of the 28th amendment and the ensuing secession.

She was now teaching, ironically, constitutional law at Penn not more than a mile from Seth's apartment. After her failed Presidential bid in 2020 and the secession that followed she quietly faded into private life and was living not far from Gretchen's apartment in the Germantown-Chestnut Hill section of northwest Philadelphia.

Being both a lawyer and an ex-Senator, Gretchen figured Seth had specifically chosen Cheshire as someone who would be both interested and sympathetic to what Seth had been involved with.

Gretchen felt like she would have an ally in Victoria Cheshire and that what Seth feared would be exposed and that might ultimately lead back to those who had killed Seth. Gretchen was feeling better. She had had enough of sitting around her apartment for the last 18 hours. It was going on 2:30 pm and Justin would be home from school soon. He insisted on going to school today, despite wishes from his mother that he stay home. He was still stunned from the murder of his father, but did not want to sit around at home all day, instead opting for some sense of normalcy. It was a very mature posture for a high school junior indeed. She decided to go out and get the fixings for Justin's favorite dinner, fried chicken and mac and cheese.

She dead bolted the door and made her way to the nearby Whole Foods, driving past the black SUV parked just down the sycamore lined street.

Chapter 86 – Philadelphia, Pennsylvania
May 9, 2023

The man in the SUV waited until Gretchen was out of site and stepped out onto the sidewalk. In a matter of seconds he was in the hallway and up the one flight to Gretchen's apartment. The mostly professional neighborhood was dead quiet at this mid-afternoon hour, with most of its residents off at work.

He went to work on the deadbolt and within 30 seconds he had successfully picked the lock and stepped inside the apartment. He was the same agent who had killed Seth and ransacked his apartment just the day before.

He began. Same routine. Every conceivable hiding place was searched. Drawers, furniture, seat cushions, floorboards, heating vents, under sinks, refrigerator, stove, over, under and behind everything was checked. Nothing.

The man stood in the center of the living room, scanning, searching, and then he saw it. One of the recessed panels in the bedroom door didn't look quite right. There was an ever so slight gap between the panel and outer frame of the door.

The man produced a switchblade knife from his pocket. With an audible click the blade sprung from its sheath as he quickly and carefully pried the panel from the doorframe. Reaching his hand down inside the panel he felt for contents. His hand came to rest on a heavy gauge folder. He pulled the folder from the inside of the hollow door and quickly opened it. Upon

seeing its contents, he nodded and said to no one
"that's it." He placed the folder in his waistband,
covered it with his jacket and slipped out the door of
the apartment leaving the deadbolt unlocked. In a
flash he was down the stairs and out the door,
stepping into the SUV, and he was gone in seconds.

Chapter 87 – Philadelphia, Pennsylvania
May 9, 2023

When Gretchen put her key in the deadbolt and noticed it was not engaged, she froze. The lock was open. She held her breath and listened carefully for any sign of activity or movement within the apartment. She stood motionless for what seemed like an eternity, but was actually only about a minute.

She slowly opened the door and peered in carefully. No sound, no movement. She opened the door a bit more and was able to see most of the room. The room was a mess, open drawers, pictures off the walls and broken open, furniture overturned and cushions strewn about.

Her mind was racing. Her pulse was pounding in her temples, and then she saw it. Her heart sank. The panel from the bedroom door had been pried off. She sprinted to the bedroom door and reached inside. "Shit!" she exclaimed. She sunk to her knees and immediately wept.

"Mom! Are you all right? What happened?" It was Justin, home from school.

Gretchen, heaving with sobs, looked up helplessly at her son.

Chapter 88 – Boston, Massachusetts
May 9, 2023

Almost within an hour of Gretchen Dudley's home being broken into by the CIA, President Pilfery's phone rang. It was the National Intelligence Director calling.

"It's done sir."

"Very well," was all The President said.

The Director sensing the President was not at liberty to speak freely, asked. "Do you want to continue surveillance on the woman?"

"Yes, thank you," The President simply stated. He hung up the phone and went back to his economic briefing with his Secretary of Commerce Lawrence Rinaldi. The President's Chief of Staff was also in attendance.

"I'm sorry Larry, let's get back to the briefing," The President said calmly, knowing that the last piece of damning evidence that existed was now under CIA control.

"Certainly Mr. President. We were reviewing the latest employment figures and about to move on to the corporate relocations for the month of April."

"Yes. Go on."

"So as I said, unemployment for SDUSA for the month of April was 11.2% up from 9.1% in March. Job losses for April were 87,000 and job losses since the start of the fiscal year on October 1, have been 502,000. Another 47 corporate relocations occurred in April. That's 121 since January first. Of those 121, a total of

22 of them were from the Standard and Poor's 500; four were from the Dow 30."

Case and Clark Pharmaceuticals of New Jersey and Joyner Technologies Corporation of Connecticut had joined earlier defectors Global Computer Corporation of New York state and Marshall Aeronautics from Washington state. These last two, CCP and JTC, were particularly painful for Pilfery as they were located right in his backyard of New York. CCP was moving to North Carolina and the Research Triangle Park area of Raleigh, Durham, and Chapel Hill. JTC was moving to Texas to join the ever growing number of companies that were relocating to the Lone Star state to avail themselves of low taxes, and the ever increasing skilled labor force that was fleeing the far west states of California, Oregon, and Washington.

Pilfery was inconsolable. Defections were rampant and unemployment was steadily rising as thousands were being thrown out of work. On top of that, many were choosing to follow their former employers to their new states with the hopes of being hired back once they were there.

The SDUSA was becoming an economic abyss. The Congress was more fractured and ineffective than ever in agreeing on legislation that would roll back corporate taxes and stem the tide of defections.

Pilfery had decided it was time to take matters into his own hands. It was time for executive action.

He immediately summoned the Attorney General, Alan Swindell, a long-time crony of Pilfery.

The President wanted to know what he could legally do to put a moratorium on any further corporate relocations.

Swindell, a Harvard trained attorney who also held an MBA from the Wharton School of Business was as smart as they come. He had been anticipating such a question and was ready with a strategy.

"Mr. President, you may recall that back in 2014, President Prentice, in order to put a halt to U.S. corporate inversions, that is, the shifting of U.S. company headquarters from the U.S. to a foreign subsidiary in order to lower their tax burden, had signed an executive order. That order allowed the Treasury Department to invoke IRS regulations that prevented U.S. companies from transferring cash or other assets to a foreign subsidiary in order for the parent to avoid paying U.S. tax. In our case, the SDUSA companies are moving their operations and headquarters to a subsidiary in the U.S. So, in the context of President Prentice's executive order, we could maintain that by moving from the SDUSA to the U.S. it's just like when a U.S. company was moving to a foreign country. The only difference being that the U.S. is now considered the foreign country."

Pilfery processed the scenario for a moment, and shot Ken Latimor a glance. "I like it," The President stated. "It's within the existing Tax laws, we have a precedent, and our courts in the SDUSA have jurisdiction, so we won't have any conservative activist judge looking to overturn it. Seems solid to me. Let's run it by the Treasury Secretary, and if he's ok with it, I'll sign the order."

"Very good, Mr. President," Swindell said with satisfaction. "It will buy us some time until the Congress can get their act together and come up with some common sense legislation that will stop the defections. I'll speak with the Treasury Secretary immediately."

As was usually the case Pilfery always found a way to get what he wanted. Now all he had to deal with was the public relations fallout from such a maneuver. The fall out would prove to be ground shaking.

Chapter 89 – Philadelphia, Pennsylvania
May 9, 2023

Gretchen Dudley had calmed down and was now napping in her bedroom. Justin was in the kitchen preparing supper. He had cleaned and prepped the chicken, and was now breading it while the oil heated in the deep fryer. Meanwhile, the macaroni had been cooked, and mixed with three kinds of cheese and a healthy helping of butter, and was now baking in the oven. Growing up with a father who wasn't around that much and a mom who worked full time to make ends meet, had taught Justin a lot about helping out. He was a very resourceful kid.

While the oil heated, he thought about what his mom had described about what Justin's Dad had said was on the hard-drive. Phone call, emails, texts, all from the last 5 years of Seth Dudley's relationship with Marcus Pilfery.

While he thought and while the chicken now fried, Justin tinkered with his iPhone. He was in the midst of downloading a video one of his friends had recommended, when he received the message: "iCloud storage full, go to settings to manage storage".

"Oh, what a pain," he said out loud. Then it struck him.

He turned toward the living room and saw his mom's cell phone sitting on the end table by the couch. "That's it," he said as he rescued the chicken from the fryer, killed the power and headed off to the bedroom to wake his mother.

Justin stood over his sleeping mother, and gently nudged her. "Mom. Wake up. I have it. I have it," he said.

Gretchen was now stirring and awoke to see her son standing over her smiling. "I have it Mom. I have it."

Chapter 90 – Philadelphia, Pennsylvania
May 9, 2023

"What do you have?" Gretchen said groggily. "What are you talking about?"

"I have the solution. I have the *replacement* for the hard-drive."

"What do you mean? Where? How?"

"Do you remember how when you and Dad got your iPhones, he didn't want to have anything to do with the cloud? He didn't understand it, didn't need it, and didn't trust it. Right?"

"Yeah. He told me to set it up for myself but leave him out."

"Yes," Justin persisted. "But I told you that wasn't a good idea. He never backed up his phone, that is until recently, and I told you it would be too risky to have no backup for all his stuff."

"Go on," Gretchen wondered.

"I had him attach his iPhone to *your* iCloud. You can do that. You can have two devices on the same cloud."

Gretchen being a little technologically challenged herself was not quite getting it.

"Mom, you have the entire contents of Dad's iPhone on your cloud. You have *all his contents*."

Gretchen eyes went wide with excitement as she hugged her son.

After a dinner of fried chicken, mac and cheese—and mountain dew for Justin. The two got to work emptying the contents of Gretchen's iCloud account onto three high capacity thumb drives that Justin had kicking around in his backpack. Justin then partitioned and isolated his Dad's emails, and text messages and saved just those to two of the drives, deleting his mom's content.

In just under two hours, the 16 year old had managed to replicate and format onto the thumb drives the entire contents of his Dad's cell phone including every email and every text he had ever gotten or sent to President Pilfery and the entire Gang of Six.

Gretchen was now ready to keep her appointment with Victoria Cheshire at 3 pm the next day.

Gretchen and Justin went out for Coldstone ice cream to celebrate. They took the thumb drives with them.

Chapter 91 – Philadelphia, Pennsylvania
May 10, 2023

"Come in Ms. Dudley, I'm Victoria Cheshire," the ex-Senator now turned law professor said warmly as she welcomed Gretchen into her office. She placed her hand over the phone receiver. "Please give me a minute while I finish up this call."

"So Ben, what are you doing in town?" Cheshire said, continuing with her call.

"Amanda is finishing up her freshman year at Villanova and I was in Washington so I thought I swing by and pick her up so we could fly home together. Her last class is tomorrow, so I thought maybe I could meet you and Paul for dinner."

"Oh, ok. I'll go you one better, why don't you come by this evening and Paul and I'll cook you dinner," Victoria countered.

"I couldn't possibly turn down a home cooked meal, sure, thanks."

"Come by about 7. I'll be leaving here about 6:30, and Paul will be home a little after 7. It'll be simple, just some pasta and shrimp, but it'll be fresh."

"Sounds great Tori. See you at 7."

Gretchen looked around the office as Cheshire hung up the phone. And what an office it was. Located in between Chestnut and Walnut streets in the heart of University City in Philadelphia, Penn Law is one of the oldest and most prestigious law schools in the country. The Professor's office was grand. High ceilings, with large dark walnut wood trim, and lined with floor to ceiling bookcases. It even had one of those charming old-time ladders on wheels that rolled along in front of the bookcases enabling you to access the higher shelves. Off in the distance the Schuylkill River can be seen as crew teams go through their afternoon training routines. The river runs through the center of Philadelphia eventually converging with the Delaware river feeding down to the Delaware Bay and out to the Atlantic Ocean.

"Thank you so much for seeing me today Professor Cheshire," Gretchen said nervously as she took a seat in front of Cheshire's desk. "I understand you knew my ex-husband during your tenure in Washington."

"Yes, I did. I met Seth on a number of occasions. I am very sorry for your loss. We were all very shocked with the news of his death," Cheshire said, avoiding the use of the word murder, although everyone knew Dudley had been brutally murdered in his own apartment.

"Thank you," Gretchen said quietly.

"Of what service can I be to you today?" Victoria asked.

Gretchen reached into her bag and produced the two thumb drives. "Seth came to me a few weeks ago very worried about something. He wouldn't say what, but he asked me to deliver this information to you," Gretchen said referring to the thumb drives. She clarified. "Seth originally had given me a hard drive containing information from his cell phone, namely all his emails, texts, and call records. But someone broke into my apartment and stole the hard drive. But I was able to recover all of Seth's information from my iCloud account. He hated technology so I had stored his information on my cloud account. He asked me to give this to you if something should happen to him."

Cheshire's eyebrows raised and she leaned forward in her chair as she intently listened. "I see," she said curiously. "Why did he wish for me to have this information?"

"He didn't say. He just said you would know what it was and what to do with it."

"Hmmm. That's odd. Let's have a look," Cheshire said as she took the thumb drives from Gretchen's hand. Cheshire turned to her laptop computer and inserted one of the thumb drives into the USB port on the side of her computer. The drive engaged and immediately appeared on her desktop. She scanned the contents, noting literally hundreds of emails, and texts, along with a listing of phone calls made and received. Immediately she recognized the phone number exchange for the Senate offices in the Capitol Building.

The emails were in date order showing the names of the senders or recipients. She saw dozens of emails to and from Marcus Pilfery, Horace Dettinger, Diane Mitchell, Angela Gutierrez, and other key Democratic Senators. She even saw a few to her email address.

Several of the email contained subject lines reading: "Secession vote count", "Senators voting no",

"Action on Kovacs", "Re: Kovacs wife DUI", and many other cryptic sounding subjects.

She pulled up the email "Action on Kovacs" and began reading. As she read she became more intently focused on the words on the screen, while Gretchen sat quietly observing.

After another 15 minutes of scanning and reading various emails, she ejected the first thumb drive and inserted the second. Again she saw a series of emails and this time there were texts to and from Seth Dudley. Miraculously, there were texts to and from Marcus Pilfery on a variety of secession related topics, and again, specific ones dealing with Senator Kovacs of West Virginia and his wife. There were even texts where Marcus Pilfery and Seth Dudley discussed Pilfery's rendezvous with both Senator Mitchell of Illinois and then Senator and now Vice-President Gutierrez.

Never before had she seen such an assortment of politically compromising material in one place. Some of it even downright criminal, or at least describing criminal activities that Seth Dudley had participated in and of which Marcus Pilfery was aware of ahead of time. It was all there, extortion, illegal campaign contributions, disbursement of money for illicit purposes.

Seth Dudley had apparently assembled all of this as some sort of "confession from the grave", were he to meet with an unfortunate ending. And he had designated Victoria Cheshire to be the recipient.

Why would he have done that, she wondered to herself. Why would he have thought I could be trusted, she thought.

Gretchen sat patiently not saying a word the entire time. Victoria next stumbled upon a series of texts with Pilfery that gave her the answer to what she had been wondering. The text read:

"Cheshire is a no vote. Look for info to discredit her and swing vote. She's going to be a hard sell. Doesn't want secession."

Victoria stopped and stared at the words: *"discredit her…"*

She thought to herself, Dudley knew I couldn't be persuaded or bought. That's why he chose me. He knew I would expose Pilfery if given the chance.

Victoria closed down the thumb drive, ejected it and turned to Gretchen. "Ms. Dudley, may I keep these?"

"Yes. Of course you may. That's what Seth wanted. He wanted you and only you to have them," Gretchen said emphatically.

"Are they useful to you?" Gretchen asked. "And Professor Cheshire, do you think they may give you a clue as to why Seth was killed and who wanted him dead?"

Cheshire looked Gretchen directly in the eye and stated, "Yes, Ms. Dudley, I truly hope so. I truly hope so."

Gretchen flashed a sad, yet hopeful smile.

Chapter 92 – Philadelphia, Pennsylvania
May 10, 2023

The man in the black SUV, parked outside the Penn Law administration building, peered down the street as Gretchen Dudley got into her car to drive home. It was going on 5 pm. Speaking into his cell phone he said, "Subject is on the move. Do I continue surveillance?"

"Who did she see?" came the response on the other end.

"Professor Victoria Cheshire," the CIA agent answered.

"Negative. Initiate surveillance of Cheshire. Await further instructions."

"Affirmative."

Chapter 93 – Boston, Massachusetts
May 10, 2023

"Damn it!" Marcus Pilfery said into the phone upon hearing the news that Gretchen Dudley had been to see Victoria Cheshire at the Penn Law School. "She must have had a back up of that hard drive stored somewhere else, probably in another location." He thought carefully while the Intelligence Director waited on the other end of the phone for instructions.

"Follow Cheshire. The damage has already been set in motion. This calls for extreme measures. Take out Cheshire. Then have your man pay Gretchen Dudley and her son a visit. They must all be taken out of the equation. They're all dangerous to me now."

"Very well, sir. We've already begun surveillance on Cheshire. We'll finish it this evening."

President Marcus Pilfery had just ordered three additional murders of U.S. citizens, and he wasn't the least bit bothered by it. He rationalized to himself that in times of war there would always be collateral damage. He was certain this was for the greater good.

Chapter 94 – Philadelphia, Pennsylvania
May 10, 2023

The cell phone of the man in the black SUV vibrated signaling an incoming call. He answered with a simple "yes".

"Continue surveillance on Cheshire. Neutralize at first opportunity. Proceed to secondary subjects. Neutralize both at first opportunity," the Intelligence Director instructed.

The man's jaw tightened as he acknowledged his orders. "Affirmative, neutralize all subjects. Two women, one child," he said emphatically offering the Director the opportunity, upon hearing the callousness of what he had just been ordered to do, to rescind the order.

"That's affirmative," the Director re-iterated.

"Understood, out."

Chapter 95 – Philadelphia, Pennsylvania
May 10, 2023

The man in the black SUV waited, as his eyes never left the Law School Administration building exit. It was past 6:30 and Cheshire was still inside. He grew impatient yet remained focused.

Then at 6:35, Victoria Cheshire emerged from the exit and made the short walk to her car, a white, mid-sized SUV. She had spent a bit more time than expected reviewing the contents of the two thumb drives Gretchen Dudley had given her earlier that afternoon. Before leaving the office, she placed the thumb drives in an office safe behind the portrait of one of her heroes, John F. Kennedy.

She'd make the drive home to Germantown in about 20 minutes. Traffic had begun to ease as the commuter hour was coming to a conclusion. She hopped onto to interstate 76, meandered north and west along the Schuylkill River and eventually exited onto to U.S. highway one north that led into Germantown. All the while the black SUV was never more than a hundred feet behind her car.

She entered her neighborhood of older style colonial homes built in the nineteen fifties. They were modest homes really, no more than 2,000 square feet and simple, yet functional.

She pulled into the driveway stopping short of the garage. She had made good time and it was just 6:50. She had received a couple of text messages on the drive home. While the car idled she glanced at the messages.

This gave the man in the black SUV a chance to stop short of the driveway, kill his lights and engine and wait concealed behind a row of arborvitae trees which lined the street. He could see that Cheshire was still in the car. The house seemed empty. No other car was in the driveway. He waited.

Suddenly Cheshire's car went silent and the door swung open. Time to move, he thought. He quietly opened his door and slid out, as he reached in his right coat pocket for the switchblade, all in one fluid motion. A motion he had probably done dozens of time in a dozen different countries around the world over a twenty-year career in the CIA.

He moved stealthily along the tree line and emerged mid-way up the driveway a mere 20 feet from where Victoria Cheshire was standing in front of the open back door of her car. She was retrieving her computer bag and a couple of textbooks and had her back turned to the man as she leaned into the back seat.

As she stood up from the inside the car, the man exploded toward her, arm up, knife open, ready to strike.

Victoria never heard him coming.

Then, came a loud crack just to the right of Victoria's head, although there seemed to be some distance between the sound and the resulting vibration in Victoria's right ear. The sound was deafening, like an explosion, accompanied by a flash of light she caught with her peripheral vision from just down the driveway.

The man, stopped, then lurched forward and crashed into the open car door just to Victoria's left. She was too startled to scream and instinctively turned away from the body that had been hurdling toward her. She spun in the direction of the man who had now sunk to the asphalt and was lying prone face down. He moaned and moved slowly as he struggled to raise himself but was unable.

He had been shot. An ugly, dark red spot was quickly forming on the man's side midway between his waist and his right shoulder. The outstretched arm raised high had provided the shooter with the perfect target exposing the ribcage and accompanying organs on the right side of the man's body.

Victoria was frozen. She looked to her left down the driveway and could scarcely believe what she saw. Ben Goodwin was double-timing it up the driveway toward Victoria, 9-millimeter pistol in his right hand at the ready, trained on the man as he struggled to move. Victoria looked at Goodwin wide-eyed, mouth agape and was unable to utter a sound.

Goodwin turned the assailant over, kicked the knife aside, and searched him for additional weapons. He was still alive, but was not going to be a further problem. The bullet had clipped his right lung and it had collapsed. The man was struggling to breath. Goodwin worked quickly and efficiently as his Marine training had taught him, and he dialed 911.

Goodwin, now breathing hard from the stress of the situation, turned to Cheshire. "Sorry I'm a little early," he said allowing a nervous smile.

Finally realizing what had happened, Cheshire collapsed into Goodwin's arms. He held her as she began to sob.

Ten minutes after the first police and EMTs had arrived, Detective Nick Brockton of homicide had arrived. He had parked in the street and walked up the driveway toward the scene. The assailant was being tended to by EMTs. They had managed to stabilize his breathing and he was being given pure oxygen. Brockton watched as the EMTs loaded him into the ambulance. Both his wrists were handcuffed to the gurney. One police officer accompanied him in the back, while another took the passenger seat up front with the driver. A squad car with two more officers led the ambulance from the scene as it headed south to Thomas Jefferson Medical Center. The man was probably a professional assassin so the Philadelphia Police were exercising extreme caution with his transport.

A forensic team was processing the area around where the man had been shot as well as down the driveway where Ben Goodwin had fired a single shot at the would be assailant. A lone shell casing was found 30 feet from where the assailant went down.

Another team was combing through the black SUV looking for evidence.

Inside the Cheshire residence, Victoria Cheshire sat on a living room sofa alongside her husband Paul who had arrived home just as the police were arriving.

Seated in an armchair opposite where the Cheshire's were sitting was Senator Ben Goodwin.

The police had taken control of his weapon upon reaching the scene as Goodwin announced he had it stashed in his shoulder holster. Goodwin had become such a recognizable national figure that both of the responding police officers immediately recognized him as the Senator from Kansas.

Brockton entered the living room where the three sat quietly waiting to make their statements. One of the officers outside had briefed Brockton before he entered.

Brockton approached Victoria Cheshire first and offered her some comfort.

"Ms. Cheshire, I'm Detective Sargent Nick Brocton, from Philadelphia homicide. I know this has been a very upsetting experience for you and I'm sorry. I'd like to take your statement in a little bit."

"Thank you Sargent, I'm ok. Just a bit shaken and a bit stunned."

"Ok ma'am. You just take it easy for a few minutes. I'm going to speak to Senator Goodwin first."

Brockton turned to Goodwin who stood to make his acquaintance. "I'm pleased to meet you Sargent Brockton. I'm Benjamin Goodwin."

"Yes, Senator. It's a pleasure to meet you. Why don't we go in the other room," Brockton said motioning to the study that was just off the living room.

The two disappeared into the study where Brockton slid the doors closed.

"I'd like to get your statement, Senator. Tell me in your own words what happened," Brockton said.

I had spoken to Victoria earlier this afternoon, and she had invited me over to have dinner with her and her husband Paul. I'm in town to take my daughter home from Villanova for the summer. She just finished up her freshman year there."

"Nova', huh? Good school. Even better basketball team," Brockton noted with a quick smile, trying to lighten the mood.

The Senator flashed a smile. "Yes, good team, indeed."

"You were saying," Brockton said to the Senator.

"Well she said to come over around 7 and we'd have dinner. I left my hotel over near the campus around 6:15 and made pretty good time on 76 east. I pulled up to Victoria's house and immediately saw a black SUV parked in the street just past the Cheshire's driveway. I saw a single man in the driver's seat and he appeared to be watching the house. I saw a white SUV in the driveway, and it looked like Victoria was still in it. A few seconds later she got out of her car and almost immediately the man stepped from the black SUV and disappeared behind the pines that line the far side of the driveway. I lost sight of him. So I got out of my car and headed toward the bottom of the driveway. I saw Victoria standing at the back door of her car and she appeared to be reaching into the back seat for something. I saw the man re-emerge from behind the pine trees. There was something in his right hand but I couldn't make out exactly what it was.

It was then that I reached into my shoulder holster for my weapon."

"Weapon sir, what kind of weapon?" The Detective asked.

"It's a 9-millimeter. An H and K VP9. I have a concealed carry permit, Sargent. Many of us in Congress do ever since Representative Scalise was wounded back in 2017. Congressional members aren't entitled to Secret Service protection, so many of us have chosen to defend ourselves. I'm ex-Marine so I know how to handle a gun."

"Well, that's pretty obvious, I'd say sir. You took this guy down with just one shot. Go on sir."

"I had my weapon pulled and suddenly the man sprinted toward Victoria, maybe he was 10 feet from her, but he was covering ground pretty quickly and he had his right hand raise up, and I could now see the blade of the knife. There was still pretty good daylight, and it was clearly a knife. He was heading right toward Victoria." Goodwin paused and swallowed. "So I shot him."

Brockton was punching notes into the note pad on his phone, as he was nodding. "Any thought of just yelling at the man to perhaps distract him or cause him to stop?"

"No thought at all Sargent. It was instinctive. I saw someone about to be assaulted from behind with a knife, so I didn't hesitate. I then approached the assailant who was now on the ground, face down, but breathing. I disarmed him and called 911."

Brockton nodded. "Senator, you served in the Marine Corp correct, sir?"

"Yes Sargent. I was a Medical Corpsman. But I saw some action. Shot a few bad guys while I was trying to evacuate some of our guys out of a few fire fights," Goodwin stated. "We weren't trained to yell at the bad guys. We were trained to stop them."

Brockton nodded again, as he raised his lower lip in affirmation. "Thank you Senator."

Chapter 97 – Boston, Massachusetts
May 15, 2023

It didn't take the FBI long to figure out who the man in the black SUV was. The registration was a phony, and the man himself was no help, choosing to say nothing. This was even after he had been accompanied by a high-powered Washington attorney who was mysteriously appointed and showed up at the hospital within 6 hours of the incident being reported all over the news outlets. Through fingerprints and facial recognition software, the man was determined to be Michael Tompkins, ex-CIA who had gone off the grid three years earlier and was rumored to be living abroad somewhere in Eastern Europe, perhaps Hungary.

The rumors were that he was an assassin for hire, still known to many within the agency, but his exact whereabouts unknown at any point in time. He was a professional ghost, a spy, who could disappear and re-appear like an apparition. It was a very handy trait indeed, when someone possessing that particular trait was needed.

Through a subpoena of cell phone records, he was eventually connected to SDUSA National Intelligence Director, William Hastings, a member of President Pilfery's National Security Council. It all began to unwind from there.

The Department of Justice issued more subpoenas and began a thorough investigation into the activities of Director Hastings. And it really began to break wide open when the FBI found the money trail. It stretched from a progressive political action committee named Patriots for Progress to a cash account residing in the SDUSA's version of the Democratic National Committee. From there it was tied to the Committee to re-elect Pilfery, which had received three large donations, each in excess of $700,000, over the past nine months. And finally from there, a total of $1.5 million of it had been placed into a Cayman island account that was under the control of the National Intelligence Agency.

It was later revealed under closed Senate testimony that the fund was used for certain black ops involving kidnapping, torture, and murder of certain local politicians in countries that were not particularly sympathetic to the goals of the Pilfery administration.

Black ops such as these were not unheard of in the world of intelligence gathering, but the disbursement that caught the eye of the Senate Committee was the one made to the account of Michael Tompkins in the amount of $1 million, that had been authorized by none other than William Hastings. The disbursement had been made two days before Seth Dudley had been murdered.

Chapter 98 – Boston, Massachusetts
August 5, 2023

The Senate investigation pressed on for most of the summer and in mid-June Director Hastings had resigned under pressure from key Democrats in the Senate and at the private urging of President Pilfery. The President began feeling the heat of the investigation bearing down on him and rumors began to swirl that he, himself might be subpoenaed to testify before Congress.

Pilfery, once the darling of such major news outlets as MSNBC and CNN, was now under almost daily attack by their panelists and pundits. There was now open and unrelenting talk of impeachment as many wondered what did the President know, and when did he know it? Chris Matthews, who always had a flair for the dramatic quipped, "President Pilfery has become almost Nixonian in his demeanor as a "bunker mentality" has taken hold of his administration. One has to ask what's next?"

It was inconceivable to many in Congress and the media that Director Hastings acted alone without the knowledge of the President. Still Pilfery hung on to hope and maintained that the murder of Seth Dudley and the attempt on the life of Victoria Cheshire had been perpetrated by some rogue element of the intelligence community at the urging of Director Hastings for some clandestine purpose of which he knew nothing.

But the final bombshell came in mid-July when Victoria Cheshire appeared before the Senate committee and brought with her the contents of the two thumb drives that had been given to her by Gretchen Dudley. Among all the dirty tricks perpetrated by Seth Dudley with the full knowledge and backing of the President of the SDUSA, none was more heinous than the extortion of the single deciding vote cast by Virginia Senator Joe Kovacs to allow the Senate to ratify the 28th amendment to the Constitution. Seth Dudley and President Pilfery had discovered the unpleasant truth about Senator Kovac's wife's DUI incident and the Senator's subsequent influence in burying the report to save his wife from what certainly would have been a lengthy prison sentence for vehicular manslaughter.

It was all there in the text messages. Dudley and the President had brazenly and recklessly documented their discussions of the extortion through their texts. And The President foolishly believed his long-time friend Seth Dudley would never reveal the truth. But something had set Dudley off so he apparently arranged for the information to make it to a trusted source were something to happen to him. Many in the media speculated that it was related to Dudley's affair with the President's wife and the President threatened to ruin Dudley. But the President obviously knew that Dudley could implicate him in the Kovacs matter. So it appeared the President could not operate with that threat hanging over his head, and probably had him killed. Again, it was all speculation, but all plausible. The media, especially Fox News ran hard with it, and covered the story around the clock.

And while there would never be conclusive proof that the President had ordered the murder of Seth Dudley, it was clear that his National Intelligence Director had because of the payment he had authorized to the assassin Tompkins. And now with the revelation of The President's involvement in the extortion of Senator Kovacs, it was clear the President would want to ensure that Dudley never released the information that implicated the President in the extortion. It was now clear that the President had motive for the murder of Seth Dudley, and may have very well been involved in ordering it. But one thing was certain. No one was counting on the fact that Dudley had managed to get proof of the extortion scheme to Victoria Cheshire after his death.

All of this aside, the SDUSA was in shambles. Unemployment in July reached 15%. Corporate relocations to the U.S. had ceased due to Pilfery's executive order curtailing them. But now companies not only were not hiring, but were cutting staff to save money. There had now been five consecutive months of job loss and the economy was shrinking. The shortages of food and other basic staples continued, and inflation was now an issue. The shortages, coupled with panic buying had caused inflation for the month of July to spike to an annualized rate of 14%. The country was teetering on depression and Congress remained paralyzed, as the various wings of the Democratic Party could not agree on a path forward.

Marcus Pilfery, for the first time in his Presidency, could see no way out of the quagmire in which the SDUSA had found itself.

The country was disintegrating economically. The media was attacking him daily. There were calls for him to be subpoenaed to testify in the investigation of Seth Dudley's murder. The evidence had already shown that he had willingly and maliciously extorted a sitting U.S. Senator for political gain, and his approval rating had sunk to an abysmal 8%, which was unheard of in modern day politics. It was just a matter of time before he would be impeached and removed from office, and then face prosecution. At worst, he would go to prison. At best, he would live the rest of his life in shame. He had even lost his wife and had ordered the killing of his best friend. There wasn't a person in the world he could turn to. He was looking into the abyss.

Now he sat alone in his office in Boston. He had asked his Secretary that he not be disturbed for the next hour.

When he had been Senator Marcus Pilfery, like so many of his colleagues in Congress, had chosen to arm himself. This was in the wake of the attack on Congressman Steve Scalise in 2017, where it was subsequently revealed how vulnerable Congressional members indeed were due to lack of security details being assigned to them.

Pilfery looked at the 9-millimeter pistol sitting in front of him on his desk. He shook his head ever so

slightly, took the gun in his hand and fired a bullet into
his mouth.

He had left no note. He had not apologized to
a single person.

Chapter 99 – Washington
August 12, 2023

In the aftermath of Marcus Pilfery's suicide, a number of predictable things had occurred. Angela Gutierrez was sworn in as the second President of the SDUSA. How sad and inauspicious, it was said by many in the media, that the first woman to hold the office of President for either the U.S. or the fledgling SDUSA had assumed office because of suicide by her predecessor. What had been hoped by millions of Americans to be an historical and celebratory occasion was instead a moment shrouded in heartbreak and anguish.

The Senate investigation into the death of Seth Dudley, and the attempted killing of Victoria Cheshire, continued and was expanded to now include the extortion of Senator Joe Kovacs. A special prosecutor was appointed by President Gutierrez, who was now under scrutiny for her alleged affair with Marcus Pilfery, leading up to her being chosen as Pilfery's running mate. The media had yet another scandal they could latch onto as the SDUSA continued to sink into the doldrums.

But a new and unforeseen event had also occurred. The remaining members of the old "Gang of Six", which now numbered just four, not including the new President, met privately with the Congressional leadership of the United States. In attendance for the U.S. were Senate Majority Leader, James Carlson of Texas, Speaker of the House, Gordon Garrison of

Kentucky, House Majority Leader Brent Locker of Wisconsin, and the senior Senator from Kansas Ben Goodwin.

Quite simply, the purpose of the meeting was to explore a pathway back to statehood in the United States for any and all of the thirteen states that had seceded.

During the nearly seven hour meeting that had gone on into the evening, the two sides used the occasion to not only chart a path and establish the process, but they also used it to vent at one another.

Senator Carlson and Speaker Gordon were particularly harsh in their criticism of their colleagues from the SDUSA for their lack of commitment to the U.S. and for causing the breakup of the greatest country the world had ever known.

"You folks ought to be ashamed of what you have done," Carlson scolded. "You undermined our Republic, and took advantage of the emotion of the voters to stir up a fever of partisanship this country has never known. And now that you've screwed things up, you want to come crawling back and become part of the United States like nothing ever happened. I've got a good mind to tell you all to go to hell!"

Ben Goodwin, who was trying to maintain some civility, took the high road. "Now Senator, we must remember that a process was used. And it's a process that was written into our Constitution and in fact is still in our Constitution and we all followed it, for better or worse, we followed it. And for that we are all to be commended. It was done without violence, without the military, and without the spilling of blood. So I say the founding fathers would say they got it right. And now we have a chance to make it right again, by coming together as our Constitution provides. So let's work together on this. The fate of two countries is riding on it."

Senator Stokely from the SDUSA had been quietly listening but now spoke up. "I appreciate the Senator from Kansas' words. I too believe we had always intended to use a process that was completely above board and within the framework of the Constitution. Our intent was noble. We wanted a better life for our citizens, yet we felt the divide in the U.S. was growing wider and that there would never be a circumstance under which we could get that better life for every American. Now I'll be the first to admit that Marcus Pilfery, God rest his wretched soul, took things way too far and allowed his lust for power to lead us down a dangerous road. But we were not all of the same mindset as Pilfery. And now we are here as Americans to try and unite us once again." He glared at Senator Carlson and said, "You do have the right to tell us to go to hell. I won't argue that, but the question needs to be, should you? There are millions of people counting on us as leaders to fix this situation, and while you certainly have no obligation to do so, it would certainly be the right thing to do for the ordinary citizens of the SDUSA who mistakenly, yet innocently trusted in leaders who just got it wrong. So I sit here today and I say if you want, sanction the four of us, deny us office, but don't turn your back on 100 million people who were just looking for a chance at a better life."

Goodwin and Stokely had succeeded in elevating the conversation to a more productive level. The group had agreed on the following approach, subject to the review of both countries' Supreme Courts for strict adherence to their respective Constitutions.

Any or all of the 13 states would be re-admitted to the United States with the same rights and privileges as before their secession subject to:

Two-thirds approval by both countries' House and Senate members,

Approval by ¾ of each of the countries' State Legislatures,

A simple majority approval by the voters of each of the 13 secession states wishing to be re-admitted to the U.S.

All had agreed that the bar for re-admittance should be set as high as it had been for secession to ensure significant commitment to the plan to re-unite the states into one Union.

Both groups agreed to take the proposal back to their members.

Within the next news cycle, reports had surfaced, that a plan had been established by both countries, for a re-unification and that Senators Ben Goodwin and Leonard Stokely were leading the re-unification efforts.

The news spread like wildfire touching off a series of spontaneous celebrations in the major cities of both countries. Apparently the people were about to speak once again.

Chapter 100 – City Tavern, Philadelphia, PA
August 19, 2023

Ben Goodwin's face lights up as he spots Victoria Cheshire coming through the door of City Tavern. City Tavern is as big a piece of American colonial history as either the Liberty Bell or Independence Hall. The famous bar was built in 1773 and was the unofficial meeting place of the first Continental Congress. It was also George Washington's favorite place to dine and drink. The original building had been destroyed in 1854, but a replica of the old building was erected in 1975. The restaurant and bar is now part of the Independence Hall National Historical Park and serves meals and drinks.

"Hey Tori, so glad to see you!" Goodwin says as he gives his friend a big hug.

"Great to see you too Ben. I didn't know you were in town."

"Sophomore year for Amanda starts Monday," the proud papa stated proudly. "She's going to declare her major too."

"Oh, and what would that be?" Victoria asked coyly.

"Pre-law. She wants to be a lawyer, and maybe serve in Congress someday. Pretty neat, huh?" Goodwin was beaming.

"But I thought you wanted her to consider Medicine, like her old man?"

"Yeah, originally I did yeah. But, she came to me yesterday. She had been watching a news report that spoke of the real possibility of re-unification. And do you know what she said to me?"

Victoria shook her head, smiling.

"She said, Dad, I want to make sure the country always stays together. I want to be a patriot like you."

Victoria melted. "Oh that's sweet. You must be so proud of her."

Ben Goodwin just smiled and nodded.

"So what are we meeting here for?" Victoria asked.

"Don't you know what this place is? I mean, you live in this city, right?"

"Yes, but maybe not for too much longer. That is, if Massachusetts chooses to go back to the United States."

"This is where George Washington and the Continental Congress used to meet. This is one of the places where are our country was conceived and born. It was built in 1773. But here's the interesting part. It was destroyed in 1854, but was re-built as a replica of the original building in 1975, just ahead of the Bi-Centennial," Goodwin said proudly.

Victoria thought for a few seconds. "That is interesting. This place got a second chance," she paused. "Just like our country is going to get a second chance."

Goodwin smiled. "That's right, Tori. Some things are simply worth a second chance."

Both the U.S. and the SDUSA Supreme Courts ruled the proposed process for states to rejoin the United States was fair and constitutional. There was, however, a little rancor in the respective Congresses. Nearly all of the members of the SDUSA voted in favor of having the states of the SDUSA rejoin the U.S. subject to a popular vote within the states themselves. On the other hand, in the U.S. Congress there was some disagreement. Some of the most conservative red states had insisted that the significant debt that the SDUSA had run up in its brief history be solely borne by those states choosing to re-enter the union. The amount was nearly $800 billion and had come about mainly from the free medical care and free tuition programs that had been put in place in the SDUSA.

After some haggling, the SDUSA had agreed to be responsible for 75% of the amount, and also agreed to abolish their free childcare program in exchange for tax credits for working families with children.

The issue was now left to the individual 13 states to decide through a simple majority popular vote.

All states, except for, amazingly California, voted to re-enter the Unites States. California had voted by the slimmest of margins, 52% to 48% to remain independent of the U.S., indicating a deep divide within its citizens.

For the 12 states that re-entered the U.S., life went on pretty much as normal, except many of the citizens who had left those states for lower taxes and better employment opportunities gradually began to move back. Some of the companies came back as well, mostly the smaller ones, but the S&P 500 companies that had left, remained in their new domiciles, choosing to avoid the cost of moving back. To that extent, the states affected like Washington, Connecticut, New York and New Jersey, would find it difficult to recover in the years following the re-unification. The damage had been done.

California, which had become a two-class, state eventually applied for and was granted re-admission to the U.S. in 2027. It would be three more years before it saw an economic turnaround and began to prosper once again.

SDUSA National Intelligence Director, William Hastings, was tried and convicted of conspiring to murder Seth Dudley, for ordering the failed attempt on the life of Victoria Cheshire, and for conspiring to murder Gretchen and Justin Dudley. He was sentenced to 30 years and died in prison.

Gretchen Dudley eventually re-married and continued to work in Advertising and lived a quiet life in North Philadelphia.

Eileen Pilfery, having moved on from her husband's suicide, re-entered school and acquired her Master's Degree in Clinical Psychology. She works as a grief counselor at Columbia Presbyterian Hospital in New York City.

Oliver Stanton left the White House in January of 2025, and re-engaged with the company he had built. He occasionally appears on Shark Tank as a guest "Shark". He was succeeded by the senior Senator from Kansas, Benjamin Goodwin, who in a never before seen gesture of bi-partisanship had chosen Victoria Cheshire to be his running mate. It was the first time in modern American history that a major party Presidential candidate had chosen a member of the other major party as a running mate.

Both moderated their political ideologies, thus setting the example for newly found cooperation in Congress.

A common sense approach, as opposed to partisan wrangling, was employed in every bill that moved through Congress, and fairness and equity became the hallmark of every new law instead of political ideology.

During their second term in office, President Goodwin and Vice-President Cheshire championed a bill that created the 29th amendment to the Constitution. It would establish two term maximums for all members of Congress. It was given little or no chance of passing into law since the members would be voting to limit their time in office. However, the example Goodwin and Cheshire had set of bi-partisan cooperation so inspired the country that the voters overwhelmingly supported the notion of term limits for Congress, and the Congress was unable to resist. After all, term limits were in place for the executive branch and for a good number of state governorships, why not for Congress?

The adoption of the amendment would prove to be beneficial in that it limited congressional lobbying efforts, and enabled the Congressional members to more often vote their conscience without having to worry about being voted out of office for standing on a common sense position.

Upon leaving office, Ben Goodwin and Victoria Cheshire remained friends and continued to vacation together with their families. They each returned to their chosen professions, and occasionally lectured on the benefits of government service.

Their ideological differences now put aside forever, the two friends, like their country, were indivisible.

The End